THE
DERBY
GAME

THE
DERBY
GAME

A History of Local Rivalries

I A N   C O L L I S

First published by Pitch Publishing, 2023

Pitch Publishing
9 Donnington Park,
85 Birdham Road,
Chichester,
West Sussex,
PO20 7AJ
www.pitchpublishing.co.uk
info@pitchpublishing.co.uk

A CIP catalogue record is available for this book
from the British Library.

ISBN 978 1 80150 423 2

Typesetting and origination by Pitch Publishing
Printed and bound in Great Britain by TJ Books, Padstow

Contents

For my wife, Lynne

Preface

A 'DERBY game' is widely known, not just in the United Kingdom but in many other countries, as a fixture between local rivals. Celebrated British football derbies include the Glasgow clashes of Celtic and Rangers, the Manchester contests between City and United, and the north London meetings of Arsenal and Tottenham Hotspur. In Italy, a match between the Roman teams of Lazio and Roma is known as the *Derby di Roma*. In Amsterdam a match between Ajax and FC Blauw-Wit would be called a *Stadsderby*. In Nairobi, AFC Leopards play Gor Mahia in the *Mashemeji Derby*, the derby of the in-laws.

As a resident of the city of Derby, I have often wondered whether there was any connection between the city's name and its use to identify a game between two local teams. A quick search through opinions posted on the internet is inconclusive. One theory suggests that a 'derby' has long been a name given to any sporting contest because of the famous Derby horserace which was founded by the 12th Earl of Derby. A 'local derby', therefore, is simply a local sporting contest.

I did not find this argument wholly convincing, so decided to dig deeper. I researched the use of the term 'derby' in a sporting context in a wide range of newspapers and journals, going back into history as far as I could. The main results of that research are set out in Chapter 13, which hopefully provides a more plausible and nuanced explanation for how the phrase has come into popular use. But in the process of this research,

I also discovered the intriguing history of what was known as 'Derby Shrovetide Football' and similar games elsewhere in the United Kingdom. It is a history full of incidents, incurred not only in the course of playing the game, but in the centuries of conflict between those who wanted to play football and those who wanted to stop them. I was also struck by how quickly local derbies became key events once association football became established and by the importance of the local derby to football fans in countless communities and countries.

Many derby games between modern-day football teams can be lively and eventful affairs. A supercharged atmosphere swirls through the watching crowd, and for many fans the local derbies are the most emotional matches of the year. Players, while supposedly 'professional', often seem unable to resist rising to the crowd's expectations. Reckless tackles seem to be obligatory. Unseemly scuffles between two players can quickly escalate into mini brawls involving most team members, carried away by the intensity of the occasion. Sometimes even managers enter the fray, unable to maintain any pretence that this is just another game with the same importance as any other.

But the historic Shrovetide football game once played for centuries by two neighbouring parishes, All Saints' and St Peter's, in the town of Derby, was much wilder. One rough but ready mob pitted its guile and muscle against the other. Rules were almost non-existent, and play would smash through fence and hedge, plunge in and out of freezing rivers and streams, and go on for hour after hour. The misrule and mischief which accompanied this annual event, as well as the fights, injuries and occasional riots, naturally led to many attempts to suppress it. National notoriety was the result.

So, this book follows the journey of the 'Derby Game', from its historic roots in mob football played by local people, to the modern-day clashes between teams whose players can come from anywhere in the world, but who still get carried away by the same 'derby' spirit.

1

The Game

FOR CENTURIES, Shrove Tuesday was the most exciting and eagerly awaited day of the year for many Derby folk. Young men, and others not so young, must have spent the night before dreaming of the lifelong honour and glory they could gain, if they could score a goal in the Shrovetide football. For the silk worker released from a 12-hour working day, for the grimy chimney sweep, for bricklayers, tanners and china painters alike, here was a day of revelry when the cares of the winter could be forgot. Publicans checked their cellars and rubbed their hands in glee at the thought of the thousands of carefree players and supporters about to engulf the town. Owners of property in the town centre fretted about whether their windows, walls and gardens would survive the following day unscathed. Pedlars checked their stocks of pies, gingerbread, fruit and nuts. For weeks before Shrove Tuesday, the annual game had been the focus of endless local debate and argument, a welcome distraction in the final weeks of a dark and dreary winter. It was the big day, something the 19th-century writer and clergyman, Rev. Thomas Mozley, recalled in his memoirs as 'THE great event of the Derby Year.'[1]

On the day itself, the atmosphere swelled before the start of the game and rippled through the town. The public houses were crammed with noisy drinkers, the pedlars were shouting their wares. Every vantage point was crowded: young boys climbed posts to sit or stand on walls and roofs, the better-off had paid householders for prime viewing spots and leaned out of upper-storey windows. In Georgian times the aristocracy – or if absent their servants – could observe discreetly from their ducal townhouses in the Market Place and Cornmarket, while the gentry could commandeer positions in the Town Hall and the Assembly Rooms. The scene before the start of the game was described by *Penny Magazine:*

> At two o'clock on Shrove Tuesday starts the sport; and as the hour approaches, the whole town seems alive with expectation. It is a universal holiday, and all ranks and ages are seen streaming towards the market-place. Here the shops are found to be shut, and the houses all around filled with spectators, men, women, and children, crowding the windows and perched upon the house-tops. The players arrive by degrees from opposite sides of the market-place, coming generally in parties of a dozen or more, each greeted as it appears by the cheers of its respective side.[2]

The throng in the centre of the Market Place would build and build. All eyes would turn to the town hall clock and as two o'clock approached the 'war cries' of the different sides started to ring out across the square; 'All Saints' for ever' would be met with a reply of 'St Peter's for ever'. From the rooftops and walls little gangs of children chanted disparaging ditties about the opposing side. The men and lads in the very centre were prepared for action; no coats or jackets, their trousers bound with strapping round their legs, coloured handkerchiefs or cloths round their heads, their arms bare:

> At the appointed hour arrives the ball, carried by the hero of last year who was lucky enough to goal it then.

The crowd of players opens to receive him; and going
into the middle of the market, he throws up the ball;
all cluster round it, and the game begins.[3]

So, what was this game that drew such crowds and created
local heroes? And where exactly is Derby? The city – it
achieved city status in 1977 as part of The Queen's Silver
Jubilee – sits slap bang in the middle of England. It is part of
the East Midlands, but only a few miles from the edge of the
West Midlands. Mozley considered it the most southerly town
of northern England. Immediately to the north of Derby, the
land starts to rise, and old houses are built of the underlying
gritstone before the limestone of the white peak landscape
takes over. A little further north and a latticework of drystone
walls leads into the Peak District National Park. Nowadays,
the Peak District, with its scenic moors and dales, is a magnet
for tourists and day-trippers but centuries ago, it must have
seemed a wild and remote place, prompting Daniel Defoe
to denounce it as a 'howling wilderness'.[4] Most of the Peak
District drains into the River Derwent and Derby was built
originally at the lowest crossing point of that river.

Today, Derby is well linked by railways and strategic roads.
It can be promoted in brochures and websites as a central
business hub. But for most of its history, Derby's 'furthest
from the sea' location meant that it was a lot more difficult
to reach than England's coastal towns, or those occupying
the banks of great rivers. Although the River Derwent runs
into the River Trent a few miles to the south, navigation
upriver from the Trent to Derby was often difficult, and
certainly did not provide a water route to anywhere further
north. While it would be wrong to think of pre-industrial
Derby as a backwater, the town was mostly left to look after
its own concerns. Perhaps this is one reason why it managed to
sustain an ancient tradition that had been extinguished many

years before in other large towns – Shrovetide football. But while Derby's relative remoteness might partly explain how this riotous game made it into the 19th century, it was a set of other extraordinary factors that gave what became known as the Derby Foot-Ball another half-century of life. We will explore these factors – events, personalities, movements – in later chapters. But for now, let's look at how the Derby Game was played.

Despite its name, Shrovetide football was very different from the game of football that is now played across the globe. There was a ball, and you could kick it if you wanted to. There were also two goals. A few of the players on each side might wear a particular colour. Everything else was different. Indeed, an article in the *Derby Mercury* in 1840 distinguishes between the manly and healthful game of football, as played in a meadow between neighbouring villages in Derbyshire, and the 'filthy and disgusting' sport played in Derby at Shrovetide.[5] The bucolic version used kicking as the main method of forcing a ball with an inflated bladder towards a goal. The Derby Game, at least by the late Georgian and early Victorian eras, was more like hug ball, with deliberate holding and shielding of the ball, while opponents sought to tear it away by any means possible.

The Derby Game had no defined pitch or playing area. Although the opposing goals were roughly a mile apart, the two 'teams' could use any route they liked to get to them. The modern city of Derby straddles the River Derwent, but its early growth was largely confined to the west bank of the river. Here, the higher ground offered greater protection from the floods that affected the lower-lying land to the east. But the watercourse that was central to historic Derby was not the Derwent; it was the Markeaton Brook. This brook provided a more manageable location for water powered mills and ran west to east through the centre of town, on its way into the Derwent. Historically, the brook seems to have been used to help define the boundaries of parishes to the north like All Saints' and St Alkmund's and those to the south like St Peter's and most of St Werburgh's. In summer the brook might wane to a few inches of water, but in winter it often had real power and frequently flooded the town.

Derby Shrovetide Football nominally pitted the parish of St Peter's, centred around St Peter's Street, against the parish of All Saints' centred around Irongate. In 1841 the population of St Peter's exceeded 10,000 people, while All Saints' had fewer than 4,500 residents. Unsurprisingly, the All Saints' side called upon support from the small neighbouring parishes of St Alkmund's and St Michael's. Residents from the parish of St Werburgh's appear to have supported either side. The key parishes were all included in the following rhyme:

> *Pancakes and fritters,*
> *Say All Saints' and St Peter's*
> *When will the ball come,*
> *Say the bells of St Alkmun;*
> *At two they will throw,*
> *Says Saint Werabo';*
> *O! very well,*
> *Says little Michael.*[6]

Markeaton Brook seems to have been the dividing line, with those to the north supporting All Saints' and those to the south connected to St Peter's. The core of each 'team' – in reality a mob of at least several hundred people – was formed by the men of these parishes. But it was also boosted by 'foot-ballers' from neighbouring parishes and villages outside Derby. Different parts of the town and outlying villages appeared to favour either one side or the other. Unusually, compared with festival football played elsewhere in the country, different colours were associated with each side: blue for St Peter's; yellow for All Saints'.

Map of Derby (West) in 1817. The goal for All Saints' was to the north west of the town centre, off Nuns Street. (Credit: Derby Local Studies Library)

In the days when the game had official approval, the ball would be thrown up at two o'clock by a local dignitary, probably the mayor. In the last few decades of the game, when opposition to the event began to grow and mayors became less keen to be associated with it, the ball was brought into the square by the victors of the previous year. The arrival and deployment of the key players was carefully choreographed beforehand. For example, if St Peter's had won the contest in the previous year, then, shortly before two o'clock, a cohort of their best men would emerge, suitably fuelled, from a nearby hostelry and carry the ball down the Morledge towards the Market Place. They would be met by a gauntlet of All Saints' players, who would close in behind them. This compressed mass would then surge into the Market Place. The St Peter's men would gravitate towards the western end of the square, presumably to be better able to block the All Saints' getting to their goal via Sadler Gate or the Cornmarket. All Saints' concentrated their forces at the eastern end to try and stop St Peter's taking the ball down to the river. The two sides faced each other with hands raised and then closed together. An observer, Thomas Broughton, recalled:

> As soon as the men with the ball reached the centre each side would close in and the game would begin in earnest. In a few minutes a forest of hands would be seen, as it was dangerous to go in unless you held them up, or you would very likely have a broken arm. Soon the surging crowd swayed from one side to the other amid the deafening shouts of the players and the earnest pressing of the supporters.[7]

There were no rules to the game, and players were free to handle, hold, kick or punch the ball as the fancy took them. Some reports claim that players tried to hide the ball in their clothing, but if this was the case the ball must have been much smaller than it was in the latter years of the game when it was around 14 inches in diameter, much larger than a modern-day football. Made of leather by local shoemakers, it was stuffed with cork shavings. The sole aim of the game was to get the ball from the Market Place to the home goal in the side's own parish – not the goal in the opposition's territory. All Saints' goal was the waterwheel on the side of Nun's Mill on the Markeaton Brook, about a kilometre west of the Market Place. By the mid-19th century, the St Peter's goal was a nursery gate on Grove Street to the north of the town, again about a kilometre away from the starting point. A goal was scored by knocking the ball three times on the 'winning post', or for All Saints' by striking the ball three times against the waterwheel, a task which could only be achieved by jumping in the mill pond. This ended the game and, according to some accounts, was celebrated by a long peal of bells from the victorious parish church.

When the game started in the Market Place, there was basically a massive scrum. It might be thought that it would have been difficult for spectators in a large crowd to know where the ball was, but there was an invaluable clue, as Rev. Mozley remembered, 'In a quarter of an hour there rose a column of steam as from a funnel up to the sky on a still day, indicating the exact spot of the ball.'[8] The column of steam rose in the cold February air from where the players were straining every muscle in their efforts to get nearer the ball. The rest of the crowd would then try to push the players towards their goal. Unsurprisingly the set-to in the Market Place could result in a bruising stalemate which might take an hour or two to resolve. The ball was large and fairly heavy and could not be thrown or kicked for more than several yards. The play – pushing, shoving, grappling, wrestling – was distinctly up close and personal. If the players with the ball managed to break out of the square and get into a narrow side street, like Sadler Gate or Irongate, then a blocking group would often be ready and waiting, and another lengthy eyeball to eyeball confrontation would be likely to ensue.

While the two goals were at a similar distance from the starting point in the Market Place, the most direct routes through the streets to these goals were rarely taken, as the narrow streets were too easily blocked by the opposing mob. Instead, as happens now at the Shrovetide game still played at nearby Ashbourne, the key players sought to get the ball into water – a tactic that soon sorts out the diehards from the blowhards. The cork shavings inside the ball helped with its buoyancy. William Hutton, who we will meet in a later chapter, tells us of his memories of the 1730s that:

> The professors of this athletic art think themselves bound to follow the ball wherever it flies; and, as Derby is fenced in with rivers, it seldom flies far without flying into the water; and I have seen these amphibious practitioners of foot-ball kicking jump into the river upon a Shrove-Tuesday when the ground was covered with snow.[9]

A common tactic used by All Saints' was to try and get the ball into Markeaton Brook and then force their way upstream, to their goal at Nun's Street Mill. Presumably, much depended on whether the brook was in full spate or had a more middling flow. St Peter's preferred the seemingly odd tactic of getting the ball into the River Derwent, which must have been bracingly cold at that time of year and to swim with the ball. This at least had the advantage of being in a downstream direction, but if pursued for too long took the ball further away from their home. No doubt this tactic helped to thin out the number of players and, if successful, resulted in a cross-country dash

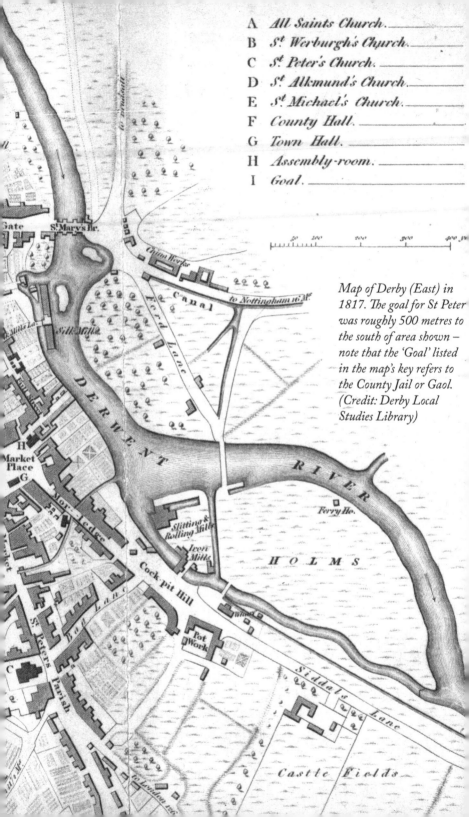

A   *All Saints Church.* _____

B   *St Werburgh's Church.* _____

C   *St Peter's Church.* _____

D   *St Alkmund's Church.* _____

E   *St Michael's Church.* _____

F   *County Hall.* _____

G   *Town Hall.* _____

H   *Assembly-room.* _____

I   *Goal.* _____

Map of Derby (East) in 1817. The goal for St Peter was roughly 500 metres to the south of area shown – note that the 'Goal' listed in the map's key refers to the County Jail or Gaol. (Credit: Derby Local Studies Library) westward towards London Road and uphill to the St Peter's goal near Grove Street. After playing the game for several centuries, the sides knew all the key places where play could be blocked or ambushed. Groups of players were stationed at or near to these strategic spots and kept informed by breathless runners of the whereabouts of the ball. Indeed, Mozley wrote in *Reminiscences* that information on the state of play was passed through the town, as if it were news 'of a flood, or a stream of lava'.[10]

If St Peter's felt particularly strong they might try a direct route, out of the Market Place, down the Cornmarket and up St Peter's Street. But this was dangerous because they had to cross Markeaton Brook. They could throw or kick the ball across, or push in force over an arched bridge. Even if they succeeded in getting the ball to the other side of the brook, the route to Grove Street would be uphill. Markeaton Brook was culverted at this point in the 1840s (being buried underneath Victoria and Albert Streets), but previously had to be crossed by St Peter's Bridge, which could easily be blocked by All Saints'. Even worse, if All Saints' got hold of the ball at this point, they would then have a straight run up Markeaton Brook to the waterwheel in Nun's Street.

Nevertheless, if play got near St Peter's Bridge, the Peterites had a trick up their sleeve. Rather than try to cross the bridge they would throw the ball to some of their players on the opposite side of the brook. Here, ready and waiting, were specialist players who would disappear with the ball into a nearby sewer and re-emerge with it in the River Derwent. An All Saints' player writing in 1830 revealed that the sewers 'are not higher than just to allow the explorers to pass on all fours; and that, in addition to a plentiful supply of decomposed dogs, cats, & etc they abound with thousands of what your more humorous correspondents would designate black game (water-rats)'.[11]

Although the plunge into cold waters must have thinned out the numbers, an observer explained, 'It is curious to see one or two hundred men up to their chins in the Derwent or brook, continually ducking each other.'[12] Getting the ball into the river was a predictable tactic for St Peter's, and accordingly the best landing places downstream would be 'invested by skirmishing parties' from All Saints' ready to block the Peterites' progress and try and wrest control of the ball.[13] One of these places must have been a spot on an open area called The Holmes (now called Bass's Recreation Ground) where the ferry operated. The 'ferry' was simply a rope stretched across the river which enabled a small boat and its occupants to be pulled from one side to the other. On Shrove Tuesday, the rope could be used to get footballers from one side to the other. If All Saints' managed to get the ball on to the east bank, they could then run north for half a mile and cross St Mary's Bridge, taking them back into town. No doubt they would be met at the bridge by St Peter's men intent on blocking any progress and who would be happy to take play back into the river.

The former player and policeman Benjamin Fearn recalled the tactics in the latter years of the game after the ball had got into the River Derwent:

> If Peter's got down towards the Siddals, they would attempt to land and work the ball up towards the goal, but it was now the policy of All Saints' to carry the ball further down and get it out on the other bank. Hundreds of people would line the river ready to oppose or assist any attempt at landing and the result was that the ball would sometimes go downstream as far as Chaddesden or almost to Alvaston. The osier beds at Chaddesden were the scene of several rare fights.[14]

If All Saints' succeeded in getting the ball out at Chaddesden, then according to Fearn, they would work the ball round getting as far north as the village of Allestree before getting back to their goal. This would have been a total round trip of at least five miles. The St Peter's 'countryside route' seems less onerous, Alvaston being a two-mile trip downstream of the Market Place and then a romp of another mile and a half by land back to the St Peter's goal. However, their exertions might well have been in vain, because as St Peter's approached their goal All Saints' could be ready and waiting:

> And even if they succeeded in reaching within a hundred yards or less of the gate the pressure of their opponents might be so great that the ball would be forced past, through the town – or better still, round the outskirts, through gardens and even houses, over walls and fences, anywhere, and at last into the mill-dam and up to the wheel.[15]

The game then could range over several miles, usually took several hours, and often lasted well into the evening. On one occasion a holder of the ball plunged into the river only to find himself surrounded by opponents. A mad chase in and out of the water then ensued, going upstream for five miles nearly to the village of Duffield after negotiating the weirs at Darley Abbey and Little Eaton. On another occasion, a player is claimed to have evaded capture by taking the ball into a sewer and making his way under a considerable part of the town. He emerged from his subterranean journey only to find a large party waiting for him.

The addition of support from outlying villages could be key to a successful outcome. In 1827, for example, play had been stuck for at least half an hour in a stalemate in a place called Old George Yard, when help arrived for St Peter's:

This consisted of a body of strong and resolute men
at least twenty in number, from Littleover, who had
already been engaged in a successful contest at kickball
with an equal party of Mickleover men. Flushed with
victory, they entered the George Yard and succeeded
in carrying the ball once more into the Morledge.[16]

Sometimes underhand tactics were employed, including
taking the cork shavings out of the ball and smuggling the
cover towards the goal underneath 'a countryman's frock or
a woman's clothing'.[17] Carts were sometimes commandeered
to help block narrow streets, false information spread about
where the ball had gone, or cries would go up for help in saving
a drowning man who turned out to be non-existent. The ball
might disappear into a factory yard, like the Rolling Mill near
the river, but if All Saints' shut the factory gates, St Peter's
would simply lift the gates off their hinges. No hedge, fence,
wall, brook or river was sufficient to stop the game.

Before each game, there must have been a lot of
organisation and planning in the respective parishes about
who was going to do what, where and when. The game at
close quarters was incredibly energy-sapping, and no one could
attempt to be continually involved throughout the several hours
that the game normally took. Even leading players would be
expected to take frequent rest breaks to regain some strength
and energy. Luckily, crowds of supporters were on hand to
provide refreshments and drag the exhausted out of harm's way,
and there are many accounts of people who had gone to the
game with the intention of just watching, ending up embroiled
in the thick of the action.

So the game would ebb and flow, running pell-mell across
fields, smashing through fences and hedgerows, pushing masses
of people up streets, getting blocked in courts and alleyways,
plunging into rivers and ponds. While players would know

that they should try and veer away from private gardens, this wasn't always possible, and many gardeners were left distraught at what a trampling horde could do.

Whoever managed, after all this herculean effort, tricks and turmoil, to goal the ball, became an instant hero. He was hoisted shoulder high through the winning parish and feted well into the night. The funds for this revelry were solicited by the winning players by knocking on houses and inviting contributions. The following day, Ash Wednesday, the whole performance would be repeated, but this time it would be a boys' only game, watched over by their bruised and battered elders.

2

Get the Bladder and Blow

FOOTBALL HAS a much longer history in the British Isles than most people suspect. Because the Football Association was formed in 1863 and the English Football League in 1888, some people assume that games of football were a Victorian invention, most probably in the public schools of the time. The real story is much more complicated. But one thing is certain, at both the casual level of a few lads or men kicking a ball around, and in the highly ritualised bouts of festival football, the game has an extensive history stretching back over many centuries.

The first written reference to football in Britain may have been made by William Fitzstephen, who was a servant of Thomas Becket, the Archbishop of Canterbury. In a work dated 1174 called *Descriptio Nobilissimae Civitatis Londiniae*, Fitzstephen described London at the time and included a section on the city's pastimes and sporting activities. He described sports such as archery, duelling, javelin throwing and wrestling and noted that after lunch on Shrove Tuesday the entire youth of the city would go out to the fields to take part in a ball game. He made it clear that every trade had its ball, and that fathers and elders would turn up to see how the boys got on. It seems that the seniors were not always able to refrain from joining in the game, as the sight of the lads playing ignited old memories and passions. Frustratingly, Fitzstephen did not describe the game itself, but it seems highly probable that it was a form of football.

In 1314, Nicholas de Farndone, Lord Mayor of the City of London, felt it necessary to proclaim:

> Whereas there is great uproar in the City, through certain tumults arising from great footballs in the fields of the public, from which many evils may perchance arise … we do command and do forbid, on the King's behalf, upon pain of imprisonment, that such game shall be practised henceforth within the City.[18]

This proclamation was issued on behalf of Edward II and was originally written in Norman French. It shows that during the period of Norman power, football had come to be so popular that it caused riots and disorder in the heart of England's capital. It is highly likely that the tumults referred to occurred during holidays like Shrove Tuesday, as these were the only times that people were free from work and able to gather together in large numbers.

But casual football kickabouts between a few friends and work-mates were not confined to holidays. Even these games could result in serious injury. Indeed, in 1321 an odd but fatal accident occurred during a football game at Shouldham Priory in Norfolk. William de Spalding, who was one of the canons responsible for running the priory, was playing football when a friend of his, also called William, ran against him. The friend inadvertently wounded himself on a sheathed knife carried by the cleric. He died six days later. No blame was attached to the canon, who was deeply upset by the death of his friend. The incident helps to show though that the game was played by people who had respected positions in the community.

In medieval times, church services were long and frequent. The hours of standing still could take a toll on the legs. Monks must have been more than grateful for the misericords, or mercy seats, to be found in some choir stalls. When folded up, the mercy seat provided a little shelf for the weary monk to lean back on. When folded down, the underneath of the misericord could not be seen, and woodcarvers appear to have been given free rein to use this bit of wood to carve what they liked. Gloucester Cathedral has 44 misericords dating from the 14th century. The carvings include mermaids, fabulous monsters and flowers but also scenes of ordinary life. One carving shows a pair of youths, contesting with feet and hands, for a ball that is bouncing between them. The carver has done his best, in the space he had to work with, to convey the impression that the two youths are running. The carving is thought to date from around 1350.

In 1365, Edward III prohibited able-bodied men from indulging in pastimes like quoits, cock fighting and football, and encouraged them to devote their leisure time to archery practice. Subsequent English kings such as Richard II and Henry IV also tried to outlaw the game. Not to be outdone, in the Football Act of 1424, James I of Scotland issued a ban across his kingdom, in a pithy Scottish style, 'Na man play at the fute-ball.'

The fact that repeated bans had to be issued shows that playing a game of football was an ingrained habit. In a poem written around 1514, two shepherds, Amintas and Faustus, discuss the respective merits of town and country life. Alexander Barclay composed the poem – his *Fifth Eclogue* – when he was a monk at a Benedictine monastery in Ely. In one lengthy section of verse, Amintas set out his appreciation for the game of football. He argued that each season of the year brings its own delights and joys, and that football is particularly beneficial in winter.

And now in winter for all the grievous colde,
All rent and ragged a man may them beholde,
They have great pleasure supposing well to dine,
When men be busied in killing of fat swine,
They get the bladder and blowe it great and thin,
With many beans and peason put within,
It rattleth, soundeth, and shineth clere and fayre,
While it is thrown and caste up in the ayre.[19]

The poem goes on to relate how players struggled to 'smite' the ball with foot or hand, and by running and leaping, they could drive away the winter cold and forget all about their work. As the poem describes, the winter period is the time for playing football. Pigs were slaughtered for meat from late autumn onwards and nothing went to waste; even the bladder could be blown up and used to play a game that would help to keep people warm. Barclay's poem, and the Gloucester carving, are evocative evidence that football was a part of mainstream life many centuries before the Victorians started to draw up rulebooks for the game.

Then, as now, the game was not confined to one particular class of people. In 1568 Sir Francis Knollys wrote a letter to Queen Elizabeth's secretary, describing a football game played at Carlisle Castle by the retinue of Mary Queen of Scots. For two hours, 20 of the Queen's supporters played a game of ten-a-side football, demonstrating a variety of skills in front of Her Majesty. Mary's retinue was made up predominantly of Scottish nobles who had followed her south in the aftermath of the Battle of Langside. Mary recorded the game in her diary. Intriguingly, in the 1980s, a ball made of cowhide and inflated with a pig's bladder was discovered behind the panelling of the Queen's Chamber in Stirling Castle, one of Mary's early residences. The castle was rebuilt a few years before Mary was born in 1542, and it is thought that while works were going on, the ball was kicked or thrown high enough for it to lodge out of reach in the castle rafters. It is now displayed in the Stirling Smith Art Gallery and Museum, and is claimed by some to be the oldest football in the world.

The Scots seemed to have had a particular liking for the game, particularly in the Borders which in the Tudor period was the most lawless part of the British mainland. The boundary between the two countries was often used by the families and clans who lived there as a way of evading justice. Despite the fact that this was a dangerous place to live, the Borders communities had a great fondness for football. Matches took place between different villages and clans. In 1601, a dispute arose during a football game at Lochton in the Merse, in Berwickshire, between the Cockburns and the Davidsons. It ended with the firing of pistols and primitive rifles called hackbuts. In the previous year, the notorious Armstrongs had shot dead Sir John Carmichael, warden of the Western Marches, while on their way home from a football match.

A description of a football game in more civilised surroundings has been found in a manuscript collection of the miracles of King Henry VI of England. The game was played at Caunton in Nottinghamshire. The description, which is in Latin, dates from the late 15th century:

> The game at which they had met for common recreation is called by some the foot-ball game. It is one in which young men, in country sport, propel a huge ball not by throwing it into the air but by striking it and rolling it along the ground, and that not with their hands but with their feet ... kicking in opposite directions.[20]

The account goes on to remark that boundaries to the game were marked out; so, this may be the earliest reference to a football field. One of the footballers was badly hurt playing the game, but miraculously King Henry VI was able to effect a cure by appearing in the footballer's dreams. It was this 'miracle' that was considered worthy of recording.

In East Anglia and Essex, a form of football called camp-ball developed and was played between the 15th and mid-19th centuries. Here some degree of organisation is apparent, because the game was not just played on common land, but on fields retained partly for that purpose. These fields, or 'camping closes', tended to be next to, or close to churches and could also be used for other community purposes. The game was played by two teams of equal numbers. Villages might play against each other, or married men might play unmarried men, or one parish might play a neighbouring parish. Icklingham, for example, a small village in Suffolk, had two camping closes, one for each of its two ancient parishes. In 1823, the soldier and writer Edward Moor wrote of camp-ball as follows:

> Goals were pitched at the distance of 150 or 200 yards from each other – these were generally formed of the thrown-off clothes of the competitors. Each party has two goals, ten or fifteen yards apart. The parties, ten or fifteen a side, stand in line, facing their own goals and each other, at about ten yards distance, midway between the goals, and nearest that of their adversaries. An indifferent spectator agreed on by the parties, throws up a ball, of the size of a common cricket ball, midway between the players and makes his escape.[21]

The game described by Moor seems something like American football, but another version of the game was played with a larger ball in which kicking it was allowed. The game's name of 'camp' did not have anything to do with tents but seems to have been derived from the German word 'kampf' meaning struggle or fight, which perhaps indicates that these were fierce contests.

In most of the country, however, there were no designated places where people could play games like football, until the advent of public parks and recreation grounds in the Victorian era. For the casual kickabout, then as now, a marked-out pitch was not a necessary prerequisite. But the enclosure of common land, and growing urbanisation, meant working people often had difficulty in finding somewhere suitable to play. In Derby, for many years the main area likely to be used for informal games, would have been the common land at Nun's Green off the Ashbourne Road. But during the 17th and 18th centuries, parts of this area started to be enclosed or developed. Consequently, it seems that any sort of open area might be used by those with a liking for a game, and nowhere was sacrosanct, even churchyards. This was bound to create conflict. Sundays were the only free time many people got, and they were also the busiest times for churches. In 1737, All Saints' Church in Derby gave instructions for notices declaring that anyone playing at games in the churchyard would be punished.

The notice could not have been successful, as the church had to issue another warning in 1742 which:

> Ordered that All Persons that play in the Church Yard shall have notice to forbear for the future and that the Parents and Masters of all such Children and Servants as follow the same practice shall have notice to discharge their Children and Servants from such practice otherwise they shall be prosecuted.[22]

In 1755, the churchwardens decided to issue a more strongly worded notice:

> Whereas an evil custom has prevailed of playing at ball in the churchyard, to the great dishonour of Almighty God, in profaning the place of his public worship to

the great damage of the church windows and to the hindrance and prejudice of persons passing about their lawful business and whereas all favourable means have been used to no purposes to stop such a wicked practice; it is therefore ordered that the church wardens of this Parish for the time being shall employ at the expenses of the Parish a proper person to discharge all persons from playing at ball henceforward in the churchyard; and in case they are obstinate to take account of their names in order that all such persons shall be prosecuted in Lichfield Court.[23]

The church beadle was a familiar figure in Stuart and Georgian times, and was the person charged with sorting out the day-to-day problems associated with running a church. Consequently, his duties could be many and varied. The All Saints' beadle, for example, was recompensed for carrying people out of church and in 1643 Samuel Houghton, then beadle, received three shillings for removing a 'strompett' from Thomas Holmes's house.[24] The beadle's main duties though seemed to have been clearing dogs and beggars out of the church. In some places, beadles were known as dog whippers or, in Derbyshire, bang-beggars, which suggests they did not rely on diplomacy alone. At All Saints', the bang-beggar was given a wig and a coat with red facings to convey his authority. The bang-beggar was the 'proper person', the churchwardens expected to enforce their ban on ball playing. But neither sternly worded notices nor the threats of the beadle, resplendent in his wig and coat, were enough to put a stop to the ball playing. In 1771, another request from the exasperated church 'ordered that the present Churchwardens take the opinion of the Council how most effectively to suppress Ball playing and gaming in the Church Yard'.[25] The churchwardens at All Saints' also issued a warning in 1769 to deter people from entering the church steeple on a Shrove Tuesday to 'gangle' the bells. [26]

The first banning order specifically against Shrove Tuesday football appears to have been made in Chester in 1533. The wording of the order is also interesting, in that clearly the Shrovetide game had been an annual event for longer than anyone could remember:

> That the said occupacions of the shoumacres which alwayes tyme out of man's remembrance have geven and delyvered yerlye upon Teuesday commonly caulyd Shroft Tuesday, otherwyse Goteddesday, at afternoune of the same unto drapers afore the mayre of the cities at the Cros uon the Rood Dee one ball of lether, caulyd a foot baule, of the value of iii s iiii d. or about to play at from thens to the Common Haule of the said cities and further at pleasure of evill disposed persons wherefore hath grete inconvenynce. [27]

The Rood Dee was a flat area of land near the city walls encircled at the time by the River Dee. The 'cros uon the Rood Dee' was a Saxon cross in the middle of this area, of which a small stump has survived to the present day. The Chester game, then, may possibly have been played for a financial reward of three shillings and four pennies. It also appears that the Shrovetide games were some sort of contest between members of different guilds, with the Shoemakers' Guild providing the ball. However, the ban must have failed in its intention as Henry Gee, the Chester mayor, tried a different approach a few years later in 1540. This time he proposed to replace Shrove Tuesday football with a running race; the mayor had a passion for horseracing, and had established the Roo Dee as a venue for his favourite sport in the previous year.

Shoemakers figure prominently in the history of festival football. In 17th-century Carlisle, only members of the Shoemakers' Guild were allowed to make a ball, and any apprentices or journeymen found playing with any other ball could be fined. In the Scottish Borders town of Duns, a game was played at Fastings Even (Shrove Tuesday), between married men and bachelors. Four balls were prepared for the game: one gold or gilt, one silver, one spotted and a fourth ball which was presented to a local patron in thanks for his hospitality. Different financial rewards were given for each goaling of the three coloured balls.

The Duns game had a habit of resulting in riot and tumult, so in 1724 John Gray, the bailie for the town, took possession of the drum which was used to summon players to the game. The loss of the drum caused considerable upset, though the game began as usual. But when the winners tried to claim victory on the stairs of the Tolbooth or Town Hall, the losers refused to accept the result without the presence of the drum. As a result, Gray found his house besieged by around 300 players, who threatened to kill him unless he gave the drum up. He refused, so the mob stoned his house, breaking many windows. Gray was having his windows repaired on Ash Wednesday, when a local woman started throwing stones and breaking them again. She was seized by town officers who set off for the Tolbooth, only to be attacked on the way by supporters of the game who managed to free her. Gray laid most of the blame for the disorder on William Horne, the local shoemaker and maker of the balls.

While concern about violent and riotous behaviour fuelled many attempts to ban large games of holiday football, concern also grew from the 17th century onwards about damage done to property, particularly glazed windows. In 1608, Manchester was a town of a similar size to Derby, having around 4,000 inhabitants. An order concerning the 'ffootebale' lamented that:

There hath been heretofore greate disorder in our towne
of Manchester, and the Inhabitants thereof greatelye
wronged and charged with making and amending of
theire glasse windows broken yearlelye and spolyed
by a company of lewde and disordered persons usinge
that unlawful exercise of playing with the ffotebale in
ye streets of said towne, breaking many mens windows
and glasse at theire plesures.[28]

The concerns about damage to property, particularly windows,
are echoed in other accounts across the country. In response,
some towns and villages seem to have made attempts to reduce
the amount of damage by moving football games out of streets
and on to fields or commons. In some places rules of play
changed to favour handball rather than football. The Borders
was a hotbed for Shrove Tuesday football, but in the 17th
century there was a shift from football to games of handball
(locally called handba' or just ba'). It seems highly probable that
this change is one reason why the Borders later provided such a
fertile nursery for the development of rugby union in Scotland.
At the time, the change to handba' probably helped to reduce
the pressure to ban the Shrove Tuesday games in some Borders
towns, although in Hawick the ba' game was still banned in
1780, before being revived in 1842.

Although the game in Derby was called football, by the
Victorian era it had become hug ball. The word football clearly
suggests that the game was originally played mostly by kicking.
As the numbers playing the game increased over the centuries,
making progress by kicking would become more difficult. So,
hugging the ball and running with it, surrounded by a phalanx
of team-mates, became the preferred style of play, and had
the added advantage of breaking fewer windows. Like the
Derby Game, most mass football events across the country
took place on Shrove Tuesday, although some towns favoured

Christmas or Easter. Indeed, in some places, Shrove Tuesday was simply called 'Football Day'. But during the 18th and early 19th centuries the number of festival football events continued to shrink as towns and villages grew and the games came into conflict with both property owners and urban development.

There is clear evidence that Shrove Tuesday football was not just a rustic tradition but was played in some large towns and cities. Usually, it is the clashes with authorities that provide the proof. Maidstone issued a ban on football, cudgel-playing and cock throwing following Shrovetide riots in 1653. In 1660, footballers ignoring a prohibition against the playing of football, broke a window in All Hallows Church in York. Action was taken against 11 alleged perpetrators who were fined 20 shillings each. This punishment was not well received; on the same day that the fines were issued a large group of men assembled armed with muskets, halberds, fowling-pieces and swords. They smashed their way into the mayor's house, and it was several hours before order was restored. The magistrates later held an inquisition into the events, heard evidence against 18 offenders and fined the ringleader £10, which was a huge sum in 1660.

In the same year, apprentices in Bristol rioted against the local ban of their Shrove Tuesday sports of football and cock throwing. In London, one piece of evidence for the tradition comes in a poem of 1716 called *Trivia: The Art of Walking the Streets of London*. The poem's author, John Gay, may be referring to a Shrovetide game when he referred to 'the furies of the football-war'. The poem describes events around Covent Garden at a time of the year when there was 'snowy ground' and apprentices had quit their workshops.

The more urbanised an area was, the more likely that Shrovetide footballers would come into conflict with the local authorities. Firstly, there was the issue of maintaining law and order. Although festival football was not confined to apprentices, they were usually at the heart of the action. The greatest concentrations of apprentices were found in the towns and cities where shoemakers, tailors, butchers, turners, coopers, clockmakers and countless other trades proliferated. Having a day when tradition required that a blind eye be turned to youthful excesses was a lot harder to sustain in a city or large town than it was in a rural village with lots of open spaces.

Secondly, there were the economic impacts from damage to property and trade. A Shrovetide game involving fewer than 100 people, in an agricultural village, might be considered tolerable. But several hundred people battling their way up a confined street of shops in a large town or city was a different matter, particularly where it brought trade to a halt and resulted in serious damage. Gradually, Shrovetide football was extinguished in the cities and the larger towns. By the late Georgian period, with the exception of Derby, Shrove Tuesday football was confined to a rapidly dwindling number of small towns and villages. By the end of the Napoleonic Wars in 1815, Derby had been, for many years, the most sizeable town where Shrovetide football was still played. It was the biggest event of its kind, and it was this together with the spread of newspapers and magazines that gave rise to its notoriety. As we will see in later chapters, the reasons for its survival were geographical, political and cultural.

3

Folklore, Fact and Fiction

WILLIAM HUTTON has plaques dedicated to his memory in both Derby and Birmingham but his origins could not have been more humble. In 1730, when just seven years old, he was apprenticed at Derby's Silk Mill. Rising each morning at five o'clock, he made his way to the building often heralded as England's first factory and took his place as the youngest of the mill's 300 employees. Here he suffered long hours in the companionship 'of the most rude and vulgar of the human race', while submitting to be caned whenever his master considered it appropriate.[29] As his legs were not long enough to reach the machines, his supervisor thoughtfully tied his feet to a special pair of clogs.

Hutton's mother died in childbirth when he was ten years old and his indolent father sought solace in drink. So, he left Derby aged 15 when his apprenticeship at the Silk Mill came to an end, and became an apprentice to his uncle, a weaver in Nottingham. After his uncle died in 1746, Hutton taught himself bookbinding by copying a local bookseller, and in 1749 borrowed money from his sister and walked to London to buy bookbinding tools. On his return he set up shop in Birmingham, a place he had once run away to in his unhappy youth. He became a successful bookseller and set up a lending library. But his fortunes really took off when he started selling cheap stationery. Hutton became wealthy enough to have two residences in Birmingham, a four-storey country mansion in Washwood Heath, as well as a townhouse-cum-shop in the High Street. In 1781 he achieved literary fame when he wrote and published the first *History of Birmingham*. The book was a great success with Hutton's plain-speaking style finding a ready audience in his adopted city.

Further books on travel, places and history followed including the *History of Derby* in 1791, in which he referred to the Derby love of football. While there are records and notices relating to attempts to ban the game which pre-date Hutton's book, his *History of Derby* was the first written description of the importance of the game in local culture. There is nothing in Hutton's account to suggest that the game he knew in his youth was a recent innovation. Indeed, he wrote as if it were something that had long been part and parcel of the lives of local people. He did not claim that the game was unique to Derby, but he did assert that there was a particular local enthusiasm for the game:

> There is also one amusement of the amphibious kind, which if not peculiar to Derby is pursued with an avidity I have not observed elsewhere, foot-ball. I have seen this coarse sport carried to the barbarous height of an election contest; nay, I have known a foot-ball hero chaired through the streets, like a successful member, although the utmost celebration of character was no more than that of a butcher's apprentice. Black eyes, bruised arms and broken shins are equally the marks of victory and defeat. I need not say this is the delight of the lower ranks, and is attained at an early period; the very infant learns to kick and then to walk.[30]

The affinity between Derby residents and football is also reflected in the piece of folklore most often associated with

Derby – the ballad of 'The Derby Ram' – the first verse of which begins:

As I was going to Derby, Sir
All on a market day,
I met the finest Ram, sir
That ever was fed on hay.

The lengthy song, which dates from at least the 17th century, goes on to detail many astonishing attributes of a huge ram and one of the subsequent verses is:

The little boys of Derby, Sir
They came to beg his eyes
To kick about the streets, Sir
For they were football size.

The folk song, like the Derby Game, is of long but uncertain antiquity. It was certainly commonplace by 1739 when mentioned in a letter by a local vicar but may have been sung for a century or more before that. By the 1830s, the local passion for football is, if anything, stronger than ever, and the events are so big and notorious that they are attracting coverage in some national papers and sports magazines. The zeal of Derby folk for this crazy game is clear, but when did it all start?

An article in the *Derby Mercury* in 1827, which provides much of our knowledge about the Derby Game, said the event had been a custom since 'time immemorial'.[31] In his *History of the County of Derby* published two years later, Stephen Glover informed readers that the origins of the game were lost in antiquity, but that there existed a tradition that a cohort of Roman soldiers marching through the town were thrust out by the local inhabitants. According to this theory the game sprang up as a way of celebrating this event. There seems little to support this suggestion, especially as Glover states that the local populace was unarmed and yet, despite this handicap, slew the Roman soldiers! Yet, the specific date of AD 217 is advanced for this supposed miracle.

A more recent suggestion in Paul Sullivan's *Bloody British History: Derby*, published in 2011, is probably even more tongue-in-cheek than Glover. This puts the date at AD 275 when a tribe of Britons, not local to the area, turned violent, chopped the Romans' heads off and started playing football with them. For some reason – which Sullivan does not explain – the locals instigated Shrovetide football as a way of celebrating this victory.

The Romans certainly built a fort in around AD 55 on high ground west of the River Derwent, just to the north of the present city centre. Then, around 25 years later they built a larger fort called Derventio, on flatter ground east of the river, in the area now known as Little Chester. Hostile tribes of Britons, like the Brigantes to the north, were not that far away, but the idea of a Roman ancestry to Shrovetide football still seems extremely fanciful, to put it mildly. It is possible though that some sort of ball game, called harpastrum, was played throughout the Roman Empire.

Another theory – advanced by the *Manchester Courier* as the most probable explanation – is that the Derby Game began as a means to celebrate a great victory of the Saxon inhabitants, led by their formidable Queen Æthelflæda, over the Danes in 917. Æthelflæda was the daughter of King Alfred the Great. She was born at a time when the Great Heathen Army of Danes and Vikings, had pushed Alfred's Anglo-Saxons out of Mercia. The Saxon settlement of Northworthy, which had been part of Saxon Mercia, was renamed as Deoraby when it came under the area of Danish control known as the Danelaw. Northworthy must have supported, or at least tolerated, Christian worship, as it was the chosen burial ground for the body of Alkmund, a Northumbrian prince who was murdered in around 800.

When her husband, King Æthelred, died, Æthelflæda took on the job of pursuing Anglo-Saxon claims to the old kingdom of Mercia. She quickly built up a reputation as a warrior queen and in September 917, Æthelflæda stormed into Deoraby at the head of her troops. A fierce and bloody battle ensued during which Æthelflæda lost four of her thanes (hereditary nobles) and hundreds of soldiers. The Danes fared even worse, and victory was declared when Æthelflæda's hand touched the remains of St Alkmund. The source for Æthelflæda's success is the *Anglo-Saxon Chronicle*. The *Chronicle* makes no reference to the heads of slaughtered Danes being used as footballs; but this did not deter the *Manchester Courier* from suggesting that such post-battle celebrations were the origins of Shrovetide football in Derby:

> The legend of the older inhabitants is to the effect that, at the sack of the town, the heads of the slaughtered Danes were, according to the brutal warfare of those days, kicked about the streets by the conquerors: and that, in memory of this triumph, the great annual game of football was established. The incidents related in history strengthen the contention, and such an explanation would account for the extraordinary manner in which the whole town took sides, the fierce rivalry of the combatants originally based upon tribal hatred being handed down to two rival parishes.[32]

Another more likely possibility is that the Derby Game simply started up at some time in the late Tudor or early Stuart period, as an entertaining way of celebrating Shrovetide. The beginnings of the game must have been unknown to those alive in Hutton's youth, otherwise he would surely have mentioned it in his account. He had several relatives of over 70 years old, so it seems reasonable to infer that the game must at least predate 1650.

In 1839 *Penny Magazine* published an article on the 'Derby Foot-ball Play'. The introduction referred to recently published descriptions of the French game of *La Soule* as played in Brittany at Shrovetide. The article stated that the French game 'reminds us strongly of the Derby foot-ball play' which was peculiar to the town.[33] Indeed, the similarities are striking. Like the Derby Game, *La Soule* was usually played between two parishes and as at Derby, the aim was to bring the ball back to a goal in the home parish. It was played during a Christian holiday over a considerable distance rather than in a confined area. Ponds or posts were favoured locations for goals, as were sites of religious importance like churches. Whether, as some have suggested, the game of *La Soule* had any links with Celtic rituals of sun worship need not concern us. But it is interesting to speculate on whether it was the French, in the form of the Normans, who introduced the game to Derby.

Following the Norman Conquest, the Normans had a strong influence over life in Derby for around 200 years. Control over local affairs passed to a Norman elite, safely protected in their castles and backed by formidable military power. At the time of the conquest in 1066, Derby, which had been a larger and more prosperous town than neighbouring Nottingham, went into immediate decline. By the time of the *Domesday Book* in 1086 it had fewer mills and 103 dwellings lay empty – some probably the forfeit of any Saxons who had fought for King Harold at Hastings – and the number of burgesses had declined from 243 to 140. It was well into the 12th century before prospects began to improve, even though it was still Norman families, like the De Ferrers, Curzons and Touchets, who controlled revenues, property and religious life. This much is true of many towns, but there are good reasons, or at least remarkable coincidences, to suggest that there is a link between the Normans and Derby Shrovetide Football.

In those days, religion was an inseparable part of everyday life. Most people had no doubt at all that Heaven and Hell were very real places and that what you thought, did and said would determine your final destination. People used religion to explain everyday events. A broken arm or a poor harvest was a punishment from God. The very purpose of life was to prepare for the afterlife by avoiding sin, carrying out good works, taking part in the sacraments, obeying the teachings of the church, and contributing goods or services to support church and monastery. The year's progress was measured out by the familiar milestones of important Christian events: Shrove Tuesday and Ash Wednesday, Lent, Easter, Ascension Day, Pentecost, All Saints' Day, Christmas. In addition, there would be special days to mark locally revered saints, whose names gave local identity to churches and religious houses. It is highly unlikely that any annual event would take place on a holy day during Norman times without the clear support of religious leaders.

The most important buildings in any town were the churches. They functioned more like community centres in those days, with people using them as meeting places to catch up on news and exchange gossip. The other important buildings were the religious houses, such as convents or monasteries. Monks and nuns provided services which today are part of the welfare state, such as rudimentary medical care, hospitality for travellers, even an element of schooling for children. The Normans were enthusiastic about Christianity. This is hardly surprising since they believed that any person who helped to fund churches, monasteries and nunneries would receive greater clemency when it came to the Day of Judgement. Accordingly, a lot of their wealth was pumped into new religious establishments as well as into church-building.

When the Norman survey of 1086 was carried out, to inform the *Domesday Book*, there were no monasteries at all in Derbyshire. During the 12th and early 13th centuries, the Normans established five new religious houses in Derby which survived in one form or another until the dissolution around 1540. The most interesting establishments in terms of tracing the origins of the Derby Game are the three religious houses that were established between 1140 and 1170. In 1140, the Church of St James was given by its patron to Cluniac monks and turned into a small priory. The Cluniacs enjoyed considerable support across England in early Norman times, but gradually came to be viewed with a certain suspicion because of the high degree of French control. Other monastic orders gained in favour. Somehow, the Cluniac Priory in Derby managed to survive until the dissolution of the monasteries under Henry VIII. The priory was located in the centre of town, on the corner of the Market Place and St James's Street, and a small hospital was added later. The location was cheek by jowl with Markeaton Brook. In fact, the Cluniacs built St James's Bridge over the watercourse, which as we know was the dividing line between the parishes of St Peter's and All Saints'.

In 1160, the Priory of King's Mead was established to provide a nunnery. The prioress was usually a member of a distinguished county family, and the nunnery was also a popular place for noble families to send their daughters to be educated. The priory was dedicated to St Mary of the Meadows and presumably this name was chosen because it also occupied a position next to Markeaton Brook. As we know, the home goal of the All Saints' Shrovetide footballers was the waterwheel at Nun's Mill. It is very likely that the mill site formed part of the priory complex. By Victorian times, Nun's Mill was the sole remaining oatmeal mill in Derby. It was demolished late in the 19th century.

Around 1170, a hospital was built on the southern edge of town along Osmaston Road. The original purpose of this hospital, which was a royal foundation, was to care for people suffering from leprosy, a disfiguring and, at the time, incurable disease, thought to have been brought back from the Holy Land by Christian crusaders. The Norman influence is again evident in the naming of the hospital after St Leonard, a French hermit. While the exact location of the hospital is unclear, local historians believe that it was close to the 19th-century street named after it, Leonard Street. It would be difficult to find a site closer to Grove Street, the home goal of the St Peter's Shrovetide football players.

The game of *La Soule*, like Derby Shrovetide Football, has only three locational requirements; a starting point situated on the boundary between two contesting parishes or villages and two goals. So, we have a Cluniac Priory in the centre of town, next to Markeaton Brook and the dividing line between the two parishes of All Saints' and St Peter's. The priory was also very close to the Market Place, which was the starting point for the game in all written records. Then we have the All Saints' goal at Nun's Mill, which was part of the Benedictine Nunnery in King's Mead. Finally, we have the St Peter's goal at Grove Street, just off Osmaston Road, which was where St Leonard's Hospital could well have been located.

This is a striking set of coincidences. We also know that the game of *La Soule* was being played in northern France in the 13th century, if not earlier. Could it be that the Norman-French, familiar with the game of *La Soule* in their homeland of northern France, established it in Derby? This possibility is boosted by the fact that the game of *La Soule* was not only tolerated by French nobility and clergy, but supported by them, with the clergy themselves sometimes throwing up the ball. In addition, the local Norman families of De Ferrers, Curzon and Touchet all hailed from the Calvados region of northern France where *La Soule* was a popular game (one ancient game played in the Cléville area of Calvados even pitted two villages separated by a river against each other, all for the prize of a sheep).

Connections elsewhere in Britain between religious sites and festival football are prolific. At Duns, for example, the church pulpit was the goal for the married men in their annual contest against the bachelors of the town. At Chester, the game began at the site of an ancient Saxon cross. So, it is possible that the claims of the Georgians and Victorians, that the Derby Game had been played for many centuries, may not have been so wide of the mark. At the very least, the close match between the location of religious houses and the Shrovetide goals strongly suggests a date before the dissolution of such institutions in 1540.

The choice of goals also suggests that a medieval origin to the Derby Game is possible. Our knowledge of the game derives solely from reports made in late Georgian and Victorian times. These reports show that the St Peter's goal was sited just off Osmaston Road, a road heading due south of the town. The goal was referred to either as a gate to a nursery ground on Grove Street, or the Gallows Baulk; indeed, the nursery ground might well have been the former site of the gallows. As played in the 19th century, the game requires the All Saints' players to jump into the bracingly cold water at the Nun's Mill pond in order to score, but the Peterites do not have to get wet to score at their goal. On first consideration this may seem unfair, but while would-be scorers must get wet, so must the defenders. Other old mob football games, like those at Kirkwall and Workington, each have one wet and one dry goal.

A clue as to the underlying reasons comes from the Shrovetide game that used to be played at Scone. According to the *Statistical Account of Scotland* published around 1795, this game pitted married men against bachelors. The aim of the bachelors was to *drown* the ball at a deep place in the river, whereas the married men aimed to *hang* the ball up on a moor. Both locations for the Scone goals were on the boundaries of the town; in fact the Scottish word 'doul' has a double meaning embracing both a 'limit' and a 'goal'.

In Derby, the goal off Osmaston Road was next to a town boundary which was first established in the 13th century and was unchanged for over 700 years, while the Nun's Mill area may have been viewed as the town's western limit during the late 12th and 13th centuries. Alternatively, of course, the two goals may simply have been chosen because they were roughly the same distance from the starting point of the game.

There is another feature of the Derby Game which also suggests an origin in a deeply religious age, and that is the custom of 'dusting'. This practice will be described in more detail in a later chapter, but briefly there are several reports from Georgian and Victorian accounts of boys throwing dust or soot over spectators or passers-by, in the tense hours before the throwing up of the ball. Again, it may be more than a coincidence that Ash Wednesday was a day when priests would sprinkle their parishioners with ashes. The ashes were produced on Shrove Tuesday by burning the palm leaves used in the previous year's Palm Sunday celebrations. The ritual was to remind everyone of the Bible's words in Genesis that man is made from dust and to dust shall return. Those who felt they had committed great sins would dress in sackcloth and present themselves before the clergy to be shriven of their sins. While by the 19th century, the practice of dusting before Derby Shrovetide Football was tremendous fun for the throwers and highly anti-social for the victims, it may have had its origins in a religious observance and be another indication of the medieval roots of the game.

Despite these various tantalising clues, there is no way of knowing when the Derby Game started up, even if it can be said with some degree of confidence that it was after 1170 and the building of St Leonard's Hospital, and before 1540 when the dissolution of the monasteries took place. If the Derby Game did begin because a Norman noble, monk or prioress transplanted the game of *La Soule* into Derby, then a date in the 12th or early 13th century seems the most probable. Indeed, there is no need to go far from Derby to find another time-honoured custom which had its roots in the Norman era and the support of both nobility and clergy.

Tutbury is a small town about ten miles from the centre of Derby, located on the Staffordshire side of the River Dove. Soon after the Norman invasion, a castle was built on the side of the river and became a major medieval fortress. Next to the church was a priory. Up until the dissolution of the monasteries, the priory played a key part in the Tutbury bull-running, which took place in August, as part of festivities to commemorate the Feast of the Assumption. The feast formed part of the annual Court of Minstrels, a ceremony which brought together travelling musicians from nearby counties. One of the obligations on the prior was to provide a bull to the town at the Feast of the Assumption. The minstrels would chase the bull through the town and could claim the animal if they could catch it. To lessen the danger of a charging bull, the tips of the bull's horns would be cut off. To make catching the bull more difficult, it would be smeared all over with soap or grease, and its ears and tail would be cut off. Finally, to make sure that it was in a vile temper, pepper was thrown up its nostrils. After a successful chase, the captured bull was then baited to death with dogs and served as part of the feast, although in later years it may have been fed and given to the poor at Christmas.

Over time the bull-running event developed into a competition between the residents of Staffordshire and Derbyshire, who competed to catch the bull within their own counties. After the dissolution of the monasteries, the Duke of Devonshire took over the responsibility for providing a bull, but the fifth duke finally brought an end to the custom in 1778. Some historians believe that the bull run began when John of Gaunt established a court of minstrels at Tutbury in 1381. Others believe that John of Gaunt had little to do with it, as it was the prior who from 1230 onwards was obliged to provide the food to celebrate the Feast of the Assumption. There appears to be no dispute though, that the custom had medieval origins. The Tutbury bull run shows how it is possible for a custom, like Shrovetide football, to be established in medieval times and to persist for several centuries.

The Shrovetide holiday included Shrove Tuesday and Ash Wednesday. Shrove Tuesday was a traditional feast day before the start of Lent on Ash Wednesday. In medieval times, many people, either through religious observance or the lack of anything else to eat, would have to endure a limited diet for the next 40 days. So Shrove Tuesday was a day to enjoy and indulge. By Victorian times, the Shrovetide holiday was a welcome opportunity for a bit of fun and frivolity, after getting through the worst days of the British winter. It provided a rare break from the drudgery imposed by six-day working weeks and the factory clock. Pancake-making, ostensibly to use up 'rich' foodstuffs, was widespread. Originally church bells were rung on Shrove Tuesday to remind parishioners to 'shrive' or confess their sins before Lent. But from at least the 16th century onwards, the bells were rung to signal the start of pancake making. Eleven o'clock in the morning (or perhaps 12 noon in the case of Derby) seems to have been the appointed time for ringing the bell, requiring apprentices to stop working and for pancake-making to begin. Some towns and villages held pancake races – the race at Olney in Buckinghamshire, for example, can trace its roots back to 1445.

But Shrovetide was also an excuse for more offensive pastimes than tossing pancakes. In addition to bull baiting and cock fighting, one of the cruel 'sports' was cock throwing. After tying a rooster to a post, participants took it in turns to throw sticks at the bird, until it fell over or died. This 'sport' was as ubiquitous a Shrovetide activity as making pancakes. The rules varied from place to place. In some areas the winner would be the thrower who could land a hit which knocked the cock down, and who could then run and pick it up before it came to its senses. Apparently, this activity was a popular pastime among children, as well as apprentices. On 5 March 1660, during the Puritan period, the bellman of Bristol walked through the streets of the city proclaiming that cock throwing and dog tossing had been banned. He was attacked by a group of rowdy apprentices and the next day, which was Shrove Tuesday, they squailed a goose and tossed cats and dogs into the air outside the Mayor's Mansion House. To squail a goose was to throw sticks at it, the sticks being weighted with lead at one end. The object was to maim the bird rather than to kill it, in order that the 'game' could last as long as possible. The Puritan ban, in any event, was a temporary reprieve for the birds, and it was not until the middle of the 18th century that authorities started to take action to stop or prevent this particular Shrove Tuesday tradition.

Bull baiting was a popular activity throughout the country and almost every town had its bull ring – a small metal hoop set into a stone. Baiting would regularly take place at Shrovetide, although it was often a feature of other holidays as well as market days and fairs. The poor beast would be tied to the fixed ring with a collar and rope and tormented by ferocious dogs. To the delight of many spectators the bulls would try to throw the dogs into the air with their horns. A skilled and experienced dog would creep in low to the ground and try and attach its jaws to the bull's nose. The Old English Bulldog, which is now extinct, was bred especially for this purpose. It was widely believed that baiting helped to tenderise the bull's beef. Indeed, Chesterfield used to have a bylaw which required every butcher in the Shambles who killed a bull, to bait the animal in the adjacent Market Place before they slaughtered the creature. Butchers who defied this regulation risked a fine of 3s 4d.

Thankfully, in the 19th century public opinion turned against sports like cock fighting, cock throwing and bull baiting. In 1822, a law was passed to prevent the cruel treatment of cattle and became one of the first pieces of legislation for animal welfare in the world. In 1835, the Protection of Animals Act made bull, bear and badger baiting, as well as cock fighting and dog fighting illegal. Ashbourne, apparently, was one of the last places in England where bull baiting took place. As society became more urbanised, the pressure to sweep away seemingly crude rural recreations intensified. However, playing at football was often lumped in with 'recreations' like bull baiting and cock throwing, as a barbarous sport that had long been indulged, but which now needed to be abolished.

With the demise of cock throwing and bull baiting, the focus on the rights and wrongs of the remaining games of festival football intensified. Unlike the cruel sports it was sometimes associated with, Shrovetide football was linked with community identity and with shared memories of what grandfathers, fathers, friends and relatives had achieved through their own strength, wit and bravery. At a time when two or three generations of a family would often live in the same parish, and often in the same street, for their entire lives, the Derby Game engendered tribal affiliation, as this rhyme recalled by an 'Old Derbeian' showed:

> Four and twenty Peter's lads went to kill a bull,
> The weakest one amongst them split him down the skull,
> Four and twenty All Saints men went to kill a snail,
> The strongest one amongst them dare not touch its tail.[34]

But the mood of modernising reform in the 19th century was a powerful one, augmented by influential economic forces. In the face of these forces, the anguish of those who wished to protect something merely because it was an ancient and time-honoured custom, counted for very little.

4

Legends of the Game

DERBY SHROVETIDE Football grew to be a major event. Thousands of people would get involved either as players, supporters or spectators. Many businesses had to close down for a day or two, and people of all ages must have looked forward to two days' holiday, even if nothing else about the event appealed to them. For a long time, none of this meant that such an event would get a mention in the local press. Apart from a few exceptions, newspaper editors rarely deemed such a lowbrow event to be newsworthy, unless there was an attempt to ban it, or if there was a fatality. Otherwise, the game took place each year without any report of it in the columns of the local newspapers; not even a short note of which side had scored the winning goal, or how long the game lasted, let alone any written recognition of the goalscorer whose name would be known throughout the town.

The class-conscious local papers were more likely to describe the meanderings of a hare as it was pursued by a pack of hounds than they were to cover an event which brought the town to a standstill every year. The *Derby Mercury* finally got round to describing a game in 1827, and did a good job of it, yet did not see any need to give accounts of future games, save those taking place in opposition to an official ban. National publications such as *Sporting Magazine* and *Penny Magazine* included correspondence describing the general characteristics

4

and nature of the Derby Game in articles in 1830 and 1839 respectively. But there was no regular reporting of each game, and very few of the thousands of those who took part in such games saw fit, or were able, to leave a written record of their endeavours. Even so, from the various reports and reminiscences of observers, we can glimpse the people who played the game and identify some of those who became local legends.

Shrovetide was traditionally an apprentice's holiday and high-spirited young men formed the core of each side, whether All Saints' or St Peter's. Shrovetide football of a very similar nature to the Derby Game is still played at Ashbourne, where strength, fitness and a degree of youthful recklessness are required qualities for those who want to be in the thick of it. Contemporary reports show that the Derby Game was mostly, but not exclusively, a young man's sport, 'The players are young men from 18 to 30 and upwards, married as well as single, and many veterans who retain a relish for the sport are occasionally seen in the very heart of the conflict.'[35] Hutton, writing about the game from his childhood memories of the 1730s, said it was 'the delight of the lower ranks'.[36] But a letter writer to *Sporting Magazine* contended that most of the players were tradesmen, shopkeepers and mechanics, 'The morning is spent in busy preparation for the impending conflict; every apprentice claims his holiday; every factory is closed; and by the hour the pancakes are frying nearly every shop is shut, and business is generally suspended for the day.'[37]

The people who were right at the bottom of Georgian and Victorian society are likely to have been too ill or infirm to consider that plunging into a freezing river was a good way of spending the afternoon and evening. It is also clear that the footballers were not just mobs of young apprentices. Tracing the background of those who were brought before the magistrates following the games in 1845 and 1846, shows that local tradesmen such as tailors, drapers, and publicans were in the thick of the action. If these records are any guide, the key participants appear to be young or middle-aged men, working in trade, with a local connection to either St Peter's or to All Saints'. This is borne out by the recollections of Benjamin Fearn, a local policeman during the game's last years, 'The game was not confined to any class, and many a sturdy trader would leave his counter and sally out with his sons to strengthen the parish of which he was an adherent.'[38]

Newspaper reports conveyed the electric sense of occasion, of a town that shut up shops, turned away customers and closed down factories, consumed by an 'all-engrossing eagerness' to see the game.[39] The inhabitants of Derby divided into two camps, each side bound together irrespective of class and status by a common cause. People who would not normally have spent more than a moment or two in each other's company suddenly became ardent friends. Prominent people in the town would be asked to contribute towards refreshments, often alcoholic, although oranges seemed to have been in abundant supply in later years but were often just used as missiles. Some employers might even reward their workers if they had done well for their side. Tunchy Shelton, a player who once worked in William Taylor's silk mill, said that he was given a new suit for his efforts for St Peter's.

Indeed, the middle and upper classes could be very active and partisan supporters. Those of higher social status attempted to stand on the edges of the main throng at the beginning of the game. However, as the game got under way, some were taken over by their zeal and enthusiasm until they found themselves in the heart of the action. *Penny Magazine* reported:

> We have indeed heard of townsmen of high standing
> and well-deserved reputation losing their spectacles,
> unused to such hard labour, in the cause; and men who

would at any other time be ashamed to appear except in
nicest dress, may, after two o'clock on Shrove-Tuesday,
be seen without a hat, with half a coat, and yet without
a blush.[40]

In addition, the game had its supporters in the upper
echelons. According to Glover, the players were encouraged
by respectable persons who took a surprising interest in the
game and urged on one party or another, and either funded
or handed out refreshments. Then, as now, betting was an
inevitable by-product of a sporting occasion. Because of this,
or perhaps due to tribal passion, some of the more opulent
inhabitants may have hired men to play on their side. A Mr
Haden, possibly a magistrate in the 1840s, used to pay to have
the ball gilded if his parish, All Saints', should win.

One of the most ardent supporters of the game was Joseph
Strutt, a major figure in Derby life in the late Georgian and
early Victorian period. Joseph Strutt's role in extending the
life of the Shrovetide game will be described later, but he was
well known to be a staunch Peterite. His impressive house
in the centre of town fell just within the parish boundary,
uncomfortably close to the flood-prone Markeaton Brook,
and a few yards from the boundary with All Saints'. He is also
reputed to have played the game. Indeed, legend has it that he
commissioned a local tailor called Hunt to fashion a buckskin
suit so he could take part without the risk of being 'denuded
of his garments'.[41]

Involvement in the proceedings was not confined to men.
Women were highly vociferous in their support, keen to help
the injured or exhausted, and willing to offer items of clothing
to those who emerged shirtless and shivering from brook or
river. Tunchy Shelton said women would wade knee-deep into
the osier beds, a comment which suggests they also played an
active part in the game. A woman seems to have been key to

thwarting the ban on the game in 1797. The town authorities were keen to prevent the Shrovetide game from starting. They stationed lines of special constables to stop the ball from being taken into the Market Place. A local nut seller, called Mother Hope, was reputed to have solved this problem by smuggling the ball in underneath her skirt. Once inside the square, she had thrown the ball to the crowd and, once under way, there was nothing the authorities could do to bring the game to a halt. There are several variants on this story. According to *Sporting Magazine*, 'an old woman of gigantic stature' with hoops underneath her skirts marched into the middle of the throng. As she made a curtsey, the ball dropped from underneath her petticoats, and the giantess retired, shouting triumphantly 'All Saints' for ever'.[42]

One of the attractions of the game, especially for those from the so-called lower ranks, was the opportunity to become a local legend. The most straightforward way of achieving celebrity status was to goal the ball. A report on the 1827 game remarked:

> Having touched with the Ball the appointed Gate Post, the champion who held the ball was immediately hoisted on the necks of his exulting companions and borne in triumph through St Peter's Parish, happier than many a bold stained conqueror who has been hailed by the plaudits of an admiring multitude.[43]

Consequently, the game attracted characters keen to make a name for themselves either by scoring a goal or by actions which went beyond the ordinary.

John Etches played the game in his youth and resumed playing again after serving in Nelson's navy, despite losing an arm in a naval battle against the French at the Battle of the Saintes in 1782. He became notorious for the zeal and energy which he displayed in the football contest and it is said that he hit people with his stump in self-defence. In 1791, he became one of Derby's first nine converts to the Baptist movement, with the converts being immersed into the River Derwent – a practice which gave the Baptists the nickname of 'Dippers'. The baptism ceremony held near to the riverside attracted onlookers, who saw that 'John was attired in his sailor's dress: Just as he was going into the water a former foot-ball companion called out from a neighbouring tree, "John, where's the foot-ball now?"[44] Etches became a committed Baptist and helped fund Derby's Brook Street Baptist Church where his memorial was incorporated into the north wall.

The legendary status of becoming a local football hero is evident from an article by Thomas Broughton published in the *Derby Mercury* in 1888, 42 years after the 'last game' of 1846. Broughton named Clem Keys as 'probably the best player, fighter and swimmer on the All Saints Side'; the Yeomans brothers who were adept at disappearing with the ball into a sewer in the Morledge and reappearing with it in the River Derwent; as well as the likes of Gibson from Littleover and big Tunchy Shelton who would lead the hardcore of the St Peter's players into the Market Place for the throwing up of the ball.[45] Others mentioned include the All Saints' players Roberts the chimney sweep and his man Jarvo, Sam Marshall and Fred Walkerdine. On the St Peter's side, players mentioned include Hinckly, Candy Hudson and another chimney sweep by the name of Fantom.

'Tunchy Shelton' was the nickname of William Williamson, a notorious Peterite in the latter years of the game. Williamson was baptised in St Peter's Church in 1812. His father had been baptised there in 1780 and married there in 1804. Three generations of Williamsons lived in close quarters in Bag Lane, a stone's throw from the church itself. His father had played the game and was an avid Peterite. Tunchy himself described being a Peterite as like belonging to a caste, and caste, for him at least, came before religion. He claimed, when interviewed in 1885, that he 'would have gladly died rather than give up St Peter's and so would many another and some have died for it'.[46]

During his lifetime, William Williamson certainly achieved such a level of local fame that everyone in Derby seems to have known who Tunchy Shelton was. This might have had something to do with his prodigious size. He was described as big of chest, strong of arm, utterly fearless and a 'ranting, roaring, tearing, swearing, leathering swash of a Derby man'.[47] His reputation must have spread beyond his native town, as William Perry, a bareknuckle boxer known as the Tipton Slasher, issued the following invitation in a national sports newspaper in 1839:

> William Perry, the Tipton Slasher, begs to inform Tunchy Shelton of Derby that he will pay his expenses of coming over the Three Horse-shoes, Tipton, to make the match. The fight to come off in six weeks from this time, or he will take his expenses of going to Derby.[48]

However, Tunchy's notoriety did not rest solely on his exploits during the Derby Game. In 1831, at the age of 19 he appeared before the Derby magistrates at the Easter Sessions, having been indicted with five other men for a riot and assault on two nightwatchmen. The two watchmen had been trying to suppress a fight in the Morledge. In the judgement of the Grand Jury, Williamson was clearly the chief troublemaker, so they let the other men off and sent Tunchy to prison for 14 days.

Six years later Williamson was in trouble again, this time appearing at the Derbyshire Summer Assizes. Joseph Clerk had been killed during an arranged prize fight between himself and Edward Dorrington. The fight took place in Littleover, then a small village or township to the west of Derby. Clerk had received such a battering that he could hardly stand. Williamson, though, had propped Clerk up and urged the heavily built Dorrington to hit him, with fatal consequences for Clerk. After hearing and reading about the case, Mr Justice Park was full of contempt for Williamson, who he felt had played a worse role in the incident than Dorrington. He was particularly dismayed that a young man's life had been lost – 'sent in an unprepared state to meet his maker' – for the sake of a few guineas. In his judgement:

> The battle fought was not occasioned by any sudden quarrel, but was fought for a sum of money, deliberately and not for some sudden and violent passion. When Clerk, the man killed, was too weak to fight, the other prisoner, Williamson, held him up, and occasioned Dorrington to strike the blow that occasioned his death.[49]

He sentenced Williamson, who had pleaded guilty, to 12 months' imprisonment and hard labour.

Undeterred by a year's confinement, Tunchy returned to the cause in the final years of the game, often leading the Peterites, with the ball under his arm, from a Morledge pub into the crowded and expectant Market Place. He claimed in an interview that all Derby lads and lasses were either All Saints' or St Peter's and, in his opinion, 'women were the worst of all'.[50] In his first game as a young lad, All Saints' had got the ball into Markeaton Brook but were beginning to tire, so Tunchy jumped in and managed to get hold of the ball. He then had a rough time of it but proved himself to be a difficult opponent. Eventually All Saints' managed to get the ball off him, by which time he had lost most of his clothes. From then on, Tunchy was hooked, always happy to put himself at the heart of the action and to use fists or head to move opponents out of the way.

One of his most vivid memories was fighting for the ball with five or six All Saints' men in the river, as hundreds of men and women lined the banks. Exhausted, he drifted downriver and hauled himself out, only to come face to face with Sir Henry Wilmot, the owner of Chaddesden Hall. Despite not having a stitch on, he managed to persuade Sir Henry to give him half a crown, which Tunchy put in his mouth as he swam back across the river. Emerging out on to the western bank, a woman lent him her flannel petticoat which he wrapped around himself. Then he saw Dick Gibson and asked him if he could borrow his smock. Unwisely Gibson refused, so Tunchy 'gave him one in the mouth'.[51] He then encountered a man who – probably fearing the same treatment as Gibson – offered him his trousers. Tunchy ripped them apart, put his head through the crotch and his arms through the legs and made his way to the Navigation Inn. In the pub, Tunchy recuperated by smoking a pipe and drinking several brandies paid for by a gentleman. Another man provided a suit of clothes which he put on in a stable. Suitably clothed and refreshed, Tunchy rejoined the fray and ended an eventful day by goaling the ball. While some may consider Williamson's tale to be far-fetched, it chimes with other accounts of the near-nakedness of many of the players.

According to Williamson, goalscorers were normally allowed to keep the ball after the game unless someone else had played particularly well and shown themselves to be a good 'water dog'. He claimed to be the holder of four or five balls. His uncompromising style is evident in his description of how he crawled with the ball, and head-butted his way through the opposition, as he progressed down a brook leading to the River Derwent. His efforts were not rewarded on that occasion as All Saints' grabbed the ball and made off with it from the river's eastern bank. They goaled it later. On another occasion he was lying exhausted downriver with a fellow player called Joe Brownsward. Joe's throat was so dry that he feared he was going to die and he begged Tunchy to spit into his mouth. Tunchy obliged, and Joe said, 'God bless you, Bill.'[52] Less endearing was the beating he dished out to a young man who accused him of turning his coat and becoming an All Saints' man – a heinous accusation.

Even though Tunchy was clearly a brute of a man who was in his element in the middle of a brawl, he displayed an awareness of the need to temper his actions with a concern for others. He once saw a respectable young man knocked down as the play swept down London Road. He went over, put his foot on the man and 'kept the rush off him', before propping him up against a wall.[53] He also received a lifelong injury when trying to rescue a young girl who was in danger of being crushed in Tenant Street. While he was trying to lift the girl over a wall, he was knocked down and his ribs were broken. A doctor strapped him up, but unfortunately the ribs never knitted back correctly.

As Tunchy Shelton demonstrated, total commitment to the cause was a prerequisite for those intent on getting to the heart of the play. For All Saints' to score a goal, they had to get the ball to the waterwheel at Nun's Mill. This meant getting into the mill dam in water which was shoulder deep. A letter writer using the pen name 'Pilarius' recalled, 'In this depth of water I have often observed two or three hundred of the parties stoutly contending for the palm of victory (most of them stripped of course) and not infrequently amidst floating masses of ice.'[54] The intensity of the passions which were evoked by the game clearly shocked many visitors. Those who had a deep familiarity with the game and the local area knew that for some it was more important than life or death. According to

'Pilarius', 'When speaking of water dogs or spaniels, I mean, the regular old-standing out-and-out veterans (of whom there are scores on either side) who, I believe, would rather lose their lives in the cause than suffer defeat.'[55]

One legend was an old-timer by the name of Tom Pym, who spotted the ball drifting along unattended by any players in the River Derwent. After venting his anger at what he considered to be the cowardice of his All Saints' side, he decided that he would plunge into the water to show how things should be done. Luckily for Tom, who was over 80 years old at the time, rescuers were able to get him out before he became another fatality.

So for centuries the Derby Game was an indelible part of local culture, a game pursued or supported with a passion that was felt to be distinctive to Derbeians, which amazed visitors and caught the eye of the national press. One anecdote, frequently retold, tells of two settlers meeting in the backwoods of America and recalling the England that they have left behind. One of the men says that he hails from Derby. His companion remarks, 'Oi don't think thee looks like a Darby mon, but I'll troy thee … All Saints' for ever!' 'St Peter's for ever!' was the instant reply.[56] Given this proof of identity, the two men shake hands united by their common heritage.

5

Mayhem and Misrule

IN FEBRUARY 1834, *The Pioneer*, a radical magazine aimed at encouraging national support for the embryonic union movement, lamented the behaviour exhibited in the Derby Shrovetide Football, 'Regardless of every thing but success in this silly exploit, different parties undergo the most astonishing inflictions; half-drowned, crushed, kicked, bruised, and, in some instances, downright killed, still the combat rages: no quarter – no mercy – nothing but barbarous recklessness and supreme folly.'[57]

Virtually all the eyewitness accounts of 'Derby Ball-Playing' stress its violent nature. A Frenchman observing the contest was reported to have remarked, 'If Englishmen called this playing, it would be impossible to say what they would call fighting.'[58] In its latter years the game was all about possession of the ball. Usually, the only way in which the ball was going to be given up by a player was if it was ripped away from them. Kicking or throwing the ball would only be a good tactic if a player was about to be engulfed or carried away by the opposing side. As Glover observed:

> The struggle to obtain the ball … is then violent, and the motion of this human tide heaving to and fro, without the least regard to the consequences, is tremendous. Broken shins, broken heads, torn coats and

lost hats, are among the minor accidents of this fearful contest, and it frequently happens that persons fall in consequence of the intensity of the pressure, fainting and bleeding beneath the feet of the surrounding mob.[59]

Anyone who witnessed the thousands of people crammed into Derby Market Place on a Shrove Tuesday afternoon never forgot the sight of the spectators hanging out of every window, the children standing or sitting on roofs and walls, the 'war cries' of each side, the growing excitement as the Town Hall clock got nearer and nearer to two o'clock. The heart-pumping, adrenalin-fuelled, no-holds-barred start to the game, following the initial throwing up of the ball, left observers astonished, as the letter from 'Pilarius' to *Sporting Magazine* describes:

> O ye Gods, what a riot! – what pulling, hauling, tearing, bawling! The ball is instantly surrounded by the "gods of war", who shortly form one solid and impenetrable mass of living clay – as closely packed together as a swarm of bees or a barrel of Yarmouth herrings – with arms erect, eyes starting out from their sockets, and mouths extended gasping for breath – just like so many madmen escaped from an Asylum.[60]

The spectacle of the Market Place at the start of the game was something that left an indelible memory. Sixty-three years after the final game, Alfred Wallis, former editor of the *Derby Mercury*, recalled that, 'For my own part, I have seen riots, involving destruction of property, and violent demonstrations against unpopular individuals, even leading to bloodshed, but nothing within my recollection has impressed me so much with its prodigious power of a contending crowd, as the first rush for the Derby football.'[61]

While the game was violent, several observers commented on how amicable much of the rivalry was. According to 'Pilarius', 'It is no unusual thing to see or hear of twenty or thirty fights in the course of the afternoon, but after this, good will and harmony are re-established, and a fresh debtor and creditor account opened for another year.'[62] The amicability was probably a result of the fact that many of the main participants, having homes or occupations in the town centre, would have been well known to each other. Also, players were united by their love for the game and a tradition which formed a central part of their identity. The game had its own unwritten code of conduct which curtailed its worst excesses. Without such a code, serious problems would quickly arise. This is shown by an incident in a game near Wakefield in 1771 when the gentlemen of Sharlston challenged their counterparts in Crofton to a one-off match for a 40-guinea wager. After the scoring of the first goal, a second ball was thrown up and two competitors met with such violence that one suffered a dislocated shoulder while the other got a broken leg. A mob then rushed into the fray, but the game had to be abandoned after an eight-year-old boy was trampled to death.

In Derby, several accounts convey how a spirit of friendliness co-existed with almost reckless determination. Oranges would be passed to those rendered desperately thirsty, care taken not to trample over fallen players, and supporters were always ready to assist the injured and infirm. Nevertheless, the game would have given an excellent opportunity for anyone with more malicious intent towards his adversaries. 'Pilarius' claimed that for the 'canaille' or common people of Derby, Shrove Tuesday was a day of reckoning: 'On this stormy day all broils and tumults, all undecided battles, and all old grudges, are sure to be brought to account and settled.'[63]

Anyone who has been in the middle of a crushing, pushing crowd will know the dangers and helplessness that come from being unable to extricate yourself from the melee. Despite the unwritten codes of care and support that were part and parcel of the Derby Game, it is a wonder that there were not a series of major tragedies instead of the black eyes, bloody noses and broken shins that are mentioned in accounts. Doctors appear to have been on hand to deal with broken bones or those knocked unconscious. In 1835 a player with a dislocated shoulder had a very painful time as helpers manipulated the ball of the shoulder back into its socket. Apparently, the injured man resumed playing. But the toll taken by the game on the health of those playing it will never be known. Physical injuries, like the broken leg suffered by 20-year-old William Wigley in the 1825 game would be immediately apparent, but the effects of plunging into freezing and possibly polluted water, would not show themselves for several days or even months. As 'Pilarius' commented, 'Only one life has been forfeited by accident for many years, though I am aware of several premature deaths by bathing at so unseasonable a time.'[64]

Indeed, there was a matter-of-fact acceptance among those who had long familiarity with the annual event that it often led to deaths in the weeks following the game. If you came away from being in the very middle of the Market Place throng without incurring a cracked rib, a broken finger or a black eye, then you could count yourself very fortunate indeed. According to the memories of a 'silver haired grandma', 'Many of the "players" suffered serious injuries. The bones of some were broken, and others ruined their health by plunging in a heated state into the ice cold waters of the river, or the brook, where the ball was often kicked or fought for.'[65]

Fist fights were commonplace but were usually less hazardous to long-term health than being trampled underfoot, submerged in freezing water or scrabbling about in sewers and drains. If the play went into the river or a brook, then 'ducking' became part of the game. Opponents were grabbed and held underwater. This could help in persuading an adversary to release the ball, or simply thinned out the numbers attempting to play. It was little wonder, therefore, that Thomas Broughton recalled players so exhausted or smothered that they had to be dragged out of the mud and revived. He also described how, 'Each night the winning side would go round the principal streets collecting money, and with this would finish the day, and often next morning the result would be torn clothes, a severe cold, a black eye and a splitting headache.'[66]

Nevertheless, despite the claims of many deaths, the records show only one directly verifiable fatality on a Shrove Tuesday. In 1796, play had taken the ball down to The Holmes, an area which formed a large, island-like piece of land surrounded by the River Derwent on one side and an offshoot stream on the other. Normally it was a popular place in Georgian times for taking an evening stroll in pleasant semi-rural surroundings, but on Shrove Tuesday it was a location where many bitter and critical battles were fought. The All Saints' side needed to get hold of the ball at The Holmes, before the Peterites advanced too far south. If the Saints could get it on to the east bank of the Derwent, they could then take the ball north and recross the river by St Mary's Bridge. Apart from a timber causeway being built to provide a towpath for the new Derby Canal, the bridge was the only place to cross the river in 1796. Once across the bridge, All Saints' would be in their own patch heading towards their goal in Nun's Street. But St Peter's knew that if their side got downriver past The Holmes, they could land the ball near Castle Fields, a large area of open land, where there was plenty of space to run south-westwards up towards their goal off Osmaston Road.

In the 1796 game, the players were diving into the River Derwent close to a boathouse – probably where a makeshift ferry boat was kept – and All Saints' were trying to drag the ball over to the eastern bank. John Snape (or Sneap, in some sources) was one of those in the water in the middle of the contest. He did not make it to either bank. Whether he was knocked out or simply succumbed to exhaustion is not known, and his body was recovered the following day. The shock of this fatality led to one of the many attempts made to stop the games from taking place.

The mayhem was not confined just to the contest itself. The holiday of Shrove Tuesday began at noon when the shops shut up for the day, so the local lads and mischief-makers had an hour or two to amuse themselves before the big event at two o'clock. One of the traditions of the occasion was for the 'rougher elements' to throw missiles at each other, before targeting strangers and the well-dressed. This practice was known as 'dusting'. The missiles could be bags of soot, ashes, or bags of colour from the dye works, and one of the most favoured weapons seems to have been wet cloths.

The impact of these dusting incidents must sometimes have been quite shocking, as I know from my own observation. Every Boxing Day morning, a raft race is held on the River Derwent starting at Matlock. The aim of the event, which began in the 1960s, is to raise funds for the Royal National Lifeboat Institute. Various homemade rafts, lashed together out of cheap or discarded materials, are manned by high-spirited crews, often sporting fancy dress. It has become something of a tradition for the crews to spray water at the onlookers crowded on the riverbanks, who in turn retaliate by throwing bags of flour or the occasional egg at the rafts. Often the flour bags get caught by a crew member and then it is the onlookers who become the target. Normally the mood is good-humoured, although it is wise to be wary of getting a soaking. However, on one occasion, I watched a man leap off one of the rafts and run up the bank, where he burst a large bag of flour over the head of a well-dressed young woman who was standing quietly watching the event. The man disappeared as quick as he had arrived, leaving the woman temporarily blinded and rigid with shock, her head and shoulders covered in a white shroud.

Alfred Wallis was editor of the *Derby Mercury* during the paper's Victorian heyday. In one of the published 'Reminiscences' of his youth, he remarked upon the special attention given to well-dressed spectators of the Derby Game by those armed with bags of coloured dyes. He pointed out that the practice of 'dusting' was not always confined to visitors or the wealthy. He recalled seeing an incident involving Jimmy Stevens in Sadler Gate, an ancient narrow street full at the time with inns, shops and a few remaining leather workers, leading to the Market Place. Stevens was standing on the doorstep of his toy shop as the players made their way down the street. He was seized by the dusters, who showered him in different dyes and 'converted him into a semblance of one of his own harlequin dolls'.[67] The astonished shopkeeper protested vociferously in high-pitched tones like those of Mr Punch. The mob debated the idea of taking him with them and giving him a wash under the Market Place pump. Thankfully, friendly hands managed to disperse his assailants and deliver him, 'more frightened than hurt', back into the care of his anxious wife.[68]

Walking or simply standing on the streets of central Derby during Shrovetide was a very hazardous thing to do for the unwary, especially, it seems, for innocent bystanders who for some reason were deliberately targeted by the mischief-makers engaged in the practice of 'dusting'. One such unwary visitor in 1815 wrote to the editor of the *Derby Mercury*:

> Sir, – I came into your town yesterday about one o'clock, and from the closed shop windows and the crowded streets, was led to imagine that some festival was about to be celebrated. Calling on a tradesman with whom I had business to transact, I soon learned from him that a great annual football match was about to commence,

... He invited me to accompany him to the market place, assuring me that I should enjoy a spectacle worth remembering ... I attended my conductor as closely as the jostling crowd would permit me. A sudden rush of people unhappily separated me from my friend, and while I was straining my eager eyes to recover sight of him, a filthy clout soaked in mud was most dextrously thrown into my face. I suppose my mouth was open as well as my eyes, for I was almost choked as well as blinded.[69]

Despite this experience, this generous visitor went on in his letter to describe his delight at the spectacle he witnessed, and the spirit and energy displayed. He noted the exultation of the spectators as shown on every face and wrote 'that women and children were at least as eager as the men'.[70]

Other observers of the event were not so delighted, including the 'silver haired grandma' previously mentioned. Continuing her recollections, she complained that:

On that day in Derby the shops were closed at noon. The streets near the Market Place were occupied by disorderly men with foul faces and fouler tongues, and unwashed boys, who hurled filthy rags and bad language at all who passed. No decent woman could go along without meeting insult.[71]

As soon as the pancake bell rang out, the holiday began, the lords of misrule were let loose, and a blind eye was turned to most forms of disorder. Indeed, even in the later years of the game, it seems that the very people, such as the local police, who should have been keeping order, were sometimes themselves participants in the game. Benjamin Fearn had a long and distinguished career in Derby Police, rising through the ranks to become an inspector. As a constable he was destined to play a starring role in the final game of 1846, when he would retain one of the balls used on that day and suffer the ignominy of being thrown over a hedge. But at heart he was a Peterite, as in 1885 the *Derby Mercury* revealed, 'So late as 1842 or 1843 Inspector Fearn might have been seen at the bottom of Friar-gate with two other officers in uniform, with "top hats", actively assisting St Peter's, while another "peeler" did his best for All Saints'.'[72]

Another apparent custom was to make football fireballs. These were made by twisting fibres of hemp or flax into a rope, reinforced with wire and woven together, to form the shape of a ball. Then the ball was covered with tar or soaked in petroleum, set alight and thrown into an unguarded street.

The passion for the game's outcome was not confined just to those taking part. Most of the spectators regarded themselves as either All Saints' or St Peter's. Tunchy Shelton claimed that if you were Derby-born, you had no choice but to be one or the other. A report in the *Derby Mercury* claimed that 'Corsican blood feuds could hardly be stronger' than the feeling that some of the supporters of each side showed for each other. Women seem to have been ardent supporters, as according to the same report:

> The mothers, wives and sisters of the combatants were at hand to stimulate them to every effort of strength, and were even heard to instruct their infants to call out "All Saints'" or "Peter's for ever". The Battle of the Boyne, though for a greater stake, was not more eagerly contested.[73]

Another account in the same newspaper described the struggle over the ball going on for hour after hour with, 'Women rushing about in a state of frantic excitement, urging on their husbands and brothers, bringing them stimulants and refreshments, lending them petticoats to cover up their naked limbs, and binding up their wounds.'[74]

Oranges were thrown from windows into the throng either as missiles or as refreshments for the two sides, while gentlemen 'swells' stood by armed with supplies of oranges, rum and brandy, urging the players on their side to 'go in and win'.[75] Despite their better intentions, however, well-dressed gents often found themselves unable to resist jumping into the fray only to re-emerge later without a jacket or hat.

The suspension of the normal rules of daily life did not end with the goaling of the ball. This achievement was followed by the scorer being hoisted on the shoulders of his fellows and paraded through the streets. This group then set off round the town soliciting money to reward their efforts, which was duly spent in public houses. According to the *Derbyshire Times*:

> The contest lasted till eight or nine at night. Sometimes it was later when the victors, bruised, blinded and bleeding, were carried on the shoulders of their companions in triumph through the excited streets, stopping at almost every door to beg money for drink. The givers were cheered, the refusers execrated.[76]

If the boyhood memories of the Rev. Thomas Mozley are any guide, the houses of the better-off, like his parents' house in the Wardwick, were a particular target, as he wrote in his memoirs, 'About nine or ten in the evening a loud cheering announced that the winning champion was at your door, on the shoulders of his paladins, claiming his guerdon.'[77] Mozley went on to remark, rather ruefully, that sometimes there were two such visits to claim this guerdon or reward.

The mayhem was not confined to Shrove Tuesday. Ash Wednesday, the day of the boys' game, could be even worse, especially for fighting. The previous day's sport left several people nursing a grudge against anyone who had injured or annoyed them during the game. Ash Wednesday presented a wonderful opportunity to right any perceived wrongs. On occasion, arrangements seem to have been made for individuals to settle their differences through boxing bouts. In addition, some men on each side took on the role of making sure that only boys played the Wednesday game. Anyone who was thought to be too old to play in the boys' game, would soon be turfed out in unceremonious fashion by self-appointed guardians, as Broughton recounted:

> The reason why there was more fighting on the Wednesday was because it was the lads' day, and men were not allowed to take part. To prevent this being done, a few of the fighting men on each side, would be on their opponent's side to see that no men played, and if they saw anyone with whiskers or beard, or anything like a man, he was dragged out. This interference often ended in a fight, and very likely the man who ought not to have played would get off with a black eye.[78]

By the mid-1840s, though, tolerance of the Shrovetide mayhem was wearing thin. A letter writer to the *Derby Mercury* in 1844 was indignant that even though he knew to keep well away from the Market Place on Shrove Tuesday, he still fell a hapless victim to the pranksters:

> I was passing down Wardwick before two o'clock on Tuesday, and was met by a band of ruffians who appeared to consider themselves outlaws. Each was prepared with a bag filled either with soot or charcoal dust, and on meeting any person who appeared

respectable they threw the bag and its contents in his face, or upon that part of his dress that suited them best.[79]

This victim was not an admirer of the game. He wanted police to protect peaceable inhabitants and he wanted 'to get rid of this annual nuisance called football'. The public mood was changing, as it was changing in the country at large. The Georgians' haphazard approach to law and order was being replaced by a vigorous Victorian appetite for organisation. After years of sporadic riots and rumbling social unrest, a greater value on law and order was beginning to make itself felt. The battle would now be over the very future of the game.

6

A Town in Turmoil

WHEN THE 19th century arrived, Derby had long been the largest town still playing host to the game of Shrovetide football. Following the arrival of the new century, the demise of old customs and sports like bull baiting and cock fighting speeded up as waves of modernisation rolled across the country. The Derby Game might well have followed them, but local events stayed the hand of those who saw such heritage as an encumbrance to an ambitious town. The events in question pitted mob against military, and worker against employer or government. A few people paid with their lives, while many became fearful of mob rule. Employers and employees learnt to band together to fight their separate causes.

The events in Derby also showed that ordinary local people were prepared to take serious risks and defy authority whether that took the form of government, council, employer or union. They demonstrated that the authorities could be harsh, ruthless and devious, and that local opinions were split on how best to deal with the grievances of the poor and labouring classes. For 25 years before the 1840s, Derby was a town in turmoil, riven by events which imprinted themselves on the local memory. One by-product was a reluctance to provoke any further unrest by banning Shrovetide football. So what were these events that inadvertently preserved the historic game?

On the early afternoon of 7 November 1817, a crowd of over 6,000 people crammed into Friar Gate, a wide street containing some fine residential properties, but also including the County Jail. Outside the jail, on a platform no more than ten feet high, swung the recently hanged bodies of three men convicted of high treason. Their names were Jeremiah Brandreth, Isaac Ludlam and William Turner. Brandreth and Turner had died relatively quickly, but the crowd had watched Ludlam struggling and convulsing for at least 15 minutes before he became still – a true diehard. At 1.15pm the three bodies were taken down and a thick timber board was balanced on a pair of foot-high supports. Two axes and two knives were shown to the crowd and sawdust sprinkled around the platform. Brandreth's body was laid across the wood, face down with his head pointing towards the spectators. The executioner raised his axe high and brought the blade down with all his force on the back of Brandreth's neck. An involuntary gasp of horror escaped from the crowd. Then, the executioner took hold of the severed head and holding it up by the hair he shouted, 'Behold the head of Jeremiah Brandreth, the traitor.'[80]

Until this point the assembled multitude had been quiet and motionless, hemmed in as they were by several companies of infantry and mounted dragoons, positioned to control the crowd and prevent any attempt to rescue the condemned men. But now the crowd reacted:

> The instant the head was exhibited, there was a tremendous shriek set up, and they ran violently in all directions, as if under the impulse of a sudden phrenzy [sic]. Those that resumed their stations groaned and hooted. The javelin-men and constables were all in motion, and a few dragoons, who had been stationed at both ends of the street, drew nearer with drawn swords.[81]

The people of Derby had just witnessed the gruesome end of three men who had been duped into insurrection by a government spy named William Oliver. In those days the Talbot Inn, in Derby's Irongate, was a well-known meeting place for those of a radical disposition, and Oliver had used the venue to infiltrate Derbyshire's activists. He persuaded the more gullible members of this group that a national uprising was imminent. Consequently, after some planning meetings in the village of Pentrich, a group of around 400 men from several nearby villages gathered on the appointed day and marched towards Nottingham, intent on persuading the soldiers there to join the uprising.

The group's march was slowed by stops to visit pubs and to persuade others to join them. They had only managed to cover 12 miles when they encountered a mounted force of light dragoons. The would-be revolutionaries fled, but around 47 were arrested and taken to what was a huge ten-day trial, held back until October so that the cream of Derbyshire's land-owning and business elite could dominate the juries, the country's top lawyers could put forward the case for the prosecution, and scores of witnesses could be called. The County Jail was not big enough to hold all the accused, and groups of prisoners held in Nottingham had to be brought into town accompanied by military escorts. The mood of local people was fractious. Crowds besieged County Hall in St Mary's Gate and sometimes it could take half an hour just to establish order inside the court. To their credit, some national newspapers were highly critical of the government's actions, particularly the fact that William Oliver was not asked to appear, despite his actions as an *agent provocateur* being well known. The government pressed on regardless, keen to make a public example through execution of the ringleaders.

Two days after the executions, Joseph Strutt wrote to his cousin Edward, conveying the horror, shock and indignation felt by local people. The poet Percy Bysshe Shelley was so moved that he issued an address to the nation, which contrasted reactions to the death in childbirth of Princess Charlotte and the deaths of the hapless Derbyshire trio. Shelley clearly thought the executions were the real national calamity rather than the death of the princess. He asked his readers to consider the feelings of the relatives of Brandreth, Ludlam and Turner, when they heard the shrieks, groans and hootings of the Derby crowd.

Times were tough and the consequences, if you stepped out of line, were harsh indeed. Here are a few examples, from one day's hearing at the Derbyshire Michaelmas Sessions of 1826. Charles Beeston, 22, stole two sacks of potatoes in Hulland; he was imprisoned for two months. James Holland, 21, stole one piece of cloth from a stack yard in Spondon; he was transported for seven years. John Wigley, 19, stole two geese and the morning after the report of the theft was found by a constable to be sitting at his bed plucking one while the other lay nearby. He was sentenced to six months of hard labour. In another case of goose-stealing, the court showed logical consistency in awarding 12 months of hard labour to George Wall, who had taken four of the birds. Samuel Varney, 26, stole five quarts of milk and two earthen vessels; for this he was transported for seven years.

The ability of a farm labourer and his family to boost their income with a handicraft like weaving or lacemaking had largely disappeared. They could no longer compete with the price of goods coming out of the factories, so the farm workers left for the towns and cities where the wages were higher, and the opportunities seemed brighter. But while the national economy prospered in the new industrial age, many manual labourers in urban areas found that their wages were still not enough to afford the rents charged for decent housing. They had no option but to move into overcrowded terraces and courts where the rents were lower. Even then it was still a struggle to feed their families, and by the 1830s an undercurrent of discontent had spread across the country.

Against this background, in 1831, the House of Commons considered a Reform Bill. The ways in which MPs were selected varied greatly across the country and bore little relation to the size of the populations they represented. Some of the so-called 'rotten boroughs' returned MPs to parliament even though they had fewer than 50 voters. The Reform Bill proposed a fairer system with representation for growing urban areas like Derby. The population of Derby Borough in 1831 was 23,627, but only around 1,500 residents were qualified to vote. Consequently, the Reform Bill was ardently supported by workers in Derby. However, although the House of Commons passed the bill, the House of Lords, dominated by Tories, voted against it by 199 votes to 158.

At about 7pm on Saturday, 8 October 1831, an express coach from *The Sun*'s newspaper office in London arrived in Derby with news of the bill's defeat in the House of Lords. This news soon caused confrontations between supporters and opponents of the bill. An angry mob forced church officials to hand over the keys to churches in their care, and the bells of All Saints', St Alkmund's and St Peter's began ringing out mourning peals. They kept ringing until 3am. Stones were hurled at businesses that had opposed the bill and angry groups visited the homes of prominent residents who were against the reforms. One of the casualties of the riots was Bemrose's bookshop. When the bill was put before parliament, the Derby printer Mozley drew up a petition against it. He placed the petition in the bookshop of William Bemrose for signatures. When the bill was defeated, the rioters wrecked Bemrose's shop, breaking all the windows, and using his books and stationery as excellent material to start a bonfire. Mozley's residence in Friar Gate also received an unwelcome visit.

The violence, however, was not confined to the town centre. A band of rioters marched over a mile out of town to the Mundy residence at Markeaton Hall. Francis Mundy had been an MP for the Derbyshire constituency for nearly ten years. The mob surrounded the building and broke most of the windows. Mrs Mundy was so terrified by the event that she did not undress for several nights afterwards. Similar damage was inflicted on the home of Sir Robert Wilmot at Chaddesden Hall, also well over a mile outside town. As a result of these various acts of vandalism and intimidation, two men were arrested and put in jail.

The following day the mayor and magistrates called a public meeting to see what might be done to prevent further rioting. Opponents of the bill demanded the release of the two men in jail. When this request was ignored, the crowd tried to break into the Town Jail in Friar Gate themselves. Uprooting a cast-iron lamp-post, they used it as a battering ram against the jail's door, securing the release of the two men imprisoned the night before, and freeing another 20. Encouraged by this success, the mob set off to the County Jail in nearby Vernon Street. This was a much tougher target. The governor of the jail was forewarned and forearmed – he had posted armed lookouts on the prison walls. At first, he tried to reason with the mob, estimated at around 1,500 people. His advice to the crowd was met with a volley of stones and he ordered his men to fire. He was then called away to deal with a disturbance inside the prison. Upon his return he found the mob to be even more determined to break into the jail, so his men fired again. This time several people were wounded and a young man, John Garner, fell. As he lay dying from a fatal wound to his abdomen, Garner told the surgeon attending him that he had just returned to the town. Garner had gone to see the damage that had been done to Markeaton Hall the previous evening. On his way home he had come across the mob outside the County Jail. He was just on the point of continuing on his way home when he was shot.

Given the severity of the situation, military help had been requested from Nottingham. A cavalry troop, the 15th Hussars, cantered into town in the afternoon and cleared the crowd away from the Market Place and the jail. The mob went off out of town and destroyed a house at Little Chester, before returning to the town centre in the evening. This time action was concentrated around All Saints' Church as the protesters pulled up iron railings around the church to use as weapons. Few properties in neighbouring Iron Gate and Queen Street escaped damage, which by now had become indiscriminate, until the hussars managed to clear the troublemakers off the streets.

The next day, Monday, 10 October, the mayor rejected a call for another public meeting and instead proposed sending a petition to the King on behalf of the town. Stalls were set up in the afternoon to collect signatures, but these only incensed protesters and were soon torn down. The magistrates had little alternative but to read the Riot Act, giving angry protesters an hour to vacate the streets before punitive force was used. The soldiers duly returned but it is clear from various accounts that the behaviour of some of the hussars was appalling. Just after noon on that day, a young man called David Aldridge decided to cross the Market Place from Morledge towards Sadler Gate. He was feeling unwell and had decided to make his way home. A mounted hussar came up close behind Aldridge and asked him, 'My lad, don't you mean to quicken your pace.'[82] Then some form of spicy verbal exchange took place between soldier and lad, for which we only have Aldridge's account. This ended with the hussar telling Aldridge that if he did not run, he would shoot him on the spot. The soldier then picked up his carbine and levelled it at Aldridge, who ran away, turning the corner of Rotten Row, a block of buildings on the west side of the Market Place. As he looked back, he saw the soldier move his firelock to his right-hand side.

Nearby, Josiah Shepherd and his friend Mr Berry were attempting to make their way out of the Market Place, when Berry saw a soldier take out a carbine and cock it. Shepherd recalled, 'A shot was fired, the ball passed through my hat, and struck a man who was on the pavement, about two yards distant from me. I did not know at first what had happened to my hat; I turned to look, and saw the man down. I heard him groan, and saw him bleeding.'[83] He had just witnessed the death of John Hickin, an innocent party, who had gone to the door of the Greyhound pub with a jug in his hand and was knocking on the door and asking for his 'allowance'. The ball had entered above his left breast and travelled as far as his right shoulder blade. But Berry and Aldridge did not stop to render assistance; shocked at this turn of events and, in fear for their lives, they fled the scene. They did not stop until they got to the bottom of Sadler Gate. There they turned into the confined space of George's Yard where only a few years before the Shrovetide footballers had been locked in battle for over half an hour. Aldridge turned to Berry and said that he thought the shot had been intended for himself. Soldiers and special constables eventually regained control of the town during Monday evening, 48 hours after disturbances first began.

At the inquests into the deaths during the Reform Bill riots, John Garner's was recorded as a justified homicide. That of Henry Haden, who was crushed in a mob intent on attacking Crompton's Bank, was recorded as accidental death. The coroner told the jury that he considered the death of John Hickin to be justified homicide, but the jury disagreed, and accidental death was recorded. Perhaps they were impressed with the evidence of Shepherd who had passed his hat to the jury – the ball had passed through the middle of the crown.

The report of the inquest into the deaths also contained crucial testimony from Constable James Allen, a man whose son would play a leading role in the final hours of the Derby Game.

Eleven people – ten men and 23-year-old Catherine Henrys – were charged with breaking into the Town Jail and releasing prisoners. They spent an uncomfortable six months becoming even more familiar with prison facilities while awaiting trial at the Spring Assizes of 1832. The trial included evidence from some of the prisoners who had been inside the jail, one of whom said that when 30 or 40 people had burst into the prison it was 'more like a foot-ball than anything else'. The judge, Sir James Parke, noted the puzzling absence of any 'respectable' witnesses given that many such people had seen the rioters attack the town jail. He apologised to the jury for this, and said he was aware of the feeling in the town but nevertheless reminded the jurors of their responsibilities, as described in a transcript of the trial:

> One circumstance, the learned judge said, had forcibly struck him during the investigation of the case before the court, it was, that, while the transaction to which it related had taken place in broad day-light, and in the presence of many respectable persons, as appeared upon the evidence, there should be no one of that character come forward on the prosecution: this looked like either having a criminal sympathy with those actively engaged in it, or that they would be afraid to appear against them; but, however that might be, he hoped the jury would dispose their duty without fear.[84]

The judge's remarks fell on deaf ears; the jury were either sympathetic to the rioters or intimidated by their supporters. They found each defendant not guilty to applause both inside and outside the courtroom. The relief was understandable because if the 11 rioters had been found guilty of a felony, they could have been sentenced to transportation.

Two other Reform Bill rioters were not so lucky. John Abell, 31, was charged with breaking and entering the house of Mrs Harrison at Little Chester and stealing the second volume of *Goldsmith's Animated Nature* (one of a four-volume set), among other diverse articles. Despite Abell's interest in natural history, he was found guilty of larceny and transported for seven years. William Atchinson, 17, was charged with stealing one pair of spectacles and a case from the property of George Haworth in Duffield Road. Two silver salt spoons and a tablespoon were also found in the lock-up after his removal to jail. He was found guilty of larceny and transported for seven years.

The Reform Bill riots provided the local ruling elite with considerable food for thought. Several had been frightened for their lives, an experience they would find it very hard to forget. They must have known that if the rioters had been successful in breaking into the County Jail, the release of the 600 prisoners within could have resulted in terrible carnage. As luck had it, the jail was in good shape having been built a few years previously to replace its ramshackle predecessor, which was now serving as the Town Jail. The local gentry and factory owners would also have been aware of the events in nearby Nottingham, where the castle had been burnt down, and Colwick Hall and a silk factory in Beeston had also been set on fire. The evidence demonstrating how fearful the local authorities had become was provided by the building works carried out to the County Jail in the aftermath of the riots. Eight Martello towers with loopholes for muskets were built along the perimeter walls of the prison. Each castle-like tower was furnished with firearms. Together with 25-foot-high walls, the new prison was a grim and forbidding addition to Derby's townscape.

A few years after the riots, Derby was the scene of yet another confrontation between a disaffected populace and their supposed superiors. The Combinations of Workmen Act of 1825 forbade the formation of trade unions in the United Kingdom. However, in 1833 around 800 Derby silk workers joined an embryonic trades union in the hope of better conditions and wages. In November, a workman at the silk mill of Peat and Frost in City Road was dismissed for producing poor-quality goods. As a response, the workforce at the mill walked out. Workmen from other mills joined in. The result was the Silk Trades' Lockout; 20 proprietors locked out their workforce unless they forswore the union. Over 2,000 workers refused to comply. Strike-breakers were imported into Derby, mostly from London, but some apparently from abroad.

The lengthy standoff of the lockout attracted national attention. The employers' strategy was clearly aimed at starving the workers into going back to work. There were daily confrontations between strikers and the 'black sheep' who had been imported to keep the mills working. The Walker family in River Street were reported to be living on potato peelings. Collections were organised in various places across the country to help support the Derby workers. The *Pioneer* (also known as *Trades Union Magazine*) ran regular updates on the situation in Derby and contained many messages of support for the strikers. In January, a funeral procession for a deceased striker took place. The vanguard of the procession was formed by over 100 hooded women dressed in white. The coffin was followed by representatives and members of different lodges including stonemasons, bricklayers, sawyers, framework knitters, weavers, tailors and shoemakers. Each wore a black and white rosette and carried sprigs of ivy leaves.

In February 1834 the union leaders attempted to stop the Derby Game. They devoted great effort in arranging alternative distractions. Their motive appeared to be to show the authorities that they had more control over ordinary working people than the council, and that they could succeed in suppressing an event which the council had failed to put down. When Shrove Tuesday arrived though, the pull of the Derby Game was too strong and the event went ahead, albeit with reduced numbers. The strike rumbled on for another couple of months. Eventually, despite the nationwide publicity and the efforts of workers elsewhere to provide funds to support the strikers, it was unsuccessful and ended on 21 April 1834. Although many workers were reinstated, nearly 600 were not.

Chartism was the dominant working-class movement of the early Victorian period, between 1837 and 1848. Chartist links with Derby were strong, partly because George Julian Harney, one of the leaders of the movement, had been imprisoned in Derby for six months for selling an unstamped newspaper called the *Poor Man's Guardian* (an unstamped newspaper was one which was sold for a price which did not include the stamp duty which the government had introduced to discourage cheap political newspapers). Harney was young and of a militant tendency. He was fond of following an earlier French fashion for revolutionaries by wearing a red cap.

After his release from a Derby jail in 1836 when aged 19, Harney returned to the town in January 1839. He met with other radicals in rooms at St Peter's Street and then, accompanied by banner-waving supporters and a 'very tolerable band', set out for Chester Green, an open space on the edge of town. According to the *Derby Mercury*, most of the inscriptions on the banners were in the 'worst possible taste'; for example, 'He who has not got a sword, let him sell his shirt and buy one.'[85] Another pithier banner, noted in the *Northern Star*, proclaimed, 'More pigs and less parsons'.[86]

Harney delivered a highly inflammatory and frequently quoted speech to the crowd at Chester Green. He began by reminding himself to the audience:

Fair women of Derbyshire, brave men of Derby! I am happy and proud once more to meet you. To many of you I am not unknown; to the rulers, the magistrates, I am not unknown. Three years ago, on a winter's evening, I was dragged from my home without the least notice and consigned to a dungeon by the magistrates of Derby, because I had committed the heinous offence of selling an unstamped newspaper – because I had striven to set the press of England free.[87]

He described how the 'Shopocracy' of Derby had stood in their doorways and windows to sneer at the morning procession through the town, but gave them a warning:

I tell these big-bellied, purse-proud, ignorant Shopocrats to look to their tills – to stick to their counters – to fawn, and crawl and creep to their Aristocratic patrons, but not to sneer at us who have too long borne with their sneers; or if they do, let them take the consequences – the day of retribution may arrive sooner than they look for.[88]

After making many references to pikes and muskets, and telling his audience that 'there was no argument like the sword', he concluded:

Time was when every Englishman had a musket in his cottage and along with it hung a flitch of bacon; now there is no flitch of bacon for there is no musket: let the musket be restored and the flitch of bacon will follow.[89]

The *Derby Mercury* sought to ridicule such protests and claimed that in Derby, agitators like Harney had 'no inflammable materials to work upon'.[90] Nevertheless, the talk of the need

for tyrants to tremble, for days of retribution, and incitement
of armed insurrection would have been deeply disturbing for
those of wealth and status, many of whom still lived in grand
houses in the centre of town. Certainly, Alfred Wallis in
recalling Derby's experiences during the Chartist agitation,
wrote that the processions of ill-dressed and half-starved
people carrying poles of bread dipped in blood, became part
of the public memory of the time.

Before 1841, the reaction of the government to local
disturbances was remarkably relaxed. Riots outside London
rarely provoked any debate in parliament, which was content by
and large to leave these matters to the Home Office and local
authorities to sort out. This does not mean that wrongdoers
got off lightly. Many ringleaders were transported, but
action was more about retribution after the event rather than
prevention. In September 1841, there was a marked change
in the wind as Lord Melbourne's Whig government was
replaced by Sir Robert Peel. Both Peel, as prime minister, and
Sir James Graham as home secretary were determined to take
a much more proactive approach to the issue of law and order.
Graham's letters and reports clearly indicate that he wants the
civil authorities to do more to curtail disturbances in their
areas. The view was shared by the Duke of Wellington who,
in a letter dated 15 August 1842, advised Graham that:

> You may rely upon the good intentions – not possibly
> upon the health and activity – of the Lords Lieutenant
> of the counties of Lancashire, Cheshire, Stafford,
> Warwick and Derby. They should each of them be
> desired to require the magistrates to perform their
> duty, and endeavour to prevent these mischievous
> proceedings by their personal exertions and presence
> with their civil force, having to support the civil power,
> such military as may be at their disposal.[91]

It is clear therefore that by 1842, local authorities such as Derby Borough Council would have been fully aware that they were expected to take whatever action they could to prevent outbreaks of mob rule. There is no evidence that Derby Shrovetide Football was ever viewed as a political event. However, what happened between 1817 and 1841 had caused more than enough trouble and turmoil in Derby, to stay the hand of those on the council who wished to see an end to the annual football game (luckily for the football historian, this meant the Derby Game persisted long enough for detailed descriptions of it to feature in newspapers and magazines). But the excitation of a mob of people, and the compliant acceptance of mischief and misrule, was increasingly at odds with the spirit of the 1840s. The government encouraged local authorities to develop police forces and to promote law and order, preferably by preventing or dissuading crime and disorder in the first place.

The newly formed borough council, dominated by members with land and business interests, was keen to show that Derby was in tune with the times, and a place where law and order, rather than mob rule, prevailed. On the one hand it would have been mindful of the distrust caused by the execution of the Pentrich rebels and how close the town's Reform Bill riots, Silk Mill lockout and Chartist unrest, had taken it to a breakdown between those who governed and those who did not. But on the other hand, the town had come close on several occasions in recent memory to mob rule, so by the mid-1840s there was little enthusiasm in the new ruling class for traditions which gave free rein to the lords of misrule. The difficulty was that many of the people who had already defied authority were also either Shrovetide footballers or supporters of the game. The authorities must have been fully aware that getting rid of the game would be no easy matter.

7

A Town Transformed

DANIEL DEFOE was a government spy, businessman and writer. He is probably best known for the novel *Robinson Crusoe*, but one of his best money-spinners was a *A Tour Thro' the Whole Island of Great Britain*. This was an account of his extensive travels across England and Scotland and was published in three volumes between 1724 and 1727. Defoe's work gave his impressions of numerous towns and counties. His impressions of Derby were favourable:

> This is a fine, beautiful, and pleasant town; it has more families of gentlemen in it than is usual in towns so remote, and therefore here is a great deal of good and some gay company: Perhaps the rather, because the Peak [District] being so near, and taking up the larger part of the county, and being so inhospitable, so rugged and so wild a place, the gentry choose to reside at Derby, rather than upon their estates, as they do in other places.[92]

It is interesting that someone so well-travelled as Defoe should consider Derby 'remote' at this time. Certainly, his observations on the number of gentry residing in the town were borne out by the evidence. Indeed, some of the grandest families in England had townhouses in Derby for many years before and after

Defoe's visit. Newcastle House on the north side of the Market Place was probably built in the 1630s for Bess of Hardwick's descendants, the earls and later dukes of Newcastle. Round the corner in the Cornmarket was Cavendish House, a not-so-little *pied a terre* for the Chatsworth branch of the family. Below this exalted level the Meynell and the Mundy families, the Leighs of Egginton and a plethora of other members of the gentry had townhouses. For the gentry, this probably had less to do with avoiding the 'inhospitable' countryside and more to do with the attractions of Derby as a pleasant place to live. Also, if you were one of the area's local bigwigs, having a home somewhere close to the Town Hall helped you to stay informed and exert influence. Similarly, if you were an earl or a duke, and you needed to be in town for some civic duty, or were simply attending the races, it was also, no doubt, very useful to have a convenient place to stop for a night or two.

But Defoe also noted a 'curiosity' which was to herald a massive transformation in the British economy and working life:

> Here is a curiosity in trade worth observing, as being the only one of its kind in England, namely, a throwing or throwster's mill, which performs by a wheel turn'd by the water; and though it cannot perform the doubling part of a throwster's work, which can only be done by a handwheel, yet it turns the other work, and performs the labour of many hands.[93]

What Defoe had seen was the huge waterwheel built by George Sorocold, to power a five-storey mill, next to the River Derwent. The silk mill was the first true factory to be built in England with several processes powered by the waterwheel and interlinking machinery. It was a precursor of a system of manufacture that was going to change the country's way of life. But despite this strange new building, Derby was slow to develop over the next century. William Hutton, writing his *History of Derby* in 1791, seemed to think the size of Georgian Derby was similar to that of Saxon Derby, although he allowed that a silk mill had been added, together with roads and a china works. Certainly, the pace of change had been very slow; he recalled an exchange he encountered in his youth when one resident challenged another regarding recent building:

> I was present in 1738, at a conversation between two natives when one challenged the other to produce an instance in Derby of a house being built on a new foundation. The affirmative, I well remember, was not proved; which shows that a very small, or rather no increase attended it.[94]

Perhaps this slow and gentle pace of change was one reason why Shrovetide football persisted in Derby, when similar games had been extinguished in most other towns. But inevitably change came to the town following the start of the 19th century and began to accelerate. In 1801, the population of Derby was only 13,154. By 1841 this had trebled to around 37,431 at a growth rate over 40 years of 284 per cent. To put this in perspective, the overall population growth rate in England over the 40-year period between 1971 and 2011 was 21 per cent. As the town entered the 1840s, residents would have been bewildered and amazed at the changes that had recently taken place and were under way. Put yourself in the shoes of someone who has been away for ten years and has returned in 1846. Indeed, imagine you are a Peterite, who hearing that the game he played in his youth is under threat, has returned on the eve of Shrove Tuesday to witness events first-hand. You take a walk around town to see what has changed in the decade you have been away.

You begin your time travel walk at the north end of the town centre outside St Mary's Catholic Church, completed a few years ago in 1839. When opened, the church was heralded by Doctor (later Cardinal) Wiseman as the most magnificent thing that Catholics had done in modern times in the entire country. As you gaze up admiringly at the tower, you are most struck by the fact that such a building could be erected at all. The previous modest Catholic chapel had to have a high wall around it, to protect it from zealous Protestants, and it is less than 20 years since the Emancipation Act signalled an end to 300 years of discrimination against Catholics. Indeed, St Mary's Church is the first major building for Catholic worship in England for hundreds of years. It is popular with the growing Irish population. The Irish have long been a component of Derby society, usually at the poorer end, but in recent years there has been a major influx prompted by the availability of work on the railways and by the Irish famine. No doubt the church is well used by families, praying for loved ones who are suffering back home, or who have emigrated overseas.

Turning round, you walk south from St Mary's towards the town centre. You have not walked more than 40 yards before you are confronted by building work which is nearing completion – a new Anglican church. The work is taking place on the foundations of previous churches on the ancient religious site of St Alkmund's. You lean back and arch your neck to view the tower and slim spire which soar to over 200 feet, clearly designed to put St Mary's, and the Catholics, in the Anglican shade. Nevertheless, the building is an elegant and striking addition to the Derby skyline.

You pursue your journey southwards into All Saints' Parish. Two hundred yards from St Alkmund's and yet another huge ecclesiastical building looms overhead, All Saints' Church. This, at least, is familiar to you, its tower of over 200 feet having been a prominent landmark for over 300 years. You have mixed feelings about this edifice. On the one hand it is clearly the most impressive building in town, but on the other it is the core of your rivals' territory. The last thing you want to hear tomorrow is the bells of All Saints' ringing out peals of victory.

You walk down Iron Gate, happy to see that this medieval street and its offshoot, Sadler Gate, are unchanged. They are nice and narrow, and therefore easily blocked. You would not admit it in public, but one reason you would never want to change sides is that since the 1820s All Saints' have had a much harder route to their goal than St Peter's. With the building of the streets, courts and factories of the West End, All Saints' have little option but to battle the ball through confined urban spaces.

At the end of Iron Gate, you enter the bustling Market Place. Approaching this large square after ten years away brings many memories flooding back; the jostling and verbal sparring with the All Saints' lads before the ball was thrown up, the surge of the crowd which lifted you off your feet, the desperate wrestling over a mass of bodies to try and make a yard or two's progress towards the ball. But you are soon jolted out of your reveries because facing you is a new bell tower which dominates the square. The tower has recently been completed; together with adjoining structures, it replaces the former Town Hall which was destroyed by fire five years ago. Near the top of the tower is a clock, which is illuminated at night and which can be seen from many places in town. Knowing the time is becoming increasingly important with railway companies pressing for adoption of Greenwich Mean Time throughout the country. You note sadly that there is no balcony in the new Town Hall from which a ball can be thrown up. The old Town Hall had a balcony which allowed civic dignitaries to come out above the crowd, wait for the appointed hour and throw the ball to the seething throng below.

People are walking through the portico beneath the new tower. You follow them through and emerge into an area where there are scores of new shops and new market areas, one for butter and eggs, one for vegetables. Turning right down a new throughfare called Albert Street, you are shocked to discover that Markeaton Brook has disappeared. The brook, which for centuries has split the old town in two, is now buried in a culvert beneath another new street, named Victoria Street, built over the top. St Peter's Bridge, which for hundreds of years has been the main link over the brook between north and south Derby, has also disappeared without trace. You find this scarcely comprehensible; in this part of the town at least, the watercourse that was the dividing line between north and south Derby, has been erased. The scene of so many struggles between All Saints' and St Peter's, the place effectively where so many games have been won or lost, has gone.

On the corner of Victoria Street and the Cornmarket is a marvellous new four-storey, stone-clad building, housing the Royal Hotel, the Athenaeum, the Post Office and the Derby and Derbyshire Bank. On entering the Athenaeum, you find reading rooms where the latest editions of some 18 different newspapers and journals are available for members to study. There is also a new Town and Country Museum which sports the dress of an American Indian chief, and a Bengal tiger, in among its collection of stuffed birds and rare minerals. This is a wonderful change, but your mood is tempered when you walk over the slight hump in the road that is now called Victoria Street. You know that you have walked over the hidden Markeaton Brook and are now in your home parish of St Peter's. Your mood is suddenly sombre because in front of you is Thorntree House, for so long the residence of Joseph Strutt, great supporter of Shrovetide football, and a Peterite through and through. The great man has been dead for over two years now, but you recall with gratitude how you once dragged yourself exhausted from the football fray, to enjoy the refreshments provided by his generosity.

Walking southwards up St Peter's Street, you come to St Peter's Church, where you were baptised and went to school in the churchyard. The ivy-covered church, where you were also married, holds many memories for you. On the same street, within sight of the church, you learnt your trade as a carpenter, and you remember celebrating football victories in the pubs in your street: the Green Man, the Barley Mow, the Durham Ox, the White Swan, the Anchor, the Old Neptune, the Nag's Head, the Marquis of Anglesea, the Old Plough and the Green Dragon, now run, you hear, by one of the infamous Williamsons.

Resisting the urge to quench your thirst, you press on up the hill to Osmaston Road. Your destination is Grove Street, because here on the edge of town is a nursery. The wooden gate that forms the entry to that nursery is the St Peter's goal. Once, during the boys' game on Ash Wednesday, when you were 12 years old, you had the ball in your hands and had the nursery gate in your sights. Running as fast as you could, lungs bursting, goaling looked a certainty, until an All Saints' foot tripped you up.

In your childhood in the 1810s, the area around here had all been countryside and gardens, a pleasant place for bird nesting or for kicking a ball around. Now plots of land along Osmaston Road are being developed. That is far from the only change, because close to the nursery is a new and wondrous attraction, the Arboretum.

Although you had been told that public admission to the Arboretum was free, you are informed by the man on the entrance gate that this only applies on a Sunday and a Wednesday. Paying a small fee, you enter a strange landscape where gravel walks meander between mounds which have been thrown up on either side. A huge variety of trees and shrubs have been planted on the mounds, presented almost like exhibits. There are seats, statues, ornamental vases, fountains and sculptures. The land used to be owned by Joseph Strutt, who had a private garden here, but he donated the 11 acres of land to the town in thanks to its inhabitants. He also paid for the land to be laid out in a manner that combines elegance with education. On leaving the Arboretum, you express your admiration to the attendant who proudly informs you of the massive crowds that flocked to see the area when it was opened in 1840. These crowds were boosted by special excursion trains, from cities like Manchester and Leeds, keen to see the astonishing novelty of a town park that is not a private place for the privileged, but open for public enjoyment.

The scale of the changes you have seen to your native town is hard for you to take in and understandably you are tired. But the attendant at the Arboretum mentioned trains. When you left Derby ten years ago there were no trains in the town. So, taking directions from the lodge keeper, you make your way eastwards towards Derby Railway Station. Walking down Litchurch Street, which is lined with newly built terraced houses, you enter a broad thoroughfare called Midland Road, at the bottom of which is a fine three-storey hotel, one of the first purpose-built railway hotels in the country. Opposite the hotel is the station. Despite the amazing changes you have already witnessed on your walk, nothing compares with what you now see. Land, which was open fields only ten years ago, and which has been used by generations of Peterites as the best route to emerge from the River Derwent and run the ball up to their goal, is now occupied by a large station. Inside the station is a single platform over 1,000 feet long built to accommodate trains to Birmingham, Sheffield and Nottingham. Originally owned by three separate railway companies, the companies have merged recently to form Midland Railway which has set up its headquarters in Derby.

Near to the station are numerous railway workshops, including a large, almost round, engine house. It is a scene of intense activity. Underneath an impressive dome held up by cast-iron columns is a 16-sided building – or roundhouse – with 16 lines of rails radiating from a 40-foot-wide turntable in the middle. The railway workers tell you the workshop can hold up to 30 steam engines. Across from the station and the workshops, again in an area which you had previously thought of as open countryside, are streets of neat, terraced houses built for railway workers. It is like a little village of its own with shops and a tavern. After such an amazing walk, the tavern is a very welcome sight, as you could do with something that hopefully hasn't changed too much – a pint of Derby ale.

***

So, after centuries of slow and leisurely change, Derby had been catapulted in the space of ten years from being a small Georgian town to a town at the forefront of the Industrial Revolution. A town which had been dominated by the local landed gentry and whose main function had been to provide a market for adjoining rural villages was fast becoming an industrial and engineering hotspot tied by revolutionary rail links to major cities like Nottingham, Sheffield and Birmingham.

Its population was changing as fast as the buildings and streets, with high levels of immigration. The owners of any vacant land within and on the edge of town must have had plenty of prospective purchasers knocking on their doors. Indeed, in some parts of the town, unscrupulous landowners and developers had squeezed the poor and desperate into cheap and nasty housing. Some of England's worst and most unhygienic housing could be found in and around St Mary's Gate, Willow Row and the burgeoning West End. A government inquiry in 1845 considered Derby to 'be almost unequalled in its neglect of drainage and sewerage'.[95] Nowhere was worse that the courts which were tucked away out of sight on back-land sites behind the main street fronts; tiny dwellings packed together and accessed off alleyways. Thirty inhabitants of six houses in a court off Walker Lane had but one privy between them; to get to this toilet they tiptoed over stepping stones to keep their feet clear of an overflowing cesspool.

The town suffered from both inadequate drainage and a poor water supply until the latter days of the Derby Game. Even in the early 1840s there were no baths for public bathing and very few sitting baths; indeed, one doctor's opinion was that bathing as an aspect of health was little understood by Derby people and 'still less practised'.[96] A consequence of this lack of provision was that the River Derwent was used by those who wished to bathe or take a swim, and some became proficient river swimmers. The Rev. Thomas Mozley recalled that while a leg injury prevented him joining other boys in games of cricket or football, he could manage to swim a mile easily in the Derwent. He also recalled the Markeaton Brook which ran behind his boyhood home in the Wardwick of the 1810s:

> At the foot of our garden ran a brook, little better than a sewer in dry weather, and something more than a flood in wet. It separated us from a little world of dirty courts, alleys, and outhouses, and always suggested malaria. We were a few yards from its confluence with another stream equally liable to inundation, and were between the two streams. A predecessor, it was said, had invited a large party to dinner, and at the appointed hour the dining room was two feet under water.[97]

It was here in the centre of town, within earshot of the ancient churches, in the cramped and stinking courtyards, in the shops and grimy factories, that the most active players of the Derby Game could be found: the chimney sweeps, whitesmiths, and joiners; the legions of framework knitters, labourers and shop assistants, who lodged and lived in a few score overcrowded streets.

So, by 1846, players and supporters of Derby Shrovetide Football not only had to contend with growing antagonism from the borough council but also had a new townscape to cope with. The culverting of part of Markeaton Brook had changed the nature of the game in central Derby. As an open watercourse, it had formed a barrier to a St Peter's crowd wanting to push south from the Market Place and advance to their goal up St Peter's Street; and it had also been a favoured water route for All Saints' to get to their goal at Nun's Street. At the same time, the time-honoured tactic of St Peter's, of getting the ball into the Derwent and drifting downstream with it before scrambling out and charging south-west, cross-country to Osmaston Road, was now compromised. A burgeoning tangle of railways, workshops and station now stood between the river and their goal near the Arboretum. This remarkable pulse of change created all sorts of difficulties to would-be Shrovetide footballers. But, as we shall see, there were still plenty of people prepared to confront whatever obstacles came between them and the game they loved.

8

Opposing Forces

THE STRUGGLE over the future of Derby Shrovetide Football was not a simple two-sided contest between a local council of stuffed shirts and a beer-swilling, football-loving rabble. The game's devotees were not just mindless ruffians but included people of intellect and enterprise. At the same time, its opponents were not all high-minded dignitaries but included trade unionists and advocates of horseracing. The combatants in the final struggles over the game embraced a surprising range of interest groups and individuals.

There is little doubt that the most influential family in Derby between 1800 and 1844 was the Strutts. In addition to their mills and factories which peppered Derbyshire's Derwent Valley, they had formed alliances through marriages with the powerful and wealthy Evans family. The Strutts were a regular presence on countless boards and committees. If they were opposed to something, like banning the ancient game of Shrovetide football, it was unlikely to happen.

The Strutt dynasty had begun with Jedidiah Strutt, a man with an eye for an opportunity. In 1759, at the age of 33, he took out a patent on a revolutionary machine for making ribbed stockings and plunged into the hosiery business, becoming a partner in several ventures in Derby and Nottingham. He had the vision to support Richard Arkwright's idea for a water-powered cotton mill and went on to help Arkwright set one up in 1771 at Cromford. It was the first water-powered cotton mill in the world and a huge step on the road to the creation of the modern factory system. Seven years later, acting on his own initiative, Jedidiah opened the second such mill, eight miles downstream of Cromford, at Belper. Further mills boosted his wealth and in 1795 he bought the imposing property of Exeter House in Derby.

Exeter House was a three-storey mansion built in the 17th century. It was perhaps the most prestigious residence in Derby town centre, occupying a prominent position with a long, walled garden next to the river. During the Jacobite Rebellion of 1745 it had been used by Bonnie Prince Charlie for his Council of War when he took the fateful decision to turn his army round and head back to Scotland. The acquisition of this prestigious residence was one measure of how far Jedidiah had come from his youth as a farmer's son. He did not have long to enjoy it; he died two years later. But he had laid the foundation for the Strutt dynasty. His sons – William, George and Joseph – all became involved in building a business empire and in various forms of social improvement. George concentrated his activities in Belper, but William and Joseph threw themselves into the improvement of Derby. William designed the first 'fireproof' mill in England – the Derby Calico Mill. He was a founding member, along with the likes of Erasmus Darwin, of the Derby Philosophical Society and became a burgess of the town when only 23 years old.

Joseph spent most of his time in the service of his native town. He lived in Thorntree House, an impressive residence on the corner of St Peter's Street, and opened up part of it as an art gallery and museum. He was also the driving force behind the funding and establishment of the Mechanics' Institute. This boasted a library and a lecture hall and offered a variety of educational classes and exhibitions. He also gave financial support to the building of the Athenaeum Building, just across the Markeaton Brook from his house. He was twice Mayor of Derby, including being the first mayor of the newly formed Borough of Derby in 1835. Joseph's popularity reached its peak when the Arboretum opened in 1840. He donated the 11 acre site to the town and provided the funds for John Claudius Loudon to lay out the site with trees, shrubs and pathways. In short, this man described in 1843 by Stephen Glover as 'excellent, enlightened and venerable' was the most eminent local person of the time.[98]

Joseph Strutt was not only known to be an ardent supporter of the Shrovetide football game but he was reputed to take part – apparently in a tailor-made protective suit of buckskin. There may be some truth in this, as the dress of an American Indian chieftain was a prize exhibit in the Town and County Museum to which Strutt had contributed exhibits, so he may have felt that buckskin gave him warrior-like qualities. There is certainly no doubt that he was a keen Peterite and a generous contributor towards the 'refreshments' enjoyed by football players. Strutt was a prominent member of the council in the 1830s and early 1840s when the issue of stopping the Shrovetide game was a bone of contention in the town. Alfred Wallis claimed that 'As long as Mr Joseph Strutt took the lead in affairs, his own love for the game was sufficient to keep it going, in despite of remonstrances from outside and opposition from within.'[99] This view was supported by Rev. Thomas Mozley, who wrote that people said the custom would last as long as Strutt did.

Strutt died in 1844, and given his status in the town, his obituary in the *Derby Mercury* was rather short and cryptic; the paper described him as occupying 'a rather conspicuous position among us' and commented that 'his feelings with respect to many questions were strong'.[100] No doubt Strutt's role as head of the local Whig-Radical party put him at odds with the Tory-supporting *Mercury*; indeed, it labelled his views as being 'ultra-Whig'. It appears, therefore, that Strutt's death was not mourned by everyone and removed a very significant obstacle in the way of those wishing to see an end to the game.

Judging from the coverage in the *Derby Mercury*, antagonism towards the Strutts seems to have grown during the 1840s. As men of property, it was easy for political opponents and mischief-makers to fling accusations that improvement schemes promoted by the Strutts were designed purely for their self-benefit. By 1846 the Strutts' main lever of influence over Derby affairs took the shape of Edward Strutt, William's son, who had been MP for the town since 1830. In 1830 the council had been dominated by Whigs. As the years passed, their control weakened and their liberal attitudes met increasingly strong resistance. By 1846 the *Mercury* was able to report, 'Mr Strutt is exceedingly unpopular in the Borough of Derby ... so unpopular as to render his expulsion as member for the town certain at no distant day.'[101] On this the newspaper proved prophetic, for Edward Strutt lost his Derby seat two years later. By the second half of the 1840s the Strutts' grip on Derby politics was in rapid decline, leaving the way clear for different factions and interests to prevail.

Other local dignitaries were not so enamoured of the Shrovetide game as Joseph Strutt, and certainly not a run of mayors in the middle part of the decade, who all showed their distaste for the tradition by word and action. By some freak occurrence, the three mayors during the final push to suppress the game between 1844 and 1848 had similar-sounding surnames: Moss, Mousley and Mozley. It was almost as if the borough council was simply working through potential candidates for the position in alphabetical order.

John Moss was a solicitor to the Derby and Derbyshire Banking Company and Mayor of Derby in 1844 and 1845. His objection to what he called a 'dirty and disgusting' game seemed to centre on concerns about property.[102] He argued that the game was so distasteful that it put off persons of property from taking up local residence. The notoriety of the game was such, that in his opinion , families did not move to live in the town because they were under the impression that 'Derby was one of the lowest and wickedest places in the kingdom'.[103] Following the failure to suppress the game in 1845, Moss referred to the behaviour of some people from a higher station in life than the football players themselves, whose obstructive attitude was not helping attempts to suppress the game. He felt that such people 'ought to have known better'.[104] It is unfortunate that we do not know who exactly Moss was referring to, or the whereabouts of Edward Strutt during Shrovetide that year.

William Eaton Mousley was elected mayor on 10 November 1845. Described as 'a masterful man fond of imposing his will on other people', Mousley was the most powerful figure on the borough council during the 1840s following the death of Strutt.[105] Although mayors normally only held office for a year, Mousley occupied the position for two years from 1845 to November 1847. He was an ambitious man who was keen to see Derby rise in importance and prosperity. He combined his civic duties with his job as a prominent local solicitor who also had a large property portfolio, including Exeter House which he bought in June 1819. Exeter House was little more than 100 yards from the Market Place where the ball was thrown up at the start of the Shrovetide football match.

One of Mousley's first actions on taking possession of his new residence was to block up the ground floor windows, possibly to avoid them being smashed during the football games, or in any of the other riotous events that took place in the 1820s and 1830s. He also made alterations of a contemporary nature to the dining room which, Lord Stanhope commented, 'will doubtless be better appreciated by Mr Mousley's convivial guests than by his antiquarian visitors'.[106] Indeed, Mousley clearly had little appreciation of heritage as he was set to sell off the oak panelling in the room used by Bonnie Prince Charlie for his War Council in 1745 in separate lots. He was only dissuaded from this course of action following an appeal by the brewer Michael Bass, the Earl of Chesterfield, and William Bemrose among others. The panelling of the drawing room was instead removed to the cellars of the Derby Assembly Rooms. (It can now be seen at Derby Museum where the former room at Exeter House has been recreated.)

Although he claimed to know next to nothing about horseracing, Mousley vigorously supported the creation of a racecourse in the town. He argued that it would be good for the health of the working classes, who he suggested should not be shut up in their manufactories from week to week without occasional exercise. In a letter to the Council, he declared that a spot of amusement in the open air would be invigorating, prevent premature old age and decay, and render the labouring classes 'more capable of discharging their duties to their employers'.[107] Mousley clearly knew how to make his points tell with an audience of mill owners and investors.

The reminiscences of Rev. Thomas Mozley about Derby and its football game feature several times in this book. He and his brother, Henry Mozley, were the sons of a bookseller and publisher, also called Henry Mozley, who introduced wholesale publishing into Derby in 1815. An 1840 edition of *Bradshaw's Railway Companion* was one of his father's publications. By 1847 when Henry Mozley Junior became Mayor of Derby, Henry Mozley and Sons was said to be the largest establishment of its kind outside London. Henry Senior had incurred ill feeling in the town when he encouraged local people to sign a petition against the Reform Bill in 1831. As a consequence, the Mozley home in Friar Gate was attacked by a mob when news broke of the bill's defeat in the House of Lords. It is little wonder, therefore, that Henry Junior was not in favour of two days of mob rule during Shrovetide. Indeed, he took a dim view of most recreations, pledging when he became mayor to bring about proper observance of the Sabbath. While it was chiefly transgressions by public houses that he had in mind, he intimated that he thought going for a walk in the Arboretum on a Sunday was not appropriate behaviour. However, he was prepared to tolerate re-establishment of horseracing, which he saw as a preferable pastime for artisans than football.

The subject of horseracing was a topic that excited fierce debate in the town. Rev. Simpson, the curate of St Peter's Church, felt so strongly on the matter that one Sunday afternoon in early August 1829 he ascended the church's pulpit and delivered a solemn warning to the assembled congregation against both the theatre and the races. He told his audience that the theatre was a place of 'grand evil' and had a 'total want of morality' – especially among females.[108] Regarding horseracing, he declared, 'Every species of profligacy abounds there, adultery, fornication, uncleanness, lasciviousness, drunkenness, blasphemy, gambling, revellings, and such like. The season of the races sounds the death knell of departing virtue, industry and sobriety, among the rich and poor.'[109] Reaching the final paragraphs of his 23-page sermon, Simpson worked himself up into a frenzy telling his parishioners that the guilt lay at their doors, and the blood was on their hands, if they let their sons, daughters, servants or apprentices go to the races. And if they were determined to go the races or the theatre themselves, he pleaded with them, 'Do not ruin your own souls! Do not crucify the Lord Jesus Christ afresh.'[110]

It is hard to read Simpson's sermon today and believe anyone took him seriously, but he represented views which were quite commonplace at the time. Indeed, to ensure that his message reached as many minds as possible, Simpson had his sermon published by Henry Mozley and Sons. Religious groups were a powerful force in the late Georgian and early Victorian era. Ministers used sermons to promulgate their opinions and values. A national society was formed to promote observance of the Sabbath, and local meetings were well attended. Like Henry Mozley Junior, some of the local clergy let it be known that they also did not approve of people walking in the Arboretum on a Sunday.

The issue of horseracing was sensitive. Derby had been without a permanent horseracing venue since the enclosure of Sinfin Moor, a few miles out of town, in 1803. Enclosure had brought an end to the sport in this location, together with attendant cock fighting and dancing. Subsequently, a site nearer to town in the Siddals had been used but railway development in the 1830s brought that to an end as well. The search was on for a new site and in 1845 an advert appeared in the *Derby Mercury* appealing for suitable land. Matters came to a head when the council called a special meeting in February 1845. An excitable audience packed into the Town Hall to hear the council debate a petition signed by around 5,000 people which put forward horseracing as a replacement for football, with the following argument:

> We, the undersigned, being impressed with a desire to secure the discontinuance of the annual game of football in the public streets and thoroughfares – provided some other more rational amusement can be secured to the working classes at a more genial season of the year – beg to suggest that the re-establishment of the Races would meet with the concurrence of a very large majority of all classes, tend to the rational enjoyment of the people, and confer great pecuniary benefit upon the town at large.[111]

The reinstatement of the sport was fiercely contested by religious groups who pointed out the evils of gambling. Four petitions were presented against the proposal. One signed by 693 'highly respectable and influential inhabitants of Derby' claimed that such sport was 'unchristian' in character.[112] The second petition was signed by 13 Nonconformist ministers of the town, a third was backed by 200 Wesleyan Methodists, and the final petition was submitted on behalf of Sunday School teachers.

Alderman Johnson spoke in favour of re-establishing the races. While acknowledging that football had been played since time immemorial and had been supported by many of the leading gentlemen of the town, he claimed that it was now viewed as 'a great public evil'.[113] There should be a substitute, he said, and he referred to a meeting with the footballers at which they had indicated that they were in favour of the races. He was supported by Alderman Fox, who argued that football was so low and degrading that it should have been swept away, as bull baiting, cock fighting and other brutal sports had been in recent years. Alderman Newton spoke against the proposal. He considered racing a far greater evil than football. While he admitted that the races were attended by persons of 'the highest rank' – presumably he had the Duke of Devonshire in mind – he claimed they were also frequented by 'swindlers, rogues, gamblers, blacklegs, drunkards and prostitutes.'[114]

Listening carefully to the debate, William Eaton Mousley bided his time, but eventually he spoke with authority and purpose. Despite being an evangelist himself, his comments on the opinions of the religious lobby were withering:

> It seemed the working classes had neither common sense nor common decency; and in fact, were unfit to be trusted alone, except the respective ministers of religion accompanied them to check their actions … If some clergymen and ministers of religion were to have their own way, everything they did not take an interest in, or of which they disapproved, must be abolished at once on the grounds of immorality.[115]

Mousley reeled off the names of the nobility who frequented race meetings: the dukes of Devonshire, Portland, Richmond, Rutland and Cleveland as well as various earls and marquises. He asked the meeting if they, too, were to be considered unmitigated blackguards. A vote was made in favour of re-establishing the races by 21 to 13. But as one contributor to the debate had pointed out, it was by no means clear that re-establishment would bring about an end to the football.

The arguments over Shrovetide football, horseracing or other amusements were played out in the local newspapers. The two main local papers were the *Derby Mercury* and the *Derby and Chesterfield Reporter*. Yet their readership was limited. In 1839 the circulation of each paper was not much over 1,000. One reason for this was stamp duty. At one point the *Reporter* cost seven pence, four pence of which was due to the duty. The duty was a tax that sought to restrict the access of working people to the press. Seven pence was a considerable sum. Skilled workers' wages varied from 20 to 30 shillings a week. Selling an unstamped newspaper could bring harsh punishment. At a Chartist meeting in Derby in 1839 (described in Chapter 6), George Harney spoke to the crowd of his personal experience of incarceration in Derby Jail for selling an unstamped paper, 'Yes, my friends, for six months I was confined in a bastille, because I dared ... to give to the working classes, that untaxed knowledge which they have a right to enjoy.'[116]

Nevertheless, the opinions of the newspapers exerted influence, for despite their limited circulation they would be read out to wider audiences and their opinions passed on by word of mouth. The *Mercury*, which had a slightly wider circulation than the *Reporter*, was decidedly against the football game, and included a lengthy diatribe against it in its edition of 22 January 1845. It asserted that no decent individual could deny that the game was a great public nuisance and contrary to the law; accordingly, the only issue was how to get rid of it.

There was a distinct whiff of collusion in the air in the mid-1840s between the *Mercury* and council leaders; more than a hint that there was a concerted campaign to shut the game down. If there was to be an organised resistance to fight back and keep the game going, it might be thought that the leaders of the working class, in the shape of the union movement, would be prime movers. But this was clearly not the case.

In the 1830s and '40s the union movement and the Chartists were keen to promote a sense of discipline and order among their supporters. Partly this was to avoid giving the authorities the excuse of restoring law and order, as a reason to send in the police or the military, to break up their public meetings. But in addition, the union movement wished to demonstrate that it was a moralising force and could do more to improve the habits of the working class than either church or gentry. Viewed from a union or Chartist perspective, the Derby Game was an unseemly display of brutish and disorderly behaviour, which reflected badly on their members. In addition, it had the unfortunate effect of mixing and uniting many people of different classes into a common cause, that of either All Saints' or St Peter's. The *Pioneer*, the national magazine of the Grand Consolidated National Trades Union, tried to drive a wedge between them in an article entitled 'Derby Ball-Playing' which informed union members, 'Your "Betters" have been foremost in this Fete, hallooing you like brute dogs to the strife. Yes, reverend creatures, full of holiness have lent a voice to brutalise the people.'[117] As we shall see in a later chapter, the union even went so far as to try and put the game down itself.

Letters to the local papers suggest growing concern during the 1830s about law and order issues. They reflected worries about the potential for mob violence following the Reform Bill riots of 1831. In February 1832 a writer identified by the initial 'W' argued in the *Derby and Chesterfield Reporter* that the Shrovetide game would not be permitted in any other large town and urged the authorities to ensure the special constables did their duty to prevent the game. 'W' described the game as 'a glaring evil' which resulted in 'an assemblage of all the blackguards in the neighbourhood'.[118] In response, a correspondent calling himself 'Pax' agreed that the game was disgraceful but advocated a more cautious approach for the time being, given the events of the preceding year. 'Pax' suggested it would be more prudent to allow the game to proceed for another year, partly because he doubted that the forces of law and order were sufficient for the task: 'Would it not require a force of more than ordinary magnitude, and discipline, to disperse "an assemblage of all the blackguards in the neighbourhood" more particularly when under the stimulating influence of liquor?'[119]

'Pax' conceded that if a large civil force could be assembled, it might possibly succeed if supported by an additional military force, but even then, success would not be achieved, 'Without bloodshed and slaughter, and perhaps renewal of the so-much-to-be-lamented riotous proceedings. To the risk of this, I cannot imagine either Mayor, or magistrates, are justified in exposing the town for the mere purpose of suppressing a game.'[120] His reference to a 'renewal of the so-much-to be-lamented riotous proceedings' was, of course, a plea to readers to remember the Reform Bill riots of the previous year.

'W', however, wrote another letter the following week accusing 'Pax' of being a secret supporter of the game, and arguing that 800 special constables should be able to deal with 200 players. This only provoked a further letter from 'Pax' who took great umbrage at being labelled 'a secret well-wisher', and questioned whether 'W' had been a spectator at recent games if he thought his assemblage of blackguards could be crushed into 'a narrow compass of 200 players'.[121] He also argued that 'W' appeared to have learnt little from the previous year, and the Reform Bill riots, if he thought there would be any fear of the lash of the law.

In February 1837, a letter to the *Derby Mercury* from an old inhabitant who had witnessed 'years after years of this unchristian play' argued that an efficient police force headed by an indefatigable superintendent should soon be able to bring the 'greatest of all disgraces' to an end.[122] The arguments in such letters reflected the increased ability of local authorities in the 1830s to address matters of law and order following legislation which had enabled the establishment of police forces. On the face of it, the writers had a good case. As we will see in a later chapter, the Highways Act of 1835 gave authorities a stronger legal basis for removing football games from the streets. At the same time, Derby now had a small full-time police force which could be supplemented if needed by swearing in special constables. Yet, notwithstanding the opposition of powerful people like Joseph Strutt, it is understandable that the council would have been hesitant to set up a confrontation between police and players.

The Reform Bill riots were still fresh in the memory and the town had also been through the bitter turmoil of the Silk Trades' Lockout in 1834 which had pitted worker against employer. Also, there was the question of scale. Whereas in a small town, a police force aided by special constables would be sufficient to put down a Shrovetide game, the situation in Derby was very different. The number of people involved as players, ardent supporters and inebriated spectators was simply too big and too volatile to be controlled by a small band of police officers and groups of untrained, undisciplined volunteer constables.

Another letter to the *Derby Mercury*, shortly after Shrovetide 1844, reflected a further source of opposition to the game – property owners. The letter was from a resident of the fast-urbanising village of Litchurch, which at the time was just outside the Borough of Derby but next to the St Peter's goal in Grove Street: 'The players trespassed upon me, destroying the fences, posts, rails and did damage to the crops growing in my garden to a very considerable amount.'[123] The resident felt aggrieved that he could not seek redress for the damage from the borough authorities. He called for suppression of the 'disgraceful and inhuman exhibition' called Derby football, cited the efforts made to suppress the Tutbury bull running and claimed that the Derby football was a more degrading and disgraceful form of amusement.[124]

The Litchurch resident could not have been the only worried property owner when Shrovetide came round each year. Even now, when Royal Shrovetide Football is played at nearby Ashbourne, the preceding hours are taken up with shopkeepers anxiously boarding up their windows, and residents moving their cars away from likely troublesome areas. Yet despite all precautions, fences can get smashed and occasionally cars can get crushed. One observer of the Derby Game wrote, 'The combined strength of the players may be inferred from the fact that strong-built walls, battlements of bridges, iron palisades, and such like barriers, are frequently levelled to earth by them.'[125] An account in the *Dundee Evening Telegraph* recalled the destruction, 'the more riotous of the multitude not hesitating at tearing up palisades, trampling down gardens, or destroying any object which retarded their path'.[126] Whilst a *Manchester Courier* article revealed, 'Great damage was done to property, the course of the play in the fields resembling that of a tornado.'[127]

Opponents of the game included property owners, promoters of horseracing, council leaders, the *Derby Mercury*, and leaders of the union movement. It is the opinions of these factions which mostly appear in print, and which have been bequeathed to posterity. It is a one-sided account. Several contributors to the debate on the future of the game purported to know what the working class or the footballers wanted, but at the time there were no published opinions of the players themselves on whether the game should continue or not. Indeed, apart from the likes of Tunchy Shelton, the thoughts of those who were in the thick of the Shrovetide action rarely see the light of day.

Account after account tells us how important the game was to Derby people, about how through their exploits on a Shrove Tuesday ordinary men could achieve lifelong fame in their hometown, and how the tales of success and subterfuge were told time and again. Yet, few of the main players were either able, or saw fit, to write any of it down. So the strength of the support for the game can only be judged by the actions and ingenuity of the local community who withstood attempts to ban the game for over 100 years.

9

Attempts to Ban

ON THE morning of 4 September 1724, a thief named Jack Sheppard was due to be hung at Tyburn for stealing a silk handkerchief, two silver spoons and three rolls of cloth. But instead, London was astonished to find that he had escaped from the death cell at Newgate prison. This was the third prison break in months by the 22-year-old. Six days later, Sheppard was rearrested and taken to a high security cell in Stone Castle. He was handcuffed and fettered, padlocked in shackles and chained down in a chamber that was barred and locked. But he escaped again and disguised as a fashionable dandy, he enjoyed two weeks of largely inebriated liberty. Back in Newgate he attracted many visitors and enjoyed a drinking match with the prizefighter James Figg. On 16 November, a massive crowd of 200,000 people attended his hanging. After his death his fame was further boosted when Daniel Defoe wrote an account of Sheppard's life – replete with characters like his accomplice Blueskin and Moll Maggot the prostitute – and an opera, *The Beggar's Opera*, based on Sheppard was launched to spectacular acclaim.

The early Georgian period was a time when feelings about law and order were somewhat conflicted. Newspapers and magazines began to appear which gloried in providing gripping accounts of both terrible crimes and gruesome punishments. Highwaymen and other criminals like Sheppard could become folk heroes if there was a good story to be told. The rise in crime, though, was also the cause of much concern, particularly as law enforcement was very different from modern times. The prosecution of criminals was largely left to the victims themselves, who were expected to organise their own criminal investigations.

In times of crisis, volunteer constables would be recruited and prevailed upon to make some effort at law enforcement. This appears to explain the intriguing entries in the accounts of the Derby Borough Chamberlain for 1731 which read:

Feb 23	*Spent at Ye Talbot examining ye football players and upon Constables and Sargeants*	2s 6d
Feb 24	*Spent at Ye Talbot at a Common Hall and ye Justices afterwards with the Constables quelling ye Riot at ye Town Gaol*	6s 0d

Clearly both a Shrovetide football game and a riot had taken place and the volunteer constables had been prevailed upon to try and quell it by arresting some of the players and rioters. Their recompense appears to have been in drinks served at 'Ye Talbot'. Quelling riots was thirsty work. The cause of the unrest can be seen in a previous entry in the chamberlain's accounts:

Feb 18	*Paid Mr Mellors for printing the proclamation against foot Ball & Riots*	2s 6d

This early attempt to ban the game is referred to in a newspaper report of 1747, but until relatively recently no contemporary evidence had been found. However, as revealed by *Derbyshire Miscellany*, the chamberlain's accounts were unearthed between 2012 and 2014 by the Derby Research Group, proving without doubt that attempts to ban the Shrovetide game had started at least 115 years before they were finally successful.[128]

One incident from the game in 1731 serves to highlight the conflicted interests of local people. The keeper of the County Jail, John Greatrex, had himself taken part in the game, despite the efforts of the mayor, Isaac Borrow, to suppress it. Consequently, much to the jailer's annoyance he found himself confined in his own prison. Unsurprisingly, as Hutton remarks in his *History of Derby*, Greatrex was able to make good on his claim that 'the prison should not hold him one night' by escaping.[129]

In February 1746, a notice was posted in the *Derby Mercury* banning any 'riotous or tumultuous meeting' for the purpose of playing football on Shrove Tuesday. One of the reasons for the ban appears to be unhappiness over the breaking of windows and people doing 'mischiefs to the persons and property of the Inhabitants'.[130] The concern about breaking windows may suggest that at that time the game was based more on kicking the ball than hugging it. Another reason for the ban appears to be to prevent people coming into town, during a time when a disease or 'contagion' was present among cattle. Interestingly, the notice made it clear that promotion of the event in adjacent counties by unnamed persons would render such action necessary. This shows that even as early as 1746, the Derby Game was of more than just local interest.

In 1796, opposition to the game grew after one of the players drowned in the River Derwent. After the inquest into the death, the jurors met in the Eagle and Child pub and took it upon themselves to submit a plea to the mayor and magistrates to prevent playing at football on a Shrove Tuesday. The submission stated that the disgraceful custom had 'no better recommendation than its Antiquity'.[131] A couple of weeks later, the mayor published a notice in the *Derby Mercury*, boldly declaring that due to the many private and public evils resulting from playing at football on Shrove Tuesdays:

> Having taken the subject matter of this address into our
> most serious Consideration, and being fully satisfied
> that many public and private evils have been occasioned
> by the custom of playing at FOOT BALL in this
> Borough on Shrove Tuesday – We have unanimously
> resolved, THAT SUCH CUSTOM SHALL FROM
> HENCEFORTH BE DISCONTINUED.[132]

Yet the second part of the same notice betrayed the weakness
of the corporation's position, and for good reason. In 1796 the
Borough of Derby had nothing remotely like a professional
police force. Despite the existence of constables and watchmen,
the business of catching criminals was largely the responsibility
of the general public. If someone witnessed a crime, he or she
was obliged by law to apprehend the perpetrator, giving chase
if necessary. It was not uncommon for a group of people to
pursue thieves or assailants through the streets. If the suspect
was caught, they would be handed over to a constable.

The constable for each parish was an unpaid volunteer,
such as a local shoemaker, shopkeeper or blacksmith. He had
no training, uniform or equipment. He could claim expenses,
for example, if he had to attend court, but relied for his income
upon his main occupation. When an arrest was made by a
constable, he would bring the suspect before a justice of the
peace, or JP. The JPs were appointed by the government and
were usually local grandees like bankers, landowners or factory
owners. Such appointments were regarded as a great honour
and conveyed certain powers, but again JPs were not paid for
carrying out their duties.

This kind of 'do-it-yourself' approach to law and
order severely constrained the borough council, so it is
understandable that a notice which started off so boldly in
banning Shrove Tuesday football had to end with the hope
that, with almost a year to think things over before the next

game, 'The Inhabitants after a dispassionate reflection upon its expediency, will voluntarily abandon the practice, nor compel us by their perseverance therein, to execute those powers which the law has given us for the maintenance of good order.'[133]

The magistrates carried through their resolve and in the week preceding Shrovetide 1797 they issued another notice headlined 'FOOT BALL PROHIBITED'. Predictably, the ban was ignored. Successful defiance of the previous ban was still in living memory, and it would have been hard for the labouring man to take such a ban seriously when the game had so many ardent supporters from the upper classes. No doubt many opinions were formed in alehouses, where pub landlords would be keen to see the games proceed for the sake of the lucrative takings that flowed from excited crowds and visitors. When Shrove Tuesday arrived the constables tried to prevent any ball from getting into the Market Place, but according to legend they were thwarted by local nut seller Mother Hope and her ploy to smuggle the ball in underneath her skirts.

The annual game carried on for another 37 years until in 1834, during the Silk Trades' Lockout, the proponents of unions sought to dissuade workers from taking part. The Grand Consolidated National Trades Union had gained significant influence over the hearts and minds of Derby workers, not least by publicising the lockout and rallying support across the country for Derby strikers. As noted in Chapter 5, the union's magazine, the *Pioneer*, was not in favour of the game. It comments that although magistrates and the military had failed to put the game down, union men had to do so. The hope – rather idealistic, it must be said – was for union men to demonstrate their moral superiority by forsaking the game. The *Pioneer* wrote, 'Magistrates cannot put a stop to it, nor military put it down. But you good men of Derby, my brothers of the Union, you must do it. When that day comes, give moralists a pill to swallow. Let Unions do what force nor gospel could achieve.'[134]

According to the *Pioneer*, these exhortations were at least partially successful in that the game of 1834 was a much smaller affair than normal. This is probably because the union movement had organised an impressive march in support of the locked-out workers. Led by a musical band, around 2,000 people took part in the march, bedecked with a variety of colourful attire: crimson bands, rosettes and scarves. Each group or trade – silk thowsters, framework knitters, sawyers, tailors, shoemakers and more – marched behind a flag or banner. The Shrove Tuesday march left Derby Infirmary and trekked four miles north to the village of Duffield, where the marchers were met by four more musical bands. Clearly this was a major event; some 8,000 to 9,000 people went along just to observe the procession. On Ash Wednesday, the march was repeated eastward to the village of Spondon. The *Pioneer* claimed that the only people who had taken part in the football game were either agricultural labourers or of 'weak mind'.[135] The magazine further argued that the most active man in the football contest had not been gifted with the power of speech since birth (given this history, it seems rather odd that the mural painted in 1986 on the side of Derby's Silk Mill pub to commemorate the lockout includes a football thrown up in the air).

On 13 January 1844, Joseph Strutt, now aged 79 and in poor health, rose from his sickbed and made the short journey from his home in St Peter's Street to the Town Hall, to cast his vote in favour of improving the town's sanitary conditions. Strutt had been involved in civic affairs for the previous 51 years, but this was his final act. He suffered a relapse on the same day and died at home.

He was a colossus in his home town. He had also been the most high-profile supporter of Shrovetide football. While alive and active his views could hardly be ignored, and his death removed a significant obstacle in front of those who wished to see the game abolished. Within a few weeks of Strutt's death, the supporters of abolition started to promote their case. On 28 February the *Derby Mercury* published a letter from a correspondent complaining about his treatment before the Shrove Tuesday game by a 'band of ruffians'.[136] In addition to the details of his encounter, he called for more action by the authorities and refers to the practice of football players knocking on doors and asking for money. He urges residents to report such incidents to the police, in the hope that this will hasten the end of the game. A week later, the *Mercury* published a letter from an exasperated Litchurch resident whose garden had been trashed during the game.

Plans to suppress the annual game started to be made soon after John Moss was elected to the position of mayor in November 1844. Despite some trepidation about the chances of success, steps were taken to gauge the public mood. The strategy that seemed most likely to be successful was to try to persuade the footballers to pursue alternative games and amusements. In return, the authorities would promise to keep the annual Shrovetide holiday. On 22 January 1845 the *Mercury* reported that a notice had been issued a few days previously stating that a public subscription was being raised to provide athletic sports and prizes. The notice claimed that a petition was being drawn up calling for the discontinuance of Shrovetide football; it also said that discussions with leading football players had secured their agreement to relinquish football and take up other sports. Subscriptions in support could be made at banks, booksellers and newspaper offices.

Following news of the notice, the *Mercury* added its own comments, saying that no decent person could be against banning the game and in a Nelsonian flourish it urged the town to 'do its duty' and cough up the money to ensure that the necessary funds for other amusements were available. As

Shrove Tuesday that year fell on 4 February, the paper warned that progress needed to be made as soon as possible. Indeed, the *Mercury*'s stance could hardly have been stronger:

> We, therefore, take the liberty of pressing the subject upon our town readers particularly, and let us add, those of our country readers also who wish well to the borough and are anxious on grounds of decency or propriety and order that the football should be ever discontinued in Derby, to send in pecuniary aid without delay.[137]

A few days later, the memorial – the Victorian equivalent of a petition – which sought the banning of the game, was submitted to the council. The petition denounced the game in the strongest, not to say hysterical, terms. It argued that a great public nuisance arose from:

> Playing at Foot Ball in the public streets and thoroughfares giving rise to the assembling of a lawless rabble, suspending business to the loss of the industrious, creating terror and alarm to the timid and peaceable, committing violence on the persons and damage to the properties of the defenceless and poor, and producing in those who play moral degradation, and in many cases extreme poverty, injury to health, fractured limbs and (not unfrequently) loss of life: rendering their homes desolate, their wives widows, and their children fatherless.[138]

But the *Mercury*'s readership was not entirely convinced of the case for banning. One correspondent took issue with the labelling of all who take part in the game as 'blackguards', pointing out that considering several thousand people took part in the game, the lack of ill feeling was remarkable.[139] Nevertheless, the petition was said to have many signatures and it included a commitment, by those signing it, to refrain from giving the players any money, pledging themselves, 'Not to give any money, support or encouragement to the players; but, on the contrary, to use our best exertions to have apprehended all persons found begging for them.'[140] Players in the Derby Game had a long tradition of soliciting money from supporters and the use of the term 'begging' to describe this custom appears deliberately demeaning. It equates a player giving his all in the cause for his parish as an unworthy beggar.

The printing of the memorial in the *Derby Mercury* was followed by a public notice stating that the game was banned.[141]

NOTICE IS THEREFORE HEREBY GIVEN

That playing at Foot Ball in the public streets and thoroughfares is contrary to law, and that all persons so playing, or encouraging others to play, or who may be found begging, will be liable to be prosecuted, and on conviction may be punished by fine and imprisonment; but although this notice is given to warn all persons of the consequences of breaking the law, the magistrates hope that after the wishes expressed by so many of the inhabitants that the playing at Foot Ball in the public streets and thoroughfares may be discontinued (especially as no holiday is to be abridged, and efforts are making to provide other sports) no person will break or incite others to break the law, but all parties will harmoniously unite in carrying these wishes into effect, and promoting the comfort, happiness and welfare of all classes.

Signed on behalf of the Magistrates
Jan 28th, 1845
JOHN MOSS, Mayor

In 1835, the Highways Act had banned the playing of football on public roads. This act had produced no discernible impact on the Derby Game for the following ten years, but it seems to be what the council was relying on in claiming that the game was contrary to law. The notice threatened fines and imprisonment not just for playing at football but also for begging.

Great effort went into banning the game in 1845. The mayor, John Moss, publicly called for its end. He and other businesspeople contributed funds towards provision of alternative amusements, including a bag race, a blindfolded foot race, and a blindfolded wheelbarrow race. If the races did not take your fancy then you could try gurning (pulling a strange face) through a horse's collar. On Ash Wednesday similar activities were on offer, together with climbing a greased pole, and a plum pudding and treacle eating competition. These games were offered on the strict understanding that they would be brought to an abrupt end if any attempt was made to play the usual Shrovetide football.

These alternatives were planned to take place on The Holmes, just outside the town centre. Negotiations were held with supporters of the football game and the council seemed confident that the alternative activities would be enough to see an end to the ancient custom. As an added incentive, the council offered to pay a total of £10 to men and £5 to boys who wished to play football, provided they did so out of town. At a time when the average weekly wage for a labouring man was 15 shillings, this was a generous offer, even though it is far from clear how the £15 allocated would have been distributed among the footballing men and boys. Lucrative prizes were also offered for each of the winners of the alternative sports: £1 for the winner of the Grand Pedestrian Hurdle Race, five shillings for the greatest distance covered in 20 hops, and seven shillings and sixpence for the winner of the bag race – provided you brought your own bag. Swarming up a greasy pole would earn you a new hat and two shillings and sixpence to spend. Two hundred free tickets were also issued for a tea festival to take place in the Mechanics' Hall, part of the Mechanics' Institute, again on the proviso that the 'disgraceful' game of football did not take place.

A few days before Shrove Tuesday, Moss met some of the leading players of the game and secured their assurance that they would go to the alternative sports and games on The Holmes. When the big day arrived events, at first, went according to plan. Thousands of people gathered at The Holmes, some keen to take part in the new games, others intrigued to see how the day would unfold. The Market Place was much quieter than on a normal Shrove Tuesday, but at two o'clock a ball was thrown up. Around 20 people started playing and their numbers quickly swelled as others joined in.

As soon as Moss heard that a football game had started in the Market Place, he cancelled the authorised alternatives and prizes straightaway. The tea festival at the Mechanics' Hall appears to have gone ahead although it was described by the Derby Temperance Society as 'not entirely successful'.[142] The day after the game, the *Derby Mercury* lost no time in expressing its dismay that the town had been disgraced by a repetition of this 'dirty, unmanly and absurd play'.[143] Police had pursued a softly-softly approach arresting only two players for taking part in the banned football game; these were two working men named Basford and Wardle. Three others were arrested and later charged with aiding and abetting: publicans Mr King and Mr Williamson, and Mr Ebenezer Davenport who for some reason was given the heftiest fine of 40 shillings plus costs. Mr Williamson, the publican at the Green Dragon in St Peter's Parish, may have been related to the Peterite leader William Williamson (aka Tunchy Shelton).

Perhaps not surprisingly then, the 1845 attempt to ban this ancient game by calm persuasion and alternative incentives had not proved sufficient. Those who had doubted that a tradition, which had existed since time immemorial, could be banned so easily, were proved to be correct. They lost no time in letting the mayor know about it. For example, the mill owner, Councillor Madeley, had much fun at a subsequent council meeting in ridiculing the idea that grinning and gurning would stop a football game. The mayor was stung by the criticism, which was hard for him to take from someone like Madeley who had not made a personal effort to help the council provide alternative amusements. John Moss was bitterly disappointed and claimed that the football leaders had broken their faith with him, at the instigation of 'persons who moved in a rather higher station of life than the football players themselves'.[144]

The names of the persons from 'a higher station of life' who encouraged the footballers in 1845 were not made public by Moss. Edward Strutt, the MP for Derby at the time, seems conspicuous by his absence from the football debate. But he must have known by this time that his standing in Derby was on the wane and if he had got involved it is hard to imagine that he would not have been vilified by the *Derby Mercury*. One of the most likely upper-class supporters is Richard Wright Haden, a wine merchant living directly on the Market Place. He was known as an ardent supporter of All Saints', having the ball gilded when they won. He was also a JP, an honoured position and therefore perhaps, in the opinion of those like Moss who wanted to end the game, someone who 'ought to have known better'.[145] But the most telling remarks in the council's debate were made by Alderman Barber, agent to his grace the Duke of Devonshire. He lamented the fact that a few ill-disposed individuals had disturbed the peace of the town and frustrated the wishes of many well-disposed people. The footballers had been given a fair opportunity to replace injury and disgrace with other games. Gentleness and conciliation had been tried but now there was only one course – 'to put the foot-ball down by force'.[146] He could hardly have known how prescient his warning would be.

10

The 'Final' Game

ON THE night of Monday, 23 February 1846, William Eaton Mousley must have gone to bed in the grand surroundings of Exeter House feeling very pleased with himself. He had only been Mayor of Derby for a few months, but he could argue that he had shown responsive leadership. He was about to deal a decisive blow against an issue that previous mayors had failed to deal with for well over a century. He had responded to the disgruntled mill and property owners that were the bedrock of local support for the Conservative Party. He had shown that he was a man for modern times.

A few weeks earlier, Councillor Pegg, a local factory owner, had spoken up at a meeting of Derby Borough Council asking if there was any intention to put down that year's football game. Mousley was cool and calculated in council debates, knowing how to use humour to telling effect. He replied that since some of those present had done their best to prevent the return of horseracing, then it seemed only fair that football should carry on. After all, he reasoned, the people must have some amusement. This reply was clearly meant to ridicule Pegg, as he had been one of those against horseracing. But Pegg was an old hand in such debates and stood his ground. He argued that something needed to be done and that it was high time that Derby stopped being 'at the mercy of a reckless and lawless mob'.[147] Pegg felt the magistrates ought to have sufficient powers to put the game down and, if not, he suggested that they could always petition the secretary of state for help. Pegg's main aim seems to have been to get rid of the Shrovetide holiday and presumably Councillor Richardson had Pegg in mind when he said there was a class of people who, 'would have the working classes shut up in factories or other places six days a week, and sent to church or chapel the seventh, throughout the year. They would deny them all recreation, unless comporting exactly with their own peculiar notions.'[148]

After the failure of the alternative games of the previous year, the council might have been tempted to put the issue on hold for a year or two, particularly after Alderman Crompton had his fellow councillors laughing when he recounted the occasion when an old woman had defied a ban and smuggled a ball into the Market Place, under her skirts, and 'delivered herself of the ball'.[149] Nevertheless, the meeting recommended that the mayor and magistrates put down the football and preserve the peace on Shrove Tuesday and Ash Wednesday. To another chorus of laughter, Mousley informed the council that there would be no swarming up poles or pudding eating competitions this time round.

The mayor sprang into action. The town's entire police force consisted of just 20 constables and a superintendent, so Mousley knew such limited manpower would have little impact on a hostile mob. To boost his forces and to show how seriously he took this matter, he had several hundred residents sworn in as special constables. Their job was to help marshal the crowds and assist the police. But Mousley also knew that he needed something more disciplined and menacing than a small police force and a large group of volunteers. He wrote to Sir James Graham, the home secretary, requesting authority to use military power if the resources of the civil authority proved insufficient to maintain law and order. Sir James agreed and on

Monday, 16 February a troop of the 5th Dragoon Guards rode over from Nottingham, with a week to make their presence well known around town before Shrove Tuesday. Their arrival must have triggered many unhappy memories of previous confrontations between mobs and military power.

To turn up the pressure on the players, Mousley issued notices banning the game and placards were posted liberally around town:

FOOT-BALL PLAY
ON SHROVE TUESDAY AND
ASH WEDNESDAY
BOROUGH OF DERBY

The Town Council and the greater part of the principal inhabitants of this Borough, having called upon the Mayor and Magistrates to put down the unlawful and riotous assemblage of persons on Shrove Tuesday and Ash Wednesday, for the purpose of PLAYING AT FOOT-BALL, by which the public peace is broken, the peaceable inhabitants put in great fear, property destroyed, banking-houses and shops closed, and public business suspended:-

NOTICE IS HEREBY GIVEN,
That the Mayor and Magistrates have found it imperative upon them, to put an end to such an unlawful assembly, and the riot and confusion arising therefrom; and if any person or persons shall assemble within the Borough of Derby for this purpose, or shall collect or attempt to collect money for the support and carrying on the same, such person or persons will be apprehended and dealt with according to law.
Dated the 17th day of February, 1846.
W. EATON MOUSLEY

The notice was printed in the *Derby Mercury*.[150] It was followed by an editorial which drew readers' attention to the efforts of the mayor to 'put an end to those scenes which have long disgraced the town of Derby'.[151] The newspaper asserted that the mayor was acting with the full support of the secretary of state, and went on to encourage the local factory owners to give their workers an additional day's holiday to enjoy the annual races, in return for giving up the football game. The *Mercury* also picked up on the council's tougher approach, warning that, 'If civil power shall be found insufficient for the purposes intended, a more efficient power will be had recourse to.'[152]

On Saturday, 21 February, with three days to go before the fateful day, a further troop of Dragoon Guards, led by Lieutenant-Colonel James Scarlett, cantered into town. The early arrival of the military was no doubt intended to remind any would-be footballers of the opposition that they might have to contend with. The 5th Dragoon Guards had been trained to be used as shock cavalry. They were provided with large warhorses and equipped with heavy swords. The dragoons' main function in battle was to smash into enemy lines, breaking up formations by hacking swathes through them, spreading chaos and terror in their wake. The regiment had helped to destroy several battalions of French infantry at the Battle of Salamanca in 1812, wielding the fearsome heavy cavalry sword. The regiment's motto was *Vestigia Nulla Retrorsum*, meaning 'Never a Step Backward'. As these troops moved through Derby in the days preceding the game, many Peterites and All Saints' men must have considered what chance they would have against the soldiers riding past on their powerful horses, as well as the guns and swords they carried.

Early on the Monday evening before the annual Shrovetide game, Mousley met with some of the leading football players. According to the *Derby and Chesterfield Reporter*, they had goaled the ball the year before – presumably this means a group of players from the parish that had scored the goal in the previous year. Consequently, one of their number would have been looking forward to the honour of throwing up the ball at the following day's game. The players surrendered the 'sacred' ball to the mayor, promising to obey the ban and to persuade their fellow players to follow suit. Mousley congratulated the players on their good sense. He said he was one of the last persons in the world to interfere with the amusements of the people, but such an 'old and barbarous custom' could not be encouraged in the present day.[153]

In return for the players' undertaking, Mousley had in fact promised very little. He had undertaken to use his influence with the manufacturers to give a day's recreation, but even if he managed to persuade the mill owners to grant this concession it would not compensate for the loss of two days' holiday. He had promised to put down a 'handsome subscription' himself so that they could have a better amusement and would encourage others to follow suit. He suggested the possibility of a railway trip. In addition, he pledged his support for re-establishing horseracing. He trusted the players would remain at work themselves on the following day, but also use their influence on their fellow players. Finally, he hoped the players' actions would spare the magistrates 'the unpleasant duty of having recourse to force'.[154]

The meeting between the mayor and footballers appears to have been quite friendly and, if the sole report on the meeting is to be believed, the players were cowed and contrite. This is understandable because Mousley seems to have skilfully prepared the ground for this meeting. In the preceding week, the Derby Race Committee had issued a public notice stating that horseracing would be re-established if the football was suppressed. No doubt many local people were keen to see the races return. On their way to the meeting the players had to walk through streets emblazoned with posters banning the football game. Well over 100 Dragoon Guards had been enjoying making their presence felt around town. The players must have spent an agonising week contemplating their chances of success against well-drilled heavy cavalry. They could see that the opposition was ready and determined and many were acutely aware from their previous experience that it was potentially deadly.

Also, the players may have been overawed by their surroundings in the new Town Hall and their meeting with the town's most powerful man. Mousley was a skilled manipulator, but when the meeting finished and the footballers emerged outside into the evening air, they may have begun to realise that they had given a lot away for very little in return. The players had not only surrendered the ball, but also given away two holidays that had been enjoyed by generations of Derby people. It is hard to imagine that families and friends would lose any time in expressing their feelings on the outcome of the meeting. The leading players were men who had already made their reputation through the game. But there were many other younger men who just wanted a chance to play and show what they could do.

So, closing his eyes on the eve of Shrove Tuesday, Mousley must have been quietly optimistic that all his preparations would pay off and that he could look forward to a fairly uneventful day. There were even some employers who had been persuaded to keep their mills and factories working as usual, instead of granting a holiday to their employees. But if Mousley was expecting a much quieter Shrovetide, then his optimism quickly evaporated the following morning as he walked the short distance from his home to the Market Place.

It was a very mild winter's day, and crowds were already starting to assemble. There was a note of rebellion in the air, particularly from groups of lads and young men. They were making it clear that they wanted a football game to go ahead. The police and special constables were told to seal off the entrances to the Market Place. But as two o'clock approached many thousands were crammed into the Morledge and other streets around the Market Place.

There was one glimmer of hope for the abolitionists. There had been no throwing of soot or filthy rags at respectable people. Two o'clock, the traditional time for throwing up the ball, arrived and went without incident. Perhaps all would be peace and harmony after all. But no, it was not to be. A huge roar erupted from the crowd as a ball was brought down Cockpit Hill into the Morledge, between the Market Place and the River Derwent. Hundreds of people in adjoining streets surged forward to see what was going on. The mob closed in upon the ball and very quickly got it into a mill stream near Mr Pegg's colour works. The police, led by Superintendent Thompson, rushed to the scene. PC Benjamin Fearn plunged into the water and after a tussle lasting several minutes emerged with the ball and handed it to his superior officer. Thompson promptly hacked the ball into leather shreds. Meanwhile, in the water a desperate struggle was going on between PC William Wragg and Henry Allen, the man who had thrown up the ball. Wragg had got hold of his adversary and was trying to drag him to the bank, but Allen managed to struggle free. He swam to the other bank and made his escape.

For the next hour the atmosphere in the Derby streets was tense. Some special constables were attacked, others were on the receiving end of insults and abuse from frustrated players and spectators, particularly youths. The magistrates withdrew the police to the Town Hall. They hoped this would help to calm things down. The tactic only provided a temporary respite. Indeed, it seemed to provide the footballers with a golden opportunity, for another ball was thrown up out of a pub on the Morledge.

This time the players acted swiftly. The ball was quickly moved out of the central streets and down to the banks of the Derwent. A detachment of police and specials rushed down to the new railway bridge to try and intercept the play. They were met by an angry mob who managed to overpower them. Mousley and some fellow magistrates cantered up to the scene of this new outbreak. They were greeted with a hail of missiles. Things were turning ugly. One of the special constables was spat upon and a brick and a bludgeon sailed through the air towards Mousley. Luckily for him, and probably for his assailant, one of these missiles narrowly missed his head but bounced off his shoulder. All the same, Mousley was left with a nasty bruise. The police dived in and got hold of his attacker, but the footballers quickly got the upper hand and freed him. Matters were clearly getting out of control and the civil authority had one last resort – to read the Riot Act.

The Riot Act enabled local authorities to declare a group of 12 or more persons to be unlawfully assembled. It was intended to be used to prevent tumults and riotous assemblies and it had some very serious consequences. Firstly, the mob had to disperse within one hour of the declaration. Secondly, the local authority could use force to clear them. Thirdly, anyone helping the authorities to move the crowd on was indemnified against legal repercussions should anyone in the crowd get injured or killed. The Riot Act had been around for well over 100 years, but its most notorious use had occurred just 27 years before 1846, in Manchester. In an event that came to be known as the Peterloo Massacre, around a dozen people were killed and hundreds injured.

The Riot Act had been used in 1831 in Derby to disperse Reform Bill rioters and two people had died and many were badly injured as a direct result of authorised actions, so local people would have been familiar with the possible consequences of defying it. Mousley's decision, therefore, to use the Act and deploy the Dragoon Guards must have been a momentous one. It shows the extent of his determination to pursue his policy of banning the game. Perhaps the brick bouncing off his shoulder had strengthened, rather than weakened, his resolve. The decision also showed how desperate he had become, as he later confessed in a report to the Home Office that he had found that the civil powers of police and volunteer constables were totally incapable of keeping the public peace. Once he had read the Riot Act, Mousley could deploy the Dragoon Guards. He did so immediately. Most of the troops, who had been held back in the Market Place, were sent down Siddals Lane (later renamed Siddals Road) towards the railway bridge.

With the dragoons approaching, the players made off into the countryside around the river and got outside the borough boundary. Troops were also stationed at both goals in case of a sudden eruption of activity. Instead, there was a welcome lull during which no one in authority knew where the ball was. Perhaps the players had given up? They had not. In the evening, there were reports of people playing near to Normanton village. In 1846, Normanton was outside the borough boundary and beyond Mousley's control. Accordingly, Sir Henry Wilmot, who was both a county as well as a borough magistrate, placed himself at the head of the military and civil forces. The game continued with around 50 Dragoon Guards in pursuit. The *Derby and Chesterfield Reporter* later remarked that the guards took the 'hedges in fine style' and onlookers thought the adventure took on a 'quite romantic character'.[155] The usual game was between the northern and southern halves of Derby. This one was now between the football diehards and the forces of law and order as represented by the police and military.

It was perhaps fortunate that the commanding officer of the 5th Dragoon Guards was James Scarlett. Somewhat unusually for military leaders at the time, he was, by several accounts, a level-headed and good-natured man, respected by both officers and the rank and file. He had taken over command from Sir John Slade in 1840. By contrast, Sir John was poorly regarded by colleagues, with 'that damned stupid fellow' and 'a disgrace to the service' being just two examples of many insults to his reputation.[156] Scarlett's instructions to his troops are not known, but sensibly they seem to have been more about trying to disperse and push the players away from the town than exacting any retribution.

But it was the local police, in the form of PCs Fearn, Messenger and Stevenson, who managed to close in on the ball. It seems the players had been using the hedges to frustrate the authorities in their attempts to get the ball. Whenever the officials closed in on someone holding the ball, the person in possession simply threw it over a hedge to a fellow player. The local police, with their knowledge of the game, were wise to this tactic. Having sighted the ball, Messenger approached on one side of a hedge with Fearn and Stevenson on the other. Messenger managed to grab hold of the man with the ball, who then immediately threw it over the hedge. Fearn was on the other side and managed to hold on to the ball for ten minutes before he was eventually overpowered. Fearn was an avowed Peterite. He had fallen into the hands of the All Saints' and they had no compunction in throwing him over the hedge. Meanwhile, Messenger had managed to hold on to his man, who was destined to spend the night in the County Jail. The game continued into darkness, only finishing when, according to a later account by Fearn, the ball was eventually 'goaled' by All Saints' at the Old Mill Wheel on Markeaton Brook.

If the exhausted participants had any time for reflection after all the excitement of the day, their thoughts must have been sobering. Mousley could hardly call the day a great success. Hundreds of constables and troops had been deployed against local citizens and still some sort of game had taken place. For the players, their thoughts may have been even more worrying. They had brazenly flouted the law and clashed with the police and military. People had been transported for less, and prison sentences certainly looked likely for those arrested. Over the next few days news of the events was covered in many newspapers across the country. Under a headline reading 'FOOTBALL RIOTS AT DERBY – THE MILITARY CALLED OUT', the *Leeds Mercury* reported, 'The almost absolute custom of driving the foot-ball through the streets of Derby on Shrove Tuesday and Ash Wednesday, were this week attended with serious riots, the military being called out and a regular chase being given to disturbers of the public peace.'[157]

Rather oddly, many similar articles seemed to be convinced that these events would be enough to put a final end to the game. But as we will see, the local council was still not convinced that it had seen off all resistance.

Despite all the efforts to stop it and the serious possibility of severe punishment for those taking part, the game of 1846 had taken place. This shows the strong, some might say fanatical, attachment of local people to this annual event. This fanaticism may be hard for some people to comprehend, but it is still clearly evident in remaining events like Ashbourne Shrovetide Football or the Atherstone Ball Game. For the players, these games are a heady mix of identity, community and bravado, with the chance to be a local hero, not just for one day, but for the rest of your life. For the youths and young men taking part in 1846, this was an event they had seen as children and heard old men tell tales about. In the period leading up to Shrove Tuesday and the weeks that followed of post-game analysis, the event was the everyday source of banter and jibe among apprentices and working people. For them, banning the game was not just a day's disappointment, it was denying them their birthright as a Derby citizen.

One citizen who had enjoyed a very eventful Shrove Tuesday was PC Benjamin Fearn. He must have had mixed feelings. On the one hand he had performed his duty with great zeal. On the other, he may have been instrumental in killing a game he enjoyed. Born in Clifton, near Ashbourne, he may have picked up Shrovetide football fever there as a boy, or as a young man after he had moved down the road to Derby when he was learning the tailoring trade in St Peter's Parish. He joined Derby Police in 1841, at a time when the idea of having a professional force was still rather a novelty. But for a man who clearly was very willing to enter the fray, this was a good career choice. This was a time when police work was low on paperwork and high on action. He started as a constable and soon became all too familiar with dealing with violent altercations. June 1843 was a typical month: while wrestling for several minutes with a drunken man he was bitten severely in the hand, and then pelted with stones by onlookers. A couple of weeks later, he was attacked by a drunken Ellen Smith, who dragged him on to a pub floor after seizing him by the hair.

In later life, Fearn admitted that as a young officer he had, together with two colleagues, actively assisted the St Peter's side during Shrovetide games, while a further officer joined in with All Saints'. His actions on the day of the 'final' game in securing the first ball and almost getting hold of the second suggest someone with a strong aptitude for the game. His profile around town undoubtedly made him well known to the players. In return, he must have known many of those in the thick of the action, and as will become clear in the next chapter, he may well have been acquainted with Henry Allen, the man who threw up the first ball and started all the mayhem. As the exhausted town went to sleep that night, at least Fearn had a memento of the game he loved. He still had the ball which Superintendent Thompson had handed back to him.

Aftermath

ASH WEDNESDAY was traditionally a day for sober reflection, particularly for those who had gone a little too wild on Shrove Tuesday. In the cold light of an early morning the events of the day before could take on a new shape drained of the heady mix of emotions, friends and foes that stirred them. On the morning of Ash Wednesday, 25 February 1846, Henry Allen, Hugh Shaw, Henry Smith, John Smith, Samuel Taft, William Tarr, William Whiting, James Wigley and Robert Wood were presented before Derby's mayor and magistrates. Some of the group were charged with violence towards the police. The remainder were charged either with playing the banned football game themselves, or exciting others to play. They were remanded until the following Saturday.

At midday, the streets around Derby Market Place were again thronged with people. Traditionally, Ash Wednesday was the day of the boys' game and no doubt many boys, as well as anxious fathers and mothers, had turned up to see what would happen. The events of the previous day, the reading of the Riot Act, the pursuit of the footballers by armed Dragoon Guards, the wrestling with police and the uncertain future of those arrested would all have been common knowledge. But the formation of another mob was the last thing the authorities wanted. Accordingly, the police and special constables were instructed to clear the streets. They must have faced some resistance as several people were rounded up and charged with obstructing the police in the execution of their duty. Nevertheless, the action was enough to prevent any attempt to start the boys' game. That evening those who had been detained by the police were taken before the mayor and then freed after giving assurances to appear when called upon.

On Thursday morning, James Bancroft, Thomas Oakley, Samuel Pipes and Luke Sharp were brought before the mayor and magistrates. They were bound to appear when called upon. A man with the surname of Kimberlain, or possibly Kimberline, claimed he had just been an innocent bystander to the events, when he had been struck on the arm by a special constable. He also said that he had told his brother to stay at work that afternoon and not get involved. On hearing this argument, Mayor William Eaton Mousley wryly commented that it was very strange Kimberlain could persuade his brother to stay away, but then commit such an error himself. It is intriguing also that Kimberlain's employer, a Mr Pipes, spoke up for Kimberlain and provided his surety on bail, especially so when it appears that his son, Samuel Pipes, according to PC Moorcroft, had been very active in inciting the mob in the Siddals area. At the same session with the magistrates, John Wood was fined seven shillings and sixpence for spitting at Mr Baker, one of the special constables on the day.

On Friday evening, Mousley attended Derby's Theatre Royal. After such a hectic and demanding week, he must have been greatly pleased to hear and receive the plaudits of the audience as he and his family took their seats in a box overlooking the stage. The event, which was under the patronage of Lieutenant-Colonel Scarlett and the Dragoon Guards, was clearly a significant event in the town's social calendar. The *Derbyshire Advertiser* reported that there was a 'brilliant and crowded audience' including several members of the gentry and principal tradesmen of the town.[158] The Band of the 5th Dragoon Guards greatly added to the evening's entertainment.

The following morning, Mousley was back at work with his fellow magistrates. Firstly they dealt with several everyday cases, then a lengthy six-hour session began as depositions and evidence were heard against Allen, Kimberlain, Shaw, Henry and John Smith, Taft, Tarr, Whiting, Wigley and Wood. Five of the defendants were let off after undertaking to keep the peace for 12 months. The rest were remanded until the Tuesday and awarded bail, with the exception of Allen. The mayor refused to take any bail for Allen, who was clearly felt to be the ringleader.

It is sad that despite their lengthy court appearances, nothing of what the accused had to say in their defence was ever published. But, using *Glover's Directory* and census information, it is possible to trace the age, homes and jobs of some of those arrested for playing football. The men were mostly young, between 19 and 30 years old, making a living from occupations such as chimney sweep, framework knitter, labourer, butcher or sawyer. The oldest was Thomas Oakley at around 35, who appears to have been a timber merchant in Siddals Lane. William Tarr, son of the publican in the Noah's Ark on the Morledge, was 19 years old and appears to have been the youngest of the accused. Most of the group, like Henry Allen, a journeyman whitesmith, were young men who perhaps thought Shrovetide 1846 was their last chance to play a game they had once considered a birthright. It is noticeable that they came from a tightly defined area. These are men who were born into and lived their lives in the confines of the inner town in Agard Street, Castle Street, Eagle Street, Sadler Gate, Siddals Lane and Nottingham Road. None of them lived more than a ten-minute walk from the Market Place.

On Tuesday, 3 March, Allen, Taft, John Smith, Wigley and Wood appeared before the mayor and magistrates for the third time in seven days. A week had now passed since the Shrovetide game and no doubt the men had spent plenty of time thinking about the possible consequences of their actions; particularly Allen, who had spent the whole time in prison. Consequently, it was a contrite group who made their appearance that day. As Mousley pointed out to them, and Allen in particular, if he pressed the serious charge for felony then they could be facing 15 years' transportation. But in view of their contrition and a promise not to offend again in the same manner, the mayor decided to press for lesser charges and proceed against them only for misdemeanour.

There may also have been another reason for Mousley to exercise some leniency. Allen, who was the most likely of those arrested to get a severe punishment, appears to have been the son of a police constable, James Allen. James was well known to the magistrates as one of Derby's first policemen. He had been one of the key witnesses to the Reform Bill riots in 1831. By 1846 his seniority was reflected in his title of magistrate's constable. If this was not embarrassing enough, it would have been common knowledge that policemen had been active participants in the game only a few years previously. Consequently, while the magistrates must have been angry that the recent game had caused so much trouble, they must also have found it difficult to justify severe punishment. After all, a few years previously the game had enjoyed the active support of some of the leading figures in the town. Whatever the reasons, the accused men were not charged with felony, but instead with unlawfully assembling with diverse other persons and committing a riot and disturbance against the peace of Her Majesty. They were committed for trial at the County Assizes. Finally, Mousley also agreed to grant bail for Allen.

The following day, in addition to its account of the various appearances before magistrates, the *Derby Mercury* contained a special statement from Mousley and his closest supporters. The statement thanked the special constables for their efforts, as well as the manufacturers and others who had kept their employees and servants fully occupied during Shrovetide, instead of letting them have time off for a holiday. The statement claimed that these joint efforts had resulted in 'nearly wholly preventing' the playing of football in public streets and thoroughfares.[159] This seems a gross exaggeration. A game had still taken place despite the strenuous efforts of the police, Dragoon Guards, and hundreds of volunteer constables. It is clear that Mousley and his allies in the local press were determined to control the narrative.

The *Mercury* expressed the thanks of the town to the mayor and magistrates 'for having rid the town of the disgraceful exhibition of foot-ball'.[160] The paper did not give coverage to complaints made elsewhere by Derby residents about the behaviour of the Dragoon Guards, billeted in local inns. Instead, it shifted the focus, 'We believe we are correct in stating that the greatest opposition to the authorities was displayed by the women and grown-up lads, who seemed either to totally disregard, or not to comprehend, the consequences of their folly.'[161]

At 11am on Monday, 16 March, Sir Robert Wilmot, baronet and high sheriff of Derbyshire, entertained a large party of gentlemen to breakfast at his stately residence at Osmaston Hall just outside Derby. The *Mercury* informed its readers that the meal was 'replete with every delicacy'.[162] Suitably fortified, the prestigious party set off at 1pm to meet the judges on their way over from Nottingham. Two hours later the cavalcade entered the town and the Commission of Assize was opened. At six o'clock the High Sheriff and a large party enjoyed a dinner at the King's Head, which was 'excellent in every respect'.[163] This was just as well, because over the next few days the Assizes would be one of the busiest ever.

In Victorian times, the courts of assize were held in county towns such as Derby and presided over by a visiting judge from a higher court in London. This arrangement saved those involved in such trials from the expense and inconvenience of travelling from the provinces to London. There were many cases to consider, including those of cases 38 to 42, the five men indicted for creating a riot in Derby on Shrove Tuesday under the pretence of playing football.

Two days later, with impeccable timing, the *Derby Mercury* published a notice on its front page containing the news that a memorial (or signed petition) had been presented to the mayor and magistrates by a James Haywood. It began:

> We, the undersigned, inhabitants of the Borough of Derby, beg to tender our thanks to the Mayor and Magistrates of the said Borough, for the promptitude, energy, and forbearance they displayed in putting an end to the disgraceful exhibition which we had been accustomed to witness in the public streets and thoroughfares on Shrove-Tuesday and Ash-Wednesday; an exhibition which was demoralizing in its tendency, physically injurious to all who participated in it, an obstruction to business, destructive of property, and a stigma upon the town.[164]

The notice went on to state that the best thanks of the town were due to the mayor and magistrates for their actions. There was then a list of around 180 signatories; typically, the signatories are aldermen, councillors, solicitors, manufacturers and traders. If one of the aims of this notice was to convince higher authorities that Mousley had the support of the town's most important people, then it could not have appeared at a better time. The very next day, Thursday, 19 March, cases 38 to 42 came before the court and Mr Justice Coltman.

The five accused men all pleaded guilty. In presenting the case, Sergeant Clarke said he had been instructed by the mayor and magistrates to bring the prosecution out of a sense of public duty. The Town Council, he said, was resolved to use every means at its disposal to put down football playing. He pointed out that the mayor had acted 'under the advice and sanction of the secretary of state' in having a military force ready to assist the special constables.[165]

Clarke described a very different situation to the 'nearly wholly prevented' line previously taken by Mousley. He said that despite all endeavours, measures and remonstrances, the prisoner Henry Allen had thrown up a ball, which had resulted in a great and tumultuous assembly. Much riot and confusion had ensued which was beyond the means of the constables to suppress. Accordingly, the mayor had read the Riot Act, the military had been called in and several people had been apprehended.

Clarke then described how Derby was a much smaller place when the game was originally practised, and went on to claim:

> At the present time the town had become very large. Persons from a distance occasionally residing in it, whose characters were unknown, availed themselves of this opportunity of injuring persons by destroying property, alarming the timid and well-disposed inhabitants, and putting a stop to all business for the greater part of two days.[166]

The years 1845 and 1846 had been a time of substantial Irish immigration into England due to the horrendous famine in Ireland caused, initially at least, by a potato blight. The early 1840s was a period of intense railway-building in Derby, which would have brought in many temporary workers. In referring to 'persons from a distance occasionally residing in it', Clarke seemed to have been hinting that Irish navvies were using the Shrovetide event as an excuse for malicious behaviour. This appears an odd statement to make given that all the defendants were local men. In addition, for as long as anyone could remember many Derby businesses had been used to shutting down during Shrovetide and granting holidays to their employees. Loss of business was nothing new.

Clarke told Coltman that he had been instructed not to press for punishment, but to instead call upon the judge's support in showing to the public that there must be an end to football-playing in Derby. Coltman duly played his part. He said that Mousley had shown great leniency and while the length of time that this custom had prevailed might have been a consideration, it was impossible to permit it any longer. He said he believed the prisoners were sincere in the feelings they had shown. Accordingly, he gave them suspended fines of £50 each, conditional upon their future good behaviour.

The guilty men ought to have considered themselves very fortunate indeed. If it were not for Mousley's request for admonishment, rather than punishment, then the sentences would have been much more severe. He could also have framed the charges in such a way that a sentence of transportation might have been on the cards. On the same day in court, Coltman gave a sentence of 15 years' transportation to William Riley, 18, for stealing £25. He also gave John Knifton, 21, four months' imprisonment and hard labour for stealing some turnips and beans. Henry Allen's actions had provoked a riot which hundreds of special constables had been unable to control and had led to the deployment of the Dragoon Guards for several hours. He was a very lucky man to have got away with one week in jail while on remand, and a few anxious weeks awaiting trial. One can only surmise whether being a policeman's son helped him escape a punitive sentence.

A year later, just before Shrovetide 1847, notices banning the football game were again posted. Mousley, who unusually was still the mayor for a second year, was as determined as ever. Scores of special constables were sworn in. They positioned themselves on the principal streets and followed their instructions not to allow any groups to assemble. With the approval of the home secretary – Mousley had made a special trip to London in the hope of seeing him – a troop of dragoons was again brought over from Nottingham. This shows that Mousley must have been fairly confident as only one troop was considered sufficient this time. A large crowd assembled around midday, but the constables managed to disperse them by insisting they return to their places of business.

In 1848 a new mayor was in charge. Not only was his name, Mozley, hardly any different to that of his predecessor in the post, but his views on Shrovetide football were also virtually identical. Indeed, within minutes of accepting the role, Henry Mozley made his position clear on the future of the football game, as he told the council that, 'He hoped it was at an end for ever; but if there was any endeavour to revive it – or if anyone thought there would be an opportunity from the change in mayoralty to renew that most degrading play – he could tell them he should firmly resist all such attempts.'[167]

Interestingly, his statement coming so soon after becoming mayor, betrays some trepidation that the game had not been extinguished. Mozley had been one of the signatories of the memorial submitted by grateful citizens in 1846 thanking Mousley for his actions in suppressing the game. Accordingly, before Shrovetide 1848, Mozley adorned the town with posters promising legal action against anyone playing football in public streets or places during Shrovetide within the Borough of Derby. The posters proclaimed that the mayor and magistrates were acting at the request of the secretary of state. In fact, Mozley had gone to considerable lengths in pestering the home secretary, now Sir George Grey, to sanction military support for the third year in a row. The 4th Royal Irish Dragoon Guards arrived a few days before Shrove Tuesday. Again, there was no attempt to start a game and no unseemly riots. Even so, for the next few years there was a military presence in the town during Shrovetide just to make sure there was no resumption of the old game.

Derby Shrovetide Football as a major event was now dead. It was killed off not just by the actions of the borough council and the triple whammy of mayors Moss, Mousley and Mozley, but by changing attitudes. In addition, the changing geography of the town must have played a part. The railways and associated infrastructure now created obstacles on the open land next to the river which had long been St Peter's preferred route to goal. Perhaps the culverting of Markeaton Brook through the town centre was a critical blow. The line of the watercourse that used to define whether a Derby resident rooted for St Peter's or All Saints' had been rubbed out.

But the love of the game could not be so easily exterminated. At two o'clock on Shrove Tuesday 1868, a crowd of around 150 from nearby factories and foundries assembled in Bridge Street, close to the Ram Inn. After driving the ball up several streets, it was taken into Markeaton Brook near St John's Church and was eventually goaled near Nun's Mill. Two years later a similar game took place in the same West End neighbourhood, this time starting in Agard Street.

In 1885, Derby County Football Club, which had formed only the previous year, held a match at the County Ground to commemorate the old game. The team representing St Peter's wore a blue ribbon, while players for All Saints' wore a yellow badge. Unfortunately, the weather was atrocious, which meant a late start with All Saints' being a man short and the mayor failing to show up. This game was played more to something like association football rules, although in honour of the old game it was decided to dispense with offside rules and to kick the ball in rather than use throw-ins. While the game was a bit of a washout, it sparked a wave of nostalgia for the Shrovetide match, and key participants were sought out for their memories. One of these was former policeman Benjamin Fearn.

By 1849, Fearn had been promoted to sergeant and in 1860 he became an inspector. In a colourful career, he dealt with assaults, robberies, poaching, election rigging, counterfeit currency, murders and con artists. On occasion he donned plain clothes and worked undercover. He also dealt with cruelty to children. On one occasion he was called upon to rescue a young girl who was being tied up every day by her stepmother when she went off to work. The starving girl was imprisoned in her home, slept on vermin-infested hay and survived by picking potato peelings out of a swill tub. On another occasion he pursued a female con artist 25 miles across country into Staffordshire. She had made off with a character called 'Flash Jack' in a horse and trap. Rushing on to the platform at Lichfield Railway Station, Fearn stopped a train that was in the process of departing so that he could make his arrest. His quarry was found to have a bundle of £5 notes concealed in her stockings. Fearn retired after 37 years' service, unfortunately permanently disabled after being assaulted in the course of his duty. A former chief constable said that 'no town in England ever possessed a better detective officer', and Derby's pub landlords presented him with a purse of 50 sovereigns as a mark of their esteem.[168] So it is not surprising that the local press sought out the reminiscences of this renowned and respected figure.

In an interview with the *Mercury*, Fearn told how his position as a young 'Peeler' or policeman in 1842 and 1843 had not stopped him getting involved on behalf of St Peter's. He told of his adventures in trying to stop the games in 1845 and 1846, of being in the thick of the action and getting thrown over a hedge by the All Saints' players, and of how he ended up as custodian of a ball used in the final game of Derby Shrovetide Football. Presumably this ball was the same one that was cut to pieces by Superintendent Thompson.

This is supported by a report in the *Derby Daily Telegraph* in 1922 which relates how an old Derby football had been passed down through generations of the Fearn family and was thought to be with descendants in Lancashire. The football was said to be of an 'extraordinary shape' – no doubt a result of the repairs needed after the treatment it received from Thompson.[169] This report means it is likely that the old Derby Shrovetide ball retained by Derby Museum is the ball that was surrendered to William Eaton Mousley by leading players on the eve of Shrove Tuesday 1846. The museum's ball is still in good condition, is perfectly round, and was gifted to the curators by the council's Estates Committee in 1889. Frustratingly, Fearn was not asked about Henry Allen, or perhaps even 40 years after the event, a veil was still being drawn over the fact that Allen was a policeman's son. With such a small force, it seems inconceivable that Fearn did not know Allen was the son of a colleague and may well have already known who he was when he saw him throw up the ball.

What happened after the demise of the old game? Well, the holiday of Shrove Tuesday quickly disappeared, but for those of a sporting inclination, there was at least some theoretical compensation, when horseracing resumed in 1848 on the new racecourse on Nottingham Road. The races were seen by many as an appropriate way to replace the more objectionable pastime of mob football. The races lasted on the site until 1939 and the Second World War.

James Scarlett, the man in charge of the horse-riding Dragoons Guards who in 1846 had cleared the Derby hedges in such fine style while pursuing Shrovetide footballers, turned out to be a hero of the Crimean War against Russia. In 1854,

Scarlett was a stout, red-faced man sporting a large white moustache and bristling white eyebrows. More importantly he was now the brigadier in charge of the Heavy Brigade. During the Battle of Balaclava, Scarlett was ordered to move his forces to a new position. However, folds in the landscape had concealed the advanced position of the Russians. Scarlett was astonished to find himself staring up the slopes of the Causeway Heights at a huge mass of Russian horsemen. Recovering his wits, Scarlett ordered his men to wheel into line. Although his force only amounted to around 700 troopers, he determined to charge uphill at the thousands above him. Meanwhile, the Russians also wheeled into line and at a steady trot, started to descend the hill.

Unfortunately, the ground to Scarlett's left was not good ground, and some readjustment was needed to get the lines together in good parade ground order. Nerves jangling, Scarlett sat on his horse, conveying an image of cool composure, waiting for his first line to get into attack formation. Up above on the heights, incredulous British observers looked down on what they must have considered would be imminent disaster. Then Scarlett gave the order for his first line of cavalry, numbering barely 300 men, to charge. Riding stirrup to stirrup with his trumpeter, the courageous brigadier plunged into the enemy head on. He slashed left and right and soon found himself supported by his remaining forces numbering about 400 in all. The Russian cavalry had ground to a halt and finding themselves attacked from all sides, broke up and retreated.

Consequently, Scarlett became associated with one of the most renowned acts of bravery by the British Army, leading one of the greatest feats of cavalry in the history of Europe. He might well still be a household name were it not for the fact that the infamous Charge of the Light Brigade occurred on the same day as his action. But in his adopted town of Burnley, he was not forgotten. When he died 17 years later in 1871, special trains brought in thousands of mourners from other nearby towns. A crowd of 60,000 people lined the streets of Burnley on a dismal December day as his funeral procession passed by.

Mousley left Exeter House soon after finishing his stint as mayor, moving a few miles away to a landed estate at Hilton where he was already lord of the manor. He sold part of the grounds of Exeter House in 1850 for stables and housing. By the time of his death in 1853, the house that had only recently been the grandest address in Derby town centre was derelict and ripe for redevelopment. The days when rich and poor lived in close proximity in towns like Derby were coming to a rapid close. When he finished his two-year stint as mayor, Mousley was congratulated as being perhaps Derby's finest mayor. He cited the putting down of the football game as being one of the principal events during his time in office, and warmly thanked both magistrates and the government for their help in this achievement.

His death sparked a glowing eulogy in the *Derby Mercury*, but subsequently his reputation took a downturn. Claims emerged that he had employed dubious methods, which had brought financial ruin to some people. The root cause for this sea-change in Mousley's esteem was a case heard by the Court of Chancery a few years after his death. The convoluted machinations of the Court of Chancery at this time were satirised by Charles Dickens in his novel *Bleak House*. The novel's story centres around a labyrinthine legal case involving contested wills. Mousley's case was similarly complicated. It also involved a cast of characters fighting over an inheritance issue. Recent research suggests Mousley was unfairly maligned by the case, and that amazingly he had been responding to requests for funds from George Stanhope, the 6th Earl of Chesterfield, when the latter was abroad or at various race meetings. Stanhope was a notorious gambler who loved and lived a party lifestyle; Mousley was both his solicitor and his agent in local property matters. By the time Mousley died, the Earl owed Mousley over £1m at today's prices.

Mousley's successor as mayor, Henry Mozley, committed suicide in 1857. Apparently he managed to shoot himself through the heart with a rifle, the ball embedding itself in the wainscoting in his bedroom. Something had upset him in the days preceding his death, but little is known about what it was.

It seems that Henry Allen, the journeyman whitesmith who provoked such tumult in 1846, may have had a much happier later life than his adversaries. The 1871 Census records him living in Derby aged 50 with his wife, two sons, daughter-in-law and three grandchildren. It also appears that old habits continued to die hard in the Allen family, for surely it is more than a remarkable coincidence that Henry and his family were living in Agard Street, the place that the very last defiant attempt to play the Derby Game took place in 1870.

12

Hell for Leather

BY 2017, Dr Dallas Burston was a rich and successful man, having made a fortune by developing pharmaceutical companies. He owned a luxurious Range Rover with a five-litre V8 supercharged engine and personalised door handles which had been hand-engraved by craftsmen in Birmingham's Jewellery Quarter. The car was finished in a bespoke red and bronze paint. This was no doubt a useful vehicle for getting around the polo club he had built on a 600-acre estate in Warwickshire including six polo grounds, a pavilion, champagne bar, club rooms, royal suite, all-weather equestrian arena and events centre seating 3,000 people. It sounds as though Dr Burston had much to be proud about, but he claimed that the proudest moment of his life came on Shrove Tuesday 2017 when he was guest of honour at a special event. An eyewitness at the same event said:

> There was elation, screaming and laughing, genuine fright and also aggression ... The significant thing that occurred was the simultaneous waves of different emotions coming from this body of people. I thought to myself where else on earth could you see that? This was what was unique about the event.[170]

The special event was the annual Royal Shrovetide Football game played at Ashbourne, a town on the edge of the Peak

District, about 13 miles from Derby. Dr Burston, as a former Ashburnian, had been asked to 'turn up the ball', a task that involves mounting a small podium near the centre of Ashbourne and at the appointed time, throwing a specially decorated ball out into a mass of people crowded below. This task is the ultimate honour for anyone raised in the town.

The eyewitness at the event was Nigel Heldreich, whose firm Wheathills had been commissioned by Burston to produce a sculpture to commemorate the game by capturing a specific moment. In his youth Heldreich had taken part in the Shrovetide game, but even though in 2017 he was 51 years old he decided to refresh his memory by getting close to the action. He pushed his way into the heaving mass of players, holding a camera on a long pole, determined to get some images which would help him fulfil his difficult brief. He suffered for his art; he was knocked over, kicked, dislocated a finger and lost a chip off his thumb bone. But in reward he got some great images. Needless to say, with this level of commitment, Heldreich and Wheathills went on to produce an outstanding piece of sculpture.

The Shrovetide game at Ashbourne has not just survived, it is thriving. But while it may be the most famous of the Shrovetide games still being played in Britain, it is not the only survivor. There are a few other towns which still have a version of Shrovetide football, as well as one or two that play at either Easter or the Christmas to New Year period. These are the remnants of a tradition of festival football which was once widespread across Britain, being played in scores of towns and villages. These are the games that 'got away'.

Concerns about loss of law and order and impacts on local economies meant that even games in little towns were under threat in the 19th century. In 1822, magistrates in the Northumberland town of Alnwick responded to complaints from local residents by passing the Alnwick Improvement Act. The residents, particularly those in the Market Place, were fed up with their doors being blocked and their property damaged by Shrove Tuesday football. The Improvement Act prohibited street activities such as bull baiting, cock throwing, bonfires and football. The football event carried on in the streets until 1827, when the Duke of Northumberland managed to get the game moved out of the streets and on to some pasture land, which he assigned for the purpose.

One of the complaints of Alnwick residents was that street football impeded traffic on the main road going north through their town to Scotland. As noted earlier, the Highways Act of 1835 gave local authorities new powers which helped to improve the maintenance of highways and prevent them from being obstructed. But the wounding blow to festival football was contained in Section 72 of the Act, which gave authorities the power to fine any persons playing football to the annoyance of any passenger. Fines of up to 40 shillings could be imposed. This Act provided a weapon which local councils throughout the country could wield. It gave them a legitimate basis to respond to local complaints and enforce a ban on football in the streets of towns and villages.

In Surrey, which was a stronghold of Shrove Tuesday football, the playing of the game was extinguished in town after town: Cheam, Epsom, Ewell and Thames Witton were just a few of the settlements where the game had gone by 1850. The most popular game in Surrey was at Kingston upon Thames, just ten miles outside the City of London. Some of the town's most wealthy residents were keen participants and treated themselves to a fine dinner after the day's exertions. The first attempt to ban the Kingston game came in 1797 when magistrates issued a ban. This was ignored and several players were arrested, but subsequently discharged by a sympathetic judge.

To the annoyance of the magistrates the game took place the following year when the cavalry at Hampton Court barracks refused to help in suppressing the occasion. In 1840 Kingston Borough Council passed a motion criticising the game, but the event was now a spectacle which was drawing large crowds, including residents of the growing London suburbs and the borough mayor at the time refused to act. The mayor of 1857 described the game as a drunken riot, and advocated that it should be removed to a park away from the main streets. This suggestion was thwarted by another member of the council, John Williams, who reminded his fellow members that Kingston was still part of 'Free England'.[171] Williams may not have been entirely disinterested, as he was landlord of the Griffin Inn where the annual Shrove Tuesday supper was held.

The game in Kingston eventually came to an end in 1867. Large numbers of police confronted would-be footballers, who took out their frustrations by stoning the homes of councillors who had opposed the game and setting fire to a hay rick. In the following years attempts were made to play Shrovetide football on a local park, but as happened in many other places which tried such relocations the game simply faded away. The torch of Shrovetide football in Surrey was now held by Dorking – a rather odd outcome, given that there is no record of any game in Dorking before 1830. But then the Dorking event was a highly eccentric affair. On the morning of Shrove Tuesday, a motley-looking group paraded through town, following a man who held aloft a T-shaped pole with two or three balls attached to it. The balls were painted, and the pole was adorned with the slogan 'wind and water is Dorking's glory'.[172] The members of the small procession wore fancy dress – including a man dressed as a woman – and their faces were daubed with soot and red ochre. They were accompanied by a drummer, fiddler and whistle players.

The Dorking game began at two o'clock. The town crier kicked the ball up near to the town church and a contest ensued between the town's Eastenders and Westenders. Bizarrely there were no goals, and the aim was simply to retain possession of the ball. The first ball was fought over by boys and the other two by adults. The most prized ball was painted gold and was the last to be contested in a game starting at 5pm. The ball often found its way into pubs off Dorking High Street where drinks would be taken. However, the game grew more heated as the church clock approached six, as a group had to have the ball in their territory in order to win.

The Dorking game, then, was a very different and comparatively tame affair compared to its Derby counterpart. Given that it seemed to lack any ancient roots, it looks a bit like a game that was dreamed up to bring in business for local hostelries. It shows, though, that the way in which Shrovetide football was played could vary considerably from place to place. Yet whatever the origins of the Dorking game were, its demise was fiercely resisted, and large numbers of police were needed to enforce a ban in 1897. Indeed, extra police were brought in on every Shrove Tuesday until 1909, when resistance finally melted away.

In Chester-le-Street in County Durham, the Upstreeters contended with the Downstreeters in a Shrovetide game that lasted well into the 20th century. As at Dorking, there were no goals and the object of the game was simply to retain possession of the ball at one end of the street or other. The game lasted several hours and was undeniably dangerous; in 1891 a footbridge over the Cong Burn collapsed due to the sheer weight of spectators. Photographs of the event from its final years shows large crowds of men and women in coats and hats eager to see the spectacle. Despite the depth of its support, the game was banned in 1932 following protests from local businesses. So although mass football events, played mostly at Shrovetide but occasionally at Christmas and Easter, were once widespread throughout the country, there are now just a handful of places which retain such a tradition. It is worth looking at these few survivors to see what similarities they share, if any, with the game once played in Derby.

The Orkney Islands, off the northern tip of the Scottish mainland, would seem an unlikely spot for mass football. In fact, both the Orkneys and the neighbouring Shetlands had a long history of such games. Now the only game that survives is at Kirkwall. Historically, the games at Kirkwall were played on common land, but have subsequently moved into the town as the common lands became enclosed. The two sides are the Up-the-Gates and Doon-the-Gates; the word 'gates' comes from a Norse word for street. The game is played both on Christmas Day and New Year's Day, and usually lasts for around five hours. As was the case at Derby, the leather ball is slightly larger than a modern-day football but a lot heavier, being stuffed with cork dust. The ball is thrown up outside St Magnus Cathedral, and to score the Doon-the-Gates must get the ball into the water at the harbour, while the Up-the-Gates must get to a place where the old town gates used to stand. The most frenetic action occurs immediately after scoring a goal, when the leading players of the winning team wrestle each other for the right to claim the ball, seen as the supreme honour. One of the customs which has an echo with latter-day reports of the Derby Game, is a pre-match procession of the two rival groups, to the throw-up point of St Magnus Cathedral.

At the other end of Scotland, a cluster of small towns in the Scottish Borders still play a version of Shrovetide football: Ancrum, Denholm, Hobkirk and Jedburgh. The history of the game in this area shows a shift from football to handball. This change probably helped to reduce complaints about damage from property owners. The balls used are much smaller than the Derby ball, with the leather casing being stuffed tightly with sphagnum moss. The small size has led to one of the key features of these games, which is smuggling the ball. Many would-be smugglers wear jackets or coats, some with special pockets. Part of the fun of the game, for both spectators and players, is trying to work out who might have secreted the ball about their person. Smuggling the ball was not unknown in the Derby Game but was much harder to do with a larger ball. It had to be slashed first and some, or all, of the stuffing removed. Also, most of the Derby players played in shirtsleeves, so if the ball did 'disappear' anyone in the vicinity wearing a coat or jacket would immediately be suspected.

In Alnwick, the move from street to field has been a long-term success. Of all the remaining games, Alnwick bears the closest resemblance to modern-day football. It has goalposts called 'hales', although these are draped in foliage. It is played on a field called the Pastures which approximates to a pitch, albeit one which is 200 yards wide and features molehills and puddles. Games usually take up to two hours and are decided on the best of three hales. The original Alnwick game did not have any goals and was a simple battle for possession, as at Chester-le-Street. Like the Derby Game, the two teams that play today are drawn from two local parishes. But this arrangement was not prevalent before the 1850s.

The only other town in north-east England with a surviving ball game is Sedgefield. There the ball is little bigger than a cricket ball, made of cork, softwood or other material with a leather covering. Historically, the players were divided into town and country and there were goals or 'allys' at both ends of town; one was a beck and the other was a pond. Unfortunately, the pond was filled in and converted into a petrol station after the First World War. Nowadays, the players are no longer split into teams. The ball is thrown up at 1pm, after it has been passed three times through a metal bull ring fixed to the ground on the corner of Sedgefield's High Street. Most early play then takes place in open spaces nearby, around St Edmund's Church. The ball may disappear for half an hour or so, as anyone holding it is said to be entitled to a free drink. Consequently, some individuals and their friends make off with the ball to a favoured inn – sometimes by car! The object of the game is to goal the ball in the beck after four o'clock, return with it to the town green and pass it three times through the bull ring. The person achieving this feat is acclaimed as the champion.

With a population of around 25,000, Workington is by far the largest town where festival football is still played. Located on the north-west coast at the mouth of the Cumbrian River Derwent, the town's geography is intricately connected with the game. The contest is between the Uppies and Downies, although other names have been used over the years. Traditionally the Downies came from homes around the town's quay and tended to be sailors or dockers, while the Uppies at the top eastern end of the town tended to be colliers. The Downies' goal is a promontory in the mouth of the River Derwent. The size of the ball used to vary considerably, but in recent years it has been a bit smaller than a modern football. Understandably the Downies are keen to get the ball into the Derwent and, once this has been achieved, they are not averse to using a boat to help them get to their goal. The Uppies prefer to keep the ball in built-up areas as they make their way towards their goal at Workington Hall.

As in the Derby Game, once a goal is scored the game is over. This is not surprising as the goals are well over a mile apart even by the most direct route. There are some major differences though. Firstly, the Workington game is played three times: on Good Friday, Easter Tuesday, and the following Saturday. Secondly, the ball is not thrown up until 6.30pm, so there is limited daylight for the games. Sadly, in recent years the Workington game has had to cope with some rather unsympathetic development on its traditional playing areas, but the game shows no sign of waning.

The game at Atherstone in Warwickshire boasts the biggest ball, 27 inches in diameter and 4lb in weight. The game used to roam beyond the boundaries of the town – locals recount tales of players stabbing the ball and hiding away in the countryside to evade detection before returning in the evening to claim victory. But since 1974 the event has been confined to Long Street, Atherstone's main commercial street. The ball is thrown up at 3pm on Shrove Tuesday by a guest of honour. For the first hour and a half, play is quite boisterous but mostly good-natured, with many people, including women and children, getting the chance to hold and kick the ball up and down the street. The biggest kicks get the most cheers. At 4.30pm everything changes after a klaxon is sounded. Play becomes extremely physical, even though there are no set sides, as small groups of friends work in concert to get hold of the ball. Once a group has taken possession, other groups will do everything they can to try and break them up. The holding group may deflate the ball to make it easier to hold on to. At 5pm the klaxon sounds again and whoever is holding the ball is declared the winner and escorted away to the Angel Inn by the stewards of the game. As at Derby, the Atherstone crowd once had a tradition for pelting well-dressed spectators with soot or flour.

Last, but certainly not least, we come to Ashbourne. Here the game has the prestigious title of Royal Shrovetide Football. The word 'Royal' was first used after the local Shrovetide committee, which long ago realised the value of making useful connections, sent a specially decorated football to celebrate the marriage, on Shrove Tuesday 1922, of Mary, the daughter of George V. Further royal connections followed in 1928 and 2003 when the ball was turned up in both years by the serving Prince of Wales. The adversaries in the Ashbourne game are the Up'Ards, born to the north of the Henmore Brook which runs roughly east to west through the town, and the Down'Ards born to the south of the brook. Historically the two goals were mills which were around three miles apart, Sturston Mill for the Up'Ards and Clifton Mill for the Down'Ards. To goal the ball, it had to be tapped three times against a mill wheel. Both mills were demolished in the 20th century, so the goal locations are now formed by purpose-built stone plinths.

In the 19th century there were several attempts to have the games moved from the streets of Ashbourne into nearby fields, and some players received fines for playing on the highway. In the 1878 game, Jimmy Harrison plunged into the pool at Clifton Mill, seized the ball and swam towards the mill wheel. The current though was strong and he sank after becoming exhausted in his attempts to score a goal. Luckily for him, help was at hand as, 'Mr Osborne, who was watching the game, immediately jumped into the water, and with great difficulty reached Harrison, who had become by that time insensible. By the utmost exertions he succeeded in reaching the bank with him and placing him in safety.'[173] However, another spectator, 19-year-old James Barker, a carter employed at the mill, saw his chance for glory. He plunged into the water and made for the ball, but soon he also got into difficulty and began to sink. At this point, 'Mr Osborne again rushed into the dam and swam towards the spot where Barker had gone down and made every effort to reach him, but unfortunately without avail. The body of Barker was afterwards discovered deeply embedded in the mud.'[174]

The *Derby Mercury* clearly believed that this incident would finally bring an end to the Ashbourne game. But the game's stalwarts were not ready to give up, even though it appears that the number of people playing in the following years declined. By 1884 the *Mercury* was able to sneer that the 'game was in a moribund state'.[175] Nevertheless the game soldiered on, albeit with some intense local acrimony between those for and against. Gradually those in favour began to win the battle of public opinion. Perhaps learning the lessons of the demise of the game in Derby, the advocates of the Ashbourne game knew that the key was to win the propaganda battle. Accordingly, they began to seek influential support and demonstrate their community spirit.

In 1891 a local dignitary was invited to turn up the ball. Previously the tradition had been for the 'captain' of either the Up'Ards or Down'Ards to have this honour. From 1891 onwards, the honour went to a celebrity or to a local worthy. Before the game 'Rule, Britannia!' was sung. Although fines were issued to 90 people for playing football in the streets, the town seemed to rally behind the players and concerts were held to raise the money needed to pay the fines. An organising committee was set up and sought ways to minimise any ill feeling.

Slowly the game came to be seen as something that united the town and made it special. By the 1920s it had gained royal endorsement and those who turned up the ball included the Marquis of Hartington and his father the ninth Duke of Devonshire, as well as Steve Bloomer, the legendary Derby County and England footballer. The apex of acceptance and respectability was achieved in 1928 when the Prince of Wales turned up the ball. At the time, Prince Edward was one of the most famous men in the world and the crowds were large and ecstatic. A special bridge over Henmore Brook was built to allow the prince to turn up the ball and view a little of the ensuing mayhem. At one point, he teased the crowd by rolling up his trouser bottoms as if he intended to join the fray.

The ball was caught by a Sheffield taxi driver called Edward Gorman. He had driven some members of the press to the event and had decided to get as close as he could to the prince. He knew nothing at all about Ashbourne football and was astonished when, after catching the ball, the crowd around him picked him up and threw him in the river. Soaking wet, Gorman got back into his taxi and drove off. Driving in wet clothes in an unheated car across the Peak District in the middle of winter is not a good idea. When Gorman entered Buxton he lost control of his vehicle and smashed into a corner shop in the town centre. When brought before the town's magistrates, his argument that his soaking in Ashbourne had affected his driving ability must have swayed their decision to dismiss the case.

The involvement of royalty and celebrities, together with the spectacle of a crazy game, helped to bring in the film crews. Soon footage of the football at Ashbourne became a regular feature on Shrovetide newsreels shown in cinemas, and then after the Second World War, on television. The future of the Ashbourne game now looks secure, although there are occasional rumblings from those unlucky enough to suffer some form of damage to property or inconvenience. Perhaps the greatest potential threat may come from development encroaching on to areas of Henmore Valley.

So, what about the Ashbourne game itself? How is it played and how similar is it to the Derby Game that was brought to a halt in 1846? The ball is slightly smaller than the Derby ball held by Derby Museum, but is slightly bigger than a modern-day football. The hand-sewn leather casing is stuffed full of cork shavings to help the ball float when taken into water. The making of the ball is only entrusted to one ball maker at a time. In May 2020, during a surge in the Covid-19 pandemic, hundreds of mourners still lined the streets for the funeral of John Harrison, aged 80, who had made the Ashbourne ball for 41 years. One of the longest-serving ball makers was John Barker, whose brother James had died at the Clifton Mill goal in 1878. Once the ball maker has finished his job, the ball is given to a local artist who then decorates it. Each year the ball gets a unique design that relates to the specially invited guest of the year. Again, there is an echo of this practice in the Derby Game as former Derby policeman Benjamin Fearn related how a Mr Haden would pay to have the ball gilded if All Saints' won the day.

As in the Derby Game, the ball is turned up at 2pm on Shrove Tuesday. Historically this took place in the Market Place but moved to Shaw's Croft during the 1860s, possibly to avoid falling foul of the Highways Act. At the time Shaw's Croft was an open meadow next to Henmore Brook. Shaw's Croft is now a public car park but is transformed on a Shrove Tuesday, when even in the most miserable weather, a crowd of well over 1,000 people congregate around the specially built podium used for turning up the ball. Again, as at Derby, Ash Wednesday used to be given over for a boys' contest but is now used for another game, with many players taking part in both. Unlike the Derby Game, the Ashbourne event is not organised on the basis of parishes, but on residence north or south of Henmore Brook. However, although it seems that the Derby Game was originally a contest between the two parishes of All Saints' and St Peter's, by the early 19th century, if not before, it had basically become a game between those north and south of Markeaton Brook.

The manner of scoring a goal in Ashbourne would be familiar to past heroes of the Derby Game, as it requires the ball to be struck three times against the purpose-built 'millstones'. In addition, the scorer must be standing in the river. At Derby, the scorer of a goal at Nun's Mill also had to be in the water to score. If a goal is scored before an appointed time (6pm in 2022) then a second ball is thrown up. Games usually last for several hours but must end before 10pm. The goaled balls become the proud possession of the person who has goaled it. If no one goals then the person who turned up the ball gets to take it home.

In common with several other of the remaining festival football games, the devotees of Ashbourne football lay claim to ancient origins. Nevertheless, there is no solid evidence for any game at Ashbourne before the 19th century. Stephen Glover, writing his *History of the County of Derby* in 1829, described the game at Ashbourne as being played in a similar manner to the game at Derby, but stated 'the institution of it there is of modern date'.[176] Indeed, the close similarity of the Derby Game to the game still played at Ashbourne, quite distinctive from those played elsewhere, suggests that the two are related. It is possible that at some point in the past, the people of Ashbourne decided to have a go at playing the same game they had observed 13 miles away in their county town. This would explain why all the essential features of the Ashbourne and Derby games are the same. But whatever its origins, we are fortunate indeed that the Ashbourne game has survived, and that every Shrovetide, the Up'Ards and Down'Ards carry on the game that refused to die.

13

Naming Rights

THERE IS no shortage of ideas for the origin of the term 'local derby'. In his book *End to End Stuff*, Les Scott suggested that derby games were so called because Victorian football supporters were expected to wear their best hat to attend a special event like a meeting between local clubs. He claimed that the 'Sunday best' hat would often be a derby hat of the bowler variety, and the change of headgear led to local clashes being called 'derbies'. Another theory is that the phrase originates from the Ashbourne Shrovetide game, presumably because Ashbourne is in Derbyshire. Then there's a suggestion that the name derives from matches between Liverpool and Everton, as the two clubs were separated by land, namely Stanley Park, once owned by the Earl of Derby. One of the factors behind this suggestion is the claim that 'a local derby' first appeared in print to describe a Liverpool versus Everton fixture. This is an inventive idea but, as will become clear, is based on a false premise. The two leading suggestions for the origin of the term, however, are either the Derby Game or the annual horserace once known as the Epsom Derby.

According to the *Oxford English Dictionary* (*OED*), the word 'derby' can be 'applied to any kind of important sporting contest' and a 'local derby' is 'a match between two teams from the same district'.[177] The *OED* cited a quotation from an article of 3 October 1914, which used the phrase 'a local derby', to describe a football match between Liverpool and Everton. While one might take issue with the word 'derby' being applied to any kind of important sporting contest, the *OED*'s definition of a local derby initially seems uncontentious, even if it conveys little impression of the emotions stirred by such events. However, the *OED* has placed these entries under a definition of 'Derby' which relates to the annual horserace established in 1780 by the Earl of Derby and which became the most noted horserace in England. So the *OED* appears to suggest that the term 'local derby' originates from the Derby horserace. It does not link the phrase to the playing of football games between local parishes in Derby.

Building on these entries in the *OED*, other agencies have put together a more rounded explanation for the term, as found for example on the Idiom Origins website:

> A local derby is a sporting contest between rivals from the same city or district and the first citation is from the early 20th century. It derives from the Epsom Derby, England's premier horserace, which was founded by the 12th Earl of Derby in 1780. For many years, the Epsom Derby was Britain's greatest sporting event and, from about 1840 onwards, any sporting event, even outside of horseracing, was known as a derby. Since the late 19th century, even without the qualifier "local", a derby was generally a contest between rivals from the same city or district. The first citation for local derby in a football context is from 1914 when the *Daily Express* described a match between Liverpool and Everton as a local derby.[178]

This type of explanation raises some questions. Firstly, if a 'derby' is simply another word for an important sporting contest, then why aren't all important football games called 'derbies' instead of matches? To follow this logic, a late-season clash between title contenders such as Chelsea and Manchester City ought to be called a 'derby'. If that were the case then yes, you could see the logic in a match between Sheffield United and Sheffield Wednesday being called a 'local derby', as this is just between two teams that from the same city. The trouble is that matches which are between teams who are not local rivals are never referred to as 'derby' games, whatever the importance of the occasion may be.

Secondly, why would a football match between local rivals take its name from a horserace? The Derby at Epsom Downs in Surrey was established in 1780 by the 12th Earl of Derby for three-year-old colts and fillies. The race soon became one of Britain's premier sporting events. It is true that the fame of the Derby appears to have resulted in the word 'Derby' occasionally being used by reporters or promoters to describe special horseracing events elsewhere in the United Kingdom. For example, in May 1861 a newspaper called the *Hull Packet* described the forthcoming Beverley, Hull and East Riding Races as 'our local derby' and had no doubt that the day 'will be availed of by large numbers of the racing community and pleasure seekers'.[179] So, the term 'local derby' does appear to have been used to a certain limited extent to describe special gala horseracing events. The newspaper reports of such events suggest that 'derby' is intended to convey a certain sense of the frivolity, as well as a lack of sobriety, that seemed to accompany such events. However, there is no hint of intense local rivalry, which is entirely understandable because there is nothing about the Epsom Derby that provides an obvious connection with the feelings stirred up by local rivalries. Also, apart from 'donkey derby' and 'roller derby' it is hard to find evidence to support the contention that sporting events in general were referred to as 'derbies'.

At the time of writing this book, the *OED*'s definition of a local derby, and its citation of the term as 'first used' in a football context in the report of a game between Liverpool and Everton in 1914, has been unchanged since 1989. However, over years since there has been an exponential growth in the range of online resources which can be searched. A simple search of the *Daily Express* alone, as far back as 1900, shows that there were several printed citations of a 'derby' game in football and other contexts before 1914. For example, reporting on a rugby game in October 1900, the *Express* commented, 'Proud Salford were silenced by their Broughton neighbours, the match being "the local Derby" and fought with amazing keenness.'[180]

In fact, numerous newspaper reports in the 1890s and 1900s described certain football matches as 'local derbies'. *Athletic News* was possibly the first to use the term in this sense. It had first been published in the 1870s as a weekly sport newspaper, with a particular emphasis on football. In October 1888 it used a headline of 'A "Derby" at Bury' as a banner to a short report about a game between Bury and Heywood, a town just over two miles to the east of Bury.[181] There is no suggestion in any of the early references to local derbies that great events are being described. The game between Bury and Heywood only attracted a crowd of around 2,000. Football at the time was still in its early stages, clubs were in their infancy and most matches were unlikely to attract attendances of more than a few thousand. But it is noticeable that during the late Victorian and Edwardian periods, whenever a reporter sought to justify the use of the term 'derby', it was not the size of the crowd that mattered but the level of rivalry between the two respective clubs. Take this example from the *Dundee Courier* in 1897:

> Manifest interest is being evinced in the western and northern districts of Dundee over the Forfarshire Cup tie between Lochee United and Dundee Wanderers. So strong has been the rivalry between the clubs for a long

time that each engagement has come to be looked upon in the nature of a local "Derby", and it goes without saying that to-morrow's contest will partake of the usual robust character.[182]

Similarly, a reporter in the *Daily Express* in March 1912 also felt the need to explain:

There are two other games around town, one of those being a kind of "local Derby" for, though Millwall are now located on the south side of the Thames, there is still a certain sort of rivalry between their supporters and the adherents of West Ham United.[183]

It is also interesting that when these reporters used the term 'Derby' they usually encased it in inverted commas. This suggests that they were identifying a special event.

Why were these late Victorian, early Edwardian reporters using the term in this way? Was it because supporters were wearing their best hats? Was it because of a link to a famous horserace? Or was it because of the notoriety and nature of the Derby Game?

We have seen that Shrovetide and festival football was played in many cities and towns across the British Isles, and still persists in a handful of small towns. But there is no doubt that for at least 100 years leading up to 1846, Derby was the largest town where a mass football game was played. During this time it achieved a notoriety that was unequalled and withstood repeated attempts to ban it. How did the game survive so long in Derby, when it had been extinguished much earlier in larger and similar-sized towns? Firstly, there must be some truth in William Hutton's claim that the game in Derby was pursued with an avidity that he had not observed elsewhere. By the time he wrote his *History of Derby*, Hutton had lived in Nottingham and Birmingham and was a well-travelled man within Britain. The Derby Game may well have been an annual event for centuries before Hutton's boyhood in the 1720s and '30s. It was certainly deeply embedded in the local culture and identity of those who lived and worked in the town. This passion helped fight off attempts to ban the game in 1731, 1746 and 1797. The fact that Derby at that time was a relatively remote town, left pretty much to its local gentry to manage, may also have helped the game to survive. It is also evident from the attempts to ban the Derby Game in 1746 that it was a game that attracted interest from outside Derby and was 'advertised' in adjacent counties.

In the early 19th century, the Industrial Revolution gathered momentum and the town suddenly started to grow. Such growth brought an end to Shrovetide games in other towns, but the support of leading local figures like Joseph Strutt, was a major obstacle to those who wanted the Derby Game to be swept away. The shock caused by the beheadings of the Pentrich rebels in 1817, the turmoil of the Reform Bill riots of 1831 and the Silk Trades' Lockout three years later also prompted a cautious approach to anything which might spark further confrontation. By the early Victorian era, the intensity of the annual Shrovetide clash between the two parts of Derby had made the town notorious for the intensity of the rivalry displayed. Take these extracts from the *London Saturday Journal* of 15 February 1840:

> The inhabitants of Derby are born foot-ball players:- the game seems interwoven with their existence; they have drunk it with their mother's milk, and it animates them through their lives. Enthusiasm is but a cold word for their attachment to it; on Shrove Tuesday it is a passion irresistible, which bears down before it every obstacle, and defies the law, the magistrates, the police

... the shouts of "St Peter's!" "All Saints'!" the clapping
of hands, the cheers, the waving of handkerchiefs and
encouraging motions from the upper windows and
roofs of the surrounding houses, is altogether such a
display of interest and enthusiasm as is rarely witnessed,
even at a horse-race; the excitement of an election, even
at the closing of the poll, is apathy compared to it; the
existence of the town might depend on the issue of
the contest.[184]

This notoriety of Derby for a football fervour which defied law,
magistrates and police was entirely unwelcome to the majority
of the town's most powerful citizens. As early as 1796, the
Derby Mercury complained that the game had existed for too
long to the 'general execration of our inhabitants'.[185] By the
1840s, several mayors and magistrates clearly felt that the
game has given the town a reputation for lawlessness which is
harmful to its economic prospects. An editorial in the *Derby
Mercury* reflected this feeling in 1845, 'A great good to the
town, both as regards its inhabitants and its reputation abroad,
would be effected were the unseemly sight annually witnessed
done away with.'[186]

In the end, it needed the energy and intelligence of
William Eaton Mousley to bring the game to an end, with
support from the secretary of state, who sanctioned military
force in the form of either the 5th or the Royal Irish Dragoon
Guards for each of four years between 1846 and 1849. No other
Shrovetide game needed such force to put it down.

Coverage in national newspapers and magazines like
Penny Magazine, the *Pioneer* and *Sporting Magazine* showed
that the Derby Game was already notorious even before the
final event of 1846. The confrontation between the Dragoon
Guards and Derby football players in 1846 was widely reported
in many papers across the country, with headlines such as

'FOOTBALL RIOTS AT DERBY – THE MILITARY CALLED OUT'.[187] One of the papers to give detailed coverage of the 1846 game was the *Northern Star*, now being edited by Chartist firebrand and ex-Derby jailbird George Harney. According to the historian and journalist Stephen Bates, the *Star* far outsold other national newspapers including *The Times*, at its peak selling 50,000 copies of each edition.

The Victorian era was a time of rising interest in the game of football. The coverage given to the sport in newspapers expanded, and arguments raged, over what the rules of football should be, and how games should be organised. One manifestation of the increasing interest was the formation in 1863 of the Football Association. The FA was to become English football's governing body; however, its initial impact on the game or the wider public was weak. Teams in the north and south of the country played to very different rules. By 1867 the FA had only ten members and internal arguments still raged over what the rules should be. Although the FA had tried to make a break from rugby, its rules still kept some of the features of that game. The goals had no crossbar and handling was allowed, but the forward pass was not. Most of the country simply ignored the FA's rules and the association came close to being dissolved.

Gradually, over the next two decades the FA began to assert its influence until it attained its position as the pre-eminent authority in the English game. If one man can be said to be responsible for this achievement then it is Charles Alcock. Alcock was an imposing figure, just shy of six feet tall and weighing in at close to 14st. He was a keen player of the game and at 16 he and his brother set up the Forest football club in Chingford, and a few years later the highly influential Wanderers club. Alcock became Secretary of the Football Association in 1871, the first player to make it on to the FA board. He possessed immense energy, transforming the FA while working for several publications as a sports journalist, and continuing his illustrious playing career. Under his guidance new rules were quickly agreed. His innovative ideas included international matches between England and Scotland, and the introduction of a sudden-death competition – the FA Cup. Indeed, Alcock played several times as captain of England, and in later life refereed several FA Cup finals.

In the world of late-Victorian football, Alcock was a pre-eminent figure. His importance was such that he has been referred to as the 'father of modern sport'.[188] In 1874, Alcock published a book called *Football: Our Winter Game*. His status within the game would have made the book essential reading for the aspiring football journalist. It included several references to the historic game of Shrovetide football played at Derby. Eight pages are devoted to repeating the coverage given in 1839 to the Derby Game by *Penny Magazine*. Any reader of this account would have been left in no doubt as to the intensity of the rivalry between St Peter's and All Saints', engendered by the Derby Game.

In 1888, the Football League was founded with 12 clubs and a second division was added in 1893. The creation of the Football Association, the agreement on rules, and the formation of leagues led to rapid expansion in the coverage of the sport by newspapers. It is inevitable that the new breed of football journalists would have been familiar with the Derby Game either from hearsay, from publications like Alcock's *Winter Game*, or from the many articles about the event that appeared in scores of provincial newspapers in 1895, as well as in the *Pall Mall Gazette*. It seems likely, therefore, that some sporting journalists compared the intense rivalry engendered by some local football matches, to the accounts they had heard or read elsewhere of the 'Derby football play'. Consequently, they started referring to such games as 'local Derbies' for that reason.

The word 'rival' is noticeably lacking in the *OED* entries explaining the term 'local derby'. But the key ingredient in the application of the word 'derby' to a football or rugby match is surely the level of local rivalry between the opposing teams, and it was the intensity of the rivalry in the Derby Shrovetide game that made it distinctive:

> There is perhaps no general feeling at the present day which can be compared with the absorbing spirit of rivalry which used to prevail with respect to these contests. Either "Peter's" or "All Saints" (or "All Hallows" as it used to be) ran in the veins of every Derbeian. The battle was "bequeathed by bleeding sire to son", and every child was born, as Mr Gilbert would say, "either a little Peterite or else a little Hallowsite".[189]

'It is this intensity which still fascinated writers over 40 years after the game's suppression. In an article published in 1886, the *Dundee Evening Telegraph* wrote, 'Many, and fierce and violent, have been the 'tussles' of the contending parties in the now put-down game of Derby.'[190] In a lengthy article in 1891 about the Derby Game the *Manchester Courier* wrote, 'It is not easy to convey an idea of the spirit in which, for many centuries, the game of football was played at Shrovetide in the public streets.'[191] A few years later, the *Pall Mall Gazette* recalled:

> The scene in the market-place resembled that in a general election in the olden time, as depicted by Hogarth. The mob was frenzied by party spirit, and in the fury of partisanship, distinguished citizens, sedate and law-abiding at all other times, gave themselves up to head-punching, wrangling, and the various other amenities of a faction fight.[192]

In newspaper reports, the use of the term 'derby' to describe a football match between intense local rivals seems to have originated in the late 1880s and grew in the following decades. Given this background, it seems more probable that the journalists of the late Victorian and early Edwardian period had the Derby Game in mind, rather than a horserace, when they started referring to matches between local rival football teams as 'derbies'. Indeed, even in modern times, for those who are immersed in football history, the link between the Derby Game and the phrase 'local derby' is regarded as self-evident. Hugh Hornby, former curator at the National Football Museum, wrote that:

> Derby ... has the distinction of providing us with a sporting term that remains in common usage today. The two teams playing on Shrove Tuesday represented the parishes of All Saints' and St Peter's (with Markeaton Brook as the boundary between them). Later in the 19th century, all football matches between teams from the same town became known as "derby" matches.[193]

Hornby's view is supported by other renowned football historians including James Walvin, Lindsey Porter and Graham Curry, as well as several historians of international reputation such as Christian Koller and Fabian Brändle. While there may never be definitive proof that the early football reporters were inspired by the Derby Game, rather than a famous horserace, in their use of the term 'derby', it is surely more than an incredible coincidence that the most notorious local rivalry in ancient football occurred in a place called Derby.

14

Promised Fury

THE FIRST local derby between two formally constituted football teams is claimed to be a game played in 1860 between Sheffield Football Club and Hallam and Stumperlowe Football Club. Sheffield FC also claim to be the first football club formed anywhere in the world. Established in 1857, the club's initial problem was finding someone else to play. At first the players had to devise contests between themselves, such as bachelors against married men. It was a year later when the club's first external fixture was arranged against a regiment garrisoned at the Hillsborough barracks. But the formation of Sheffield FC proved to be the catalyst that prompted the members of Hallam Cricket Club, which had been in existence since 1804, to form their own football club. The newly formed club challenged Sheffield FC to play them on Boxing Day at their Sandygate ground, then situated a mile or so from the urban edge of Sheffield.

It was a cold but beautiful day, as a clear blue sky and a snow-covered playing surface showed off the respective colours of the two teams: red and white for Sheffield, blue for Hallam. The game was billed as 16-a-side but the weather conditions prevented some members of each team from turning up. Nevertheless, there was a good turnout of spectators who were 'extremely liberal with their plaudits' and 'equally unsparing in their sarcasm'.[194] The players needed to concentrate hard simply to remain upright on the tricky playing surface, but the game was played in a friendly spirit and there were no accidents or major incidents. Sheffield FC won 2-0.

Just two years later, though, the friendly spirit had evaporated. In a game at the Bramall Lane cricket ground, which lasted for three hours and fielded teams of 13, an incident sparked an aggressive response from both players and spectators. Major Creswick, playing for the reds of Sheffield, had got the ball but was being blocked by Shaw and Waterfall for the blues of Hallam. Creswick was being held back by Waterfall and received a blow from Creswick. According to the reporter from the *Sheffield Independent*, the blow was accidental, but clearly Waterfall did not agree, for the paper recounted:

> Waterfall, however, ran at the Major in the most irritable manner, and struck at him several times. He also threw off his waistcoat and began to "show fight" in earnest. Major Creswick, who preserved his temper admirably, did not return a single blow. They were surrounded by partisans, and for a few minutes there was every appearance of a general fight amongst players and spectators. The advice of older and cooler heads prevailed, the field was cleared, and play again resumed.[195]

These games were played under Sheffield Rules, which were devised originally by Sheffield FC. Under these rules, throw-ins and corner kicks were features of the game, catching the ball was allowed, as was pushing of other players, but there was no such thing as offside. Other football clubs, which now began to form in the Sheffield area, readily accepted the rules. The question that arises is why did these important developments in the sport of football take place in Sheffield?

One reason undoubtedly takes the shape of Nathaniel Creswick, the major who was involved in the unseemly fisticuffs during the so-called 'Battle of Bramall Lane'. Creswick was one of those characters who seemed to throw himself wholeheartedly into whatever he did. Two days after Sheffield FC's first snowbound match against Hallam FC, he and some friends were walking across the ice on a reservoir in the Crookes area of the city. A youth called Thomas Bardwell got into difficulties after skating upon thin ice where the water flowed into a dam. The ice gave way and he sank into water which was 15 to 20 feet deep. Creswick got hold of a wooden rail and threw it to Bardwell, but he was too weak to retain hold of it. Creswick then lowered himself on to the ice, crawled to the edge and seized hold of Bardwell before he was about to go down for the third time. Then the ice broke and Creswick slid into the water. Clinging with his left hand to the remaining ice shelf, he managed to keep the youth afloat with his other arm until helpers lowered a gate into the water, enabling the pair to scramble out of danger.

Within a fortnight of his icy escapade, Creswick found himself standing in the grand surroundings of Sheffield's Cutlers' Hall. He was presented with a silver salver as a token of the city's recognition of his valour. However, he may have had mixed feelings about this gift as he worked for a silver plate company. Creswick also found time for plenty of other pursuits. In addition to founding Sheffield FC, he was a justice of the peace for Derbyshire, and founded Sheffield's first golf club and the Hallamshire Volunteer Rifle Corps, rising to the rank of colonel.

The second reason that Sheffield was so influential in taking football forward was that its promoters were pushing at an open door. South Yorkshire and Derbyshire had enjoyed a strong football culture for many years. As we saw in Chapter 1, in the middle of the Derby Game of 1827, the deadlock reached between All Saints' and St Peter's was broken by a party of Littleover men who had arrived on the scene after beating 'an equal party of Mickleover men' from their adjacent village in a game of 'kickball'.[196] The contest between equal parties suggests organised football with rudimentary rules. Indeed, in 1840 an article in the *Derby Mercury* described the Derbyshire custom of football which it said was played with great spirit at that time:

> The contest usually lies between two neighbouring villages. A field large enough is selected, and an equal number of persons on each side make the match. The ball, filled with a bladder previously inflated is then thrown up in the centre of the meadow, and on either party being able, by kicking, to force it to a certain place called the goal, gains the triumph. This is a manly and healthy exercise compared to the filthy and disgusting sport carried on in Derby at Shrovetide, where the ball, instead of being freely kick'd, is hugg'd by a set of fellows pulling and tearing in all the luxury of dirt and heat.[197]

From other newspaper reports, it is evident that football was a children's game throughout Derbyshire, from Repton and Shardlow in the south of the county to Brampton, Bolsover and Staveley in the north. The interest in the annual adult game between Middleton and Wirksworth brought both towns to a standstill and inspired a local publican to write a ballad in its honour. A similar grassroots (pardon the pun) football culture existed in neighbouring South Yorkshire. Men were fined for playing football on the Sabbath and complaints were made about boys playing football in the streets. The national newspaper *Bell's Life* was used for the issuing of sporting challenges, and in 1843 the village of Totties approached the neighbouring village of Thurlstone to meet them for a game of six- or eight-a-side football at Shrovetide. According to the newspaper, the purpose of this challenge was to continue an earlier contest between 'six of the celebrated players' of each village which had resulted in a goalless stalemate.[198]

So it is not surprising that having sowed the first seed by forming Sheffield FC, the organised sport of football mushroomed within the area. There was no shortage of willing players, or of eager spectators. Together with William Prest, a local wine merchant and captain of Sheffield Cricket Club, Creswick devised the Sheffield Rules. During the 1860s and '70s the rules were quickly adopted not only by other football clubs in South Yorkshire, but by clubs and associations in the wider north and Midlands area. By 1867, when a local entrepreneur called Thomas Youdan organised the world's first football tournament, the Sheffield Rules were the dominant code for the game in England. Down in London, the recently formed Football Association had published its own rulebook in 1863. For a time it looked as though two forms of football might develop, one in the north and the other in the south. Arguments about the rules raged on, with both sides making frequent amendments, but thanks to the loyalty of the Sheffield Football Association to the national FA an agreement on a common set of rules was finally reached in 1877.

Although the early games between Sheffield FC and Hallam FC may now be claimed by today's websites as local 'derbies', they were not so regarded at the time. Sheffield FC moved its home base from ground to ground and might have been better named as the Nomads. In 1860, Hallam FC's ground was nearly a mile's walk from the urban edge of Sheffield and indeed the *Sheffield Daily Telegraph*'s report of that first match in 1860 referred to the Hallam team as 'the country players'.[199] (Hallamshire was the historical name given to the land rising up from the River Sheaf towards the Peak

District, and much of it was yet to become a leafy suburban escape from the noise, smoke and dust of the city's steel works).

These were not clubs that sprang out of working-class communities. Instead, they were the creations of Sheffield's elite: doctors, solicitors, architects and manufacturers with enough leisure and wealth to devote their time to various improving pursuits. Like many early football clubs, one of the main motives was probably to provide a competitive way for cricketers to keep fit during the winter.

The number of football clubs in Britain grew significantly from the 1860s to the 1890s and while the initial impetus for their formation may have come from well-to-do 'gentlemen', the working class were keen to join in. Churches, public houses and businesses often sponsored or helped to establish new clubs. Class differences led to tensions. By 1865 Sheffield FC was not very interested in playing local teams. It appears that the club preferred to travel to play games against middle-class opposition, rather than local teams of working-class players. While one reason may have been to test their players against better opposition, the club's thinking may well have been influenced by the fractious relationship at the time, between Sheffield's industrial workforce and their masters.

Many of the working practices in the steel mills were archaic, but the different trades were resistant to change. The workers had to endure long hours in awful conditions. A cutlery worker starting work at 14 years old would develop 'grinder's asthma' from breathing in fine metal particles. By the time he was 20, he would be short of breath and find it painful to straighten up from a hunchbacked position. Local trade unionists became militant, none more so than William Broadhead, secretary of the Saw Grinders' Union. He enforced rigorous compliance with trade union policy among his members. This included intimidation and attacks on any members who associated with nonmembers. He also instigated a series of attacks from 1859 to 1866 upon employers and non-unionists. These attacks included sabotage, gunpowder bombings and shootings. The authorities found it hard to bring Broadhead to justice, despite a campaign by the *Sheffield Daily Telegraph* against him. No one was brave enough to testify against him or admit their role in various outrages, until Disraeli's government appointed a Royal Commission in 1867 and guaranteed to give witnesses immunity from prosecution. Broadhead eventually had to confess to instigating the murder of one man and a long string of other outrageous incidents.

A match between Sheffield or Hallam against a team representing the Saw Grinders' Union might well have qualified as the first real football derby, but alas it never took place. It is perhaps impossible to pinpoint precisely when the first football derby between two fully constituted clubs imbued with a distinct and local identity took place. But by the late 1870s there is no doubt that such games were happening. The interest in organised football in certain areas of late Victorian Britain was growing at an exponential rate. One of these areas was Lancashire. Blackburn alone had at least 12 active football clubs in 1877. The clubs came from different origins, they played each other on a regular basis, some folded, some continued, others merged. But gradually, some clubs grew stronger, drew a regular following, and began to develop rivalries.

One of the most intense early rivalries was between Blackburn Rovers and Darwen FC. Darwen occupies an area of moor just three miles from the centre of Blackburn, but in 1878 it had its own borough and MP, and a Latin motto of *Absque Labore Nihil* which means 'Nothing without Labour'. It was a typical stone-built Lancashire mill town, built on graft, and it had a football team to match. Darwen FC was founded in 1870. While the initiative to set the club up had come from

190

local businessmen and former public schoolboys, most of the men recruited to play came from the town's cotton mills. These locally born 'Darreners' turned out wearing trousers cut off at the knee and sometimes held up by braces. Adopting the passing style of play pioneered by Queen's Park in Scotland, they quickly built up a reputation. They also induced two Scotsmen to move south to join them, Fergie Suter and James Love. They achieved national fame in 1879 when it took Old Etonians three attempts to beat them in the quarter-final of the FA Cup, Darwen having to make the arduous and expensive journey to the Oval in London on each occasion.

Darwen's local rivals were Blackburn Rovers, who were envious of their neighbours' success. Both teams then reached the final of the Lancashire FA Challenge Cup and a crowd of 10,000 turned up to watch Darwen win 3-0. A larger crowd turned out in late 1880 to watch a friendly match between the two teams at Rovers' home ground of Alexandra Meadows. Passions were inflamed because Darwen's star player, Fergie Suter, had defected to join Rovers. Indeed, Rovers had recruited several players from other clubs. Darwen had responded to Suter's defection by vowing to rely on 'Darren lads bred and born'.[200]

The game had been the talk of the two towns in the preceding days. The ground was packed, and every vantage point around had been taken by fans unable to get in. Play in the first half was littered with fouls while sections of the crowd exchanged verbal abuse. Shortly after half-time with the score standing at 1-1, Suter charged wildly into one of his former team-mates, Tom Marshall. Suter had a lightweight build and Marshall pulled him on to his back like a sack of coal. He then pulled Suter over his head until he was holding the Scotsman by his ankles. Reports vary as to whether he threw Suter into the crowd or just dangled Suter's head in the mud. Whatever he did, it was enough to prompt a pitch invasion and a general fight involving both players and spectators. The referee had to abandon the match 40 minutes before time.

Britain's papers were full of condemnation for the events in the Blackburn versus Darwen 'friendly'. The *Belfast Morning News* was one of many papers containing a report calling the game 'most exciting and most disgraceful'.[201] A week later the country's leading sports paper, *Athletic News*, remarked that it had received five reports of the now-famous match and about 200 letters on the subject which it would have needed a special edition to publish in full. Interestingly, the paper's front page writer suggested that football alone was not solely to blame for the ugly scenes:

> I was not at all astonished to hear that the match between Darwen and Blackburn Rovers ended in a "scene". My only surprise would have been if the game ended quietly and in peace. Darwen and Blackburn have always nursed a deal of strong feeling with respect to one another, and any impression as to the rivalry between their respective football clubs being the primary cause of it is altogether mistaken and inaccurate.[202]

So, with this game, the 'local derby' had well and truly arrived as part of association football; an outlet for community identity and pride channelled into two teams battling over local superiority. Unsurprisingly, the rivalry between Darwen and Blackburn grew increasingly bitter and matches in the next few years were frequently marred by fighting among supporters. Club officials were only too happy to upset the plans of their rivals. In 1881, Darwen postponed a Lancashire Challenge Cup tie with Rovers so they could play an FA Cup fixture. In retaliation, Rovers cancelled the rescheduled match at short notice to play a friendly against Nottingham Forest.

Derby Market Place (c.1842): the starting point of the Derby Game where the ball was thrown up to the massed crowd every Shrove Tuesday. (Credit: Derby Museums Trust)

William Hutton, shown here selling books from his Birmingham bookshop, described the passion of Derby people for football in his History of Derby. *(Credit: Classic Image/ Alamy Stock Photo)*

Bull-baiting was another popular way of spending Shrove Tuesday in the Georgian era. It was finally banned in 1835. (Credit: Chronicle/Alamy Stock Photo)

Nun's Mill, Derby – the goal for St Peter's. A goal was scored by jumping in the pond and striking the ball three times against the mill wheel. (Credit: Derby Museums Trust)

Derby Gaol. The rounded Martello towers with gun slits were added after the Reform Bill riots of 1831. (Author)

Mural commemorating the silk trades lockout of 1834, on the wall of the Silk Mill Public House. Derby Shrovetide football was still played despite pressure from unions. (Author)

Spencer Bailey, Curator Collections Manager at Derby Museums, with a Derby Shrovetide football — possibly the ball surrendered by the players on the eve of Shrove Tuesday 1846. (Author)

A lithograph by Henry Burn showing a view of Derby from the east in 1846, the year of the final Shrovetide Game. On the left bank is the area known as The Holmes where many games were won or lost. (Credit: Derby Local Studies Library)

BOROUGH OF DERBY.

CAUTION.

The Mayor and Magistrates of this Borough, having been requested by the Secretary of State to take efficient measures to prevent Persons assembling on Shrove-Tuesday, or Ash-Wednesday, for the purpose of

PLAYING AT

FOOT-BALL,

Notice is therefore hereby given, that if any Persons shall be found in the Public Streets, Passages or other Public Places within this Borough, for the purpose of Playing at Foot-Ball, or for any other riotous or unlawful object, such Persons will be Prosecuted and dealt with according to law.

HENRY MOZLEY, Mayor.

Town-Hall, Derby,
March 3rd, 1848.

Printed by Wm. Bemrose, Derby.

Notice of 1848 banning Derby Shrovetide Football: the third year in which the Secretary of State sanctioned military support to suppress the game. (Credit: Derby Local Studies Library)

Atherstone Ball Game Shrovetide 2020. (Credit: P A Images/Alamy Stock Photo)

Ashbourne Shrovetide 2010. Play in the brook that divides Up'Ards from Down'Ards. (Credit: P A Images/Alamy Stock Photo)

Fergus Suter, one of the first professional footballers. His foul in a game in 1880 between Darwen and close neighbours, Blackburn Rovers, prompted a pitch invasion. (Credit: Pictorial Press Ltd/ Alamy Stock Photo)

On New Year's Day 1930, Dixie Dean emerges from the tunnel with Elisha Scott in the Merseyside derby. (Credit: Trinity Mirror/Mirror/ Alamy Stock Photo)

Kai Johansen leaps for joy after scoring for Rangers in the 1966 Scottish Cup Final against 'Old Firm' rivals Celtic. (Credit: Trinity Mirror/Mirror/Alamy Stock Photo)

Pre-match choreography by fans in the Milan derby, the Derby della Madoninna, *between AC Milan and Inter Milan, 1 March 2022. (Credit: Insidefoto di andrea staccioli/Alamy Stock Photo)*

These actions resulted in both teams being thrown out of the competition.

Sadly, Darwen's decline was as swift as their rise. Their feats were soon eclipsed by neighbouring teams. Another working-class team, Blackburn Olympic, finally broke the dominance of the public school and varsity set when they beat Old Etonians to win the FA Cup. Then Blackburn Rovers went on to win the cup three times in a row. Darwen were humiliated in 1890 when they travelled the short distance to Ewood Park, Rovers' new ground. Rovers had just won their fourth FA Cup and only saw fit to field three of their first-choice players. The visiting fans went on the rampage, ripping up goalposts and corner flags, breaking windows and generally trying to do as much damage as they could to the ground. Although elected to the Football League in 1891, Darwen lost a game by the record-breaking margin of 12-0 to West Bromwich Albion in the following year. The 1898/99 season was to be their last as a Football League team, when they recorded 18 defeats in succession.

Darwen's spell in the limelight may have been relatively short, but their success and their strong roots in the local community had ignited a football mania that was to spread to the rest of Lancashire and then to the rest of the country. It is hard, nowadays, to appreciate how novel the growing interest in football was in the 1880s. But many observers at the time were seriously worried about the passions raised, the 'win at all costs' mentality displayed in games, and the inability of some people to talk about anything else.

The formation of the Football League in 1888 highlighted the importance of the game in Lancashire. Even though the league was the idea of William McGregor, a director of Aston Villa, six of the original 12 founding clubs came from Lancashire: Accrington, Blackburn Rovers, Bolton Wanderers, Burnley, Everton and Preston North End. Four clubs were from the industrial heartlands of the West Midlands: Aston Villa, Stoke City, West Bromwich Albion, and Wolverhampton Wanderers. The remaining two clubs were from further east: Notts County, one of the country's oldest clubs, and Derby County.

Casual football games on fields and waste ground had no doubt continued in Derby following the banning of the Shrovetide games in the late 1840s. On a more formal level, Derby School, which had moved into a former Strutt residence, became a public school in the 1860s and quickly achieved a national reputation for its football. Several clubs sprang up and competed for local supremacy, the most competitive being Derby Town, Derby Junction, and Derby Midland. In 1884, the final of the first Derbyshire Cup, between Derby Midland and Staveley, was held at the county cricket club's ground in Derby. The event attracted a crowd of 7,000 people, 3,000 more than the attendance achieved at that year's FA Cup Final at the Oval in London.

Excited by the possible financial benefits of the Derby public's appetite for the game, the cricket club quickly set up the Derbyshire County Football Club. Renamed the following year as Derby County, the club caused a major upset by knocking the mighty Aston Villa out of the FA Cup. This feat was eclipsed three years later in 1888, when Derby Junction got as far as the quarter-final of the FA Cup and drew Blackburn Rovers. Derby Junction were originally formed as a team for former pupils of Junction Street School. They played their home games at the Arboretum field and the Rovers players were dismayed when they saw the state of the frost-damaged pitch. The 'Juncs', however, were in their element and won 2-1 to reach the semi-final. The result was greeted with wild celebrations and football reporters who had considered the tie to be a mere formality had to apologise, 'But who would have been bold enough to predict that Blackburn Rovers, thrice winners of the National Cup, would be knocked out of the competition by Derby Junction – a team of Derby lads, that up to Saturday were almost unknown to the football world.'[203]

A crowd of 5,000 had turned up to watch the match, and the architects of the Football League could have been in no doubt that a club from Derby would make a fitting founder member. The excitement caused by Derby Junction's success and the formation of Derby County had stirred up memories of the fervour surrounding the old Shrovetide games. The renewed enthusiasm for football in Derby at this time also fired the imagination of a young lad called Steve Bloomer, who was to go on to become England's first football superstar. Bloomer's goals for Derby County meant they could compete with the best clubs in the land and the new organised form of football became the town's new obsession.

The formation of the Football League gave a further boost to the sport by giving more meaning to contests than ad hoc friendly matches could do. But the rise in the popularity of football in the late Victorian era is most easily tracked by the attendance figures for the FA Cup Final. When Blackburn Rovers played West Bromwich Albion at the Oval in 1886 they attracted 15,000 fans, with 12,000 going to the replay at Derby County's ground, the first time an FA Cup Final had been played outside of London. In 1892 the attendance was 32,800, in 1896 it was 48,800, and in 1899 a massive crowd of 73,800 at Crystal Palace watched Sheffield United beat the hot favourites, Derby County, 4-1.

Football mania was no longer restricted to the mill towns of Lancashire but had taken a permanent hold on much of the nation. Undoubtedly, the creation of the half-holiday on Saturday afternoons, which had become widespread after 1875, fuelled the interest. Football promised the possibility of an exciting, thrill-packed escape from the dull monotony of factory life. Newspapers were ready to fan the flames, happy not just to report on games, but to offer pre-match opinions and relay gossip about different players and clubs.

The term 'local derby' did not start to be widely used in the newspapers to describe a football match until the turn of the century. In 1880 many towns had several football clubs who spent much of their time playing each other. It is noticeable that until the late 1890s these matches were very rarely referred to as 'derbies', despite the competing teams being mostly very local to each other. But, as national leagues developed in England and Scotland, and as the number of teams thinned out, the branding of a local game as a 'derby' took on more meaning, particularly as a way of promoting a game, as the following extract from the *Dundee Courier* suggests: 'The local "Derby" takes place in Dundee to-morrow, when Wanderers meet the First Leaguers in Carolina Port. With the name "Derby" is usually associated all that is keen and exciting, and circumstances point to the application being realised in every way.'[204]

By the start of the Edwardian era, the number of clubs vying to represent their borough, town or city had been greatly reduced; many had merged and others fell by the wayside. Many towns now had one principal club, and the bigger cities like Birmingham, Liverpool, Manchester, Nottingham, Sheffield and Stoke had two Football League clubs. The Football League had expanded its reach outside of Lancashire, Yorkshire and the Midlands to include Middlesbrough, Newcastle and Sunderland in the north-east. But in London, the only Football League team was Woolwich Arsenal, and their nearest competitor was Luton Town.

Most of the larger football clubs south of Birmingham played in the Southern League, set up in 1894 on the initiative of Millwall Athletic. With fewer clubs and a preponderance of league fixtures, a local clash between clubs became a more unusual event, and consequently more worthy of mention. In addition, several of these surviving clubs had often been in existence for 20 years or more, and had built up a history and a following, aware of previous successes, failures and incidents. Under a heading of 'To-morrow's Local Derby' a 1909 article in the *Yorkshire Telegraph* already felt the weight of history:

> Interesting as Saturday's matches undoubtedly are everything sinks into commonplace besides the big encounter at Bramall Lane, where Sheffield United and Sheffield Wednesday meet of the 31st time under League auspices, and the 60th encounter under all conditions. Looking back reveals many a struggle of note, and recalls the names of players who have added lustre to the good name of Sheffield clubs. Long may their memory live.[205]

Newspaper reports referring to some games as 'derbies' significantly increased during the Edwardian period. Fixtures attracting this epithet included Manchester City v Manchester United, The Wednesday v Sheffield United, Nottingham Forest v Notts County, Fulham v Chelsea, Liverpool v Everton, Portsmouth v Southampton and Millwall v West Ham. The relevant local derby for each club now often became the biggest attraction of the season.

In 1909, a football gossip columnist commented on the 'dramatic leap to popularity' football had made in London, after a derby between Chelsea and Tottenham attracted a crowd of 60,000 people. The reporter, B. Bennison, found more 'life and colour, more thrill in the mighty congregation of folk' than in the actual game. He described the scene:

> Here were people tightly wedged in the most wonderful of all club grounds with little or no thought of anything but a possible victory of their favourites: one felt that

real football counted nothing to them – they were out because of promised fury; every man was steeped in local prejudice.[206]

In his report, Bennison went on to lament the quality of football in London and wondered what size of crowd might be drawn to see a team with the skills of an Everton.

Even as early as 1894, fixtures between Everton and Liverpool were drawing crowds of around 40,000. In the Edwardian period other local derby fixtures emerged as major crowd-pullers. In Manchester, the Old Trafford meetings of United and City saw attendances rise steadily from 30,000 in 1907, to the 60,000 in 1910 who saw a hard-fought game in an atmosphere of intense excitement. On Christmas Day 1911 in London, a crowd of 47,109 saw Tottenham thrash Woolwich Arsenal 5-0, with an estimated 10,000 locked out. The pull of the local derby was by now a national phenomenon.

15

Trouble and Strife

THE INTENSE rivalry shown in the Derby Shrovetide games between north Derby in the guise of All Saints' and south Derby in the shape of St Peter's was built up over hundreds of years. But it seems that local games of association football led to rivalries being developed very rapidly, or perhaps they just exposed underlying grudges between different local communities. Ill feeling was not confined to the cities and large towns, it could occur almost anywhere. In 1907, for example, a game between the small neighbouring Cornish towns of Helston and Porthleven had to be abandoned after spectators invaded the pitch; in Yorkshire disciplinary action had to be taken against seven players from the picturesque town of Knaresborough after disgraceful scenes in their game against Starbeck St Andrew's, a team from nearby Harrogate.

One of the most intense and long-standing rivalries in English football is between Millwall and West Ham United. Millwall Rovers Football Club was formed in 1885 by workers at J.T. Morton's Canning and Preserve factory on the Isle of Dogs in the East End of London. Ten years later, a shipbuilding company called Thames Ironworks, about a mile downriver of Millwall, formed a football club of the same name: Thames Ironworks Football Club. The driving force behind the club's establishment was Dave Taylor, a foreman at the works who was a local football referee. His idea was to form a works team.

Three years later they turned professional, and in 1900 wound up the Ironworks club and relaunched as West Ham United. In 1910, Millwall FC (who had now dropped 'Rovers' from their name) moved south of the Thames to New Cross, but no doubt retained the loyalty of many supporters in the Isle of Dogs.

The two clubs often played each other before 1914. Their fans were drawn from East End neighbourhoods bordering the Thames, and from the dockyards and businesses that lined the river. In a game at Upton Park in 1906, Millwall's right-winger Alf Dean was badly injured after being hurled against a metal advertising hoarding. This provoked a fight among spectators at one end of the ground, just one of several to take place during the game. Another Millwall player also had to be stretchered off. The match was played in a frenzied and antagonistic spirit which was shared by both players and supporters. A reporter commented, 'Happily for the reputation of professional Association Football there are not many games in which the element of roughness is so liberally introduced.'[207]

Various theories have been put forward in explanation of the animosity between Millwall and West Ham. One of these is that the businesses behind the formation of the clubs were in competition for contracts. This seems highly doubtful, as Thames Ironworks built ships like HMS *Dreadnought*, while J.T. Morton produced canned and preserved foods.

Another theory is that of a rift between dockland workers during the General Strike of 1926. This action, across Britain as a whole, was called by the Trades Union Congress in protest over poor pay and working conditions. Millions of people took part in the nine-day strike. The London dockers joined the strike and it is often claimed that Millwall-supporting dockers in the Isle of Dogs did not take part, unlike their West Ham-supporting counterparts concentrated around the Royal Docks. Again, there seems to be no basis for this story. Firstly, reports clearly show intense animosity for many years before the General Strike. Secondly, while there was tremendous turmoil across London during the General Strike, there seems to have been great solidarity among its dockers. Of course, this has not stopped West Ham fans referring to Millwall supporters as 'scabs'.

It seems more likely that animosity between the two clubs originally arose out of the nature of the local area, and particularly the way in which work was organised there in the first decades of the 20th century. Many local people did not have a permanent job but had to make do with casual employment, turning up at the docks or at factory gates and trying to get a few days' work. Success in this often depended on who you knew, so any friendships or family connections were very important. Often, people would work for the same company as their relatives, so loyalty to family, friends and firm was helpful, if not vital, to putting food on the table, and for some, support for a local football club was an extension of this. It seems the same fierce loyalty was also given to both clubs. The East End was a tough area where a degree of verbal and physical belligerence might be needed just to get inside the factory gates. It paid to be a bit mouthy and handy with your elbows.

Whatever the cause for the original animosity, the rivalry between the clubs' supporters is still keenly felt, although meetings between West Ham and Millwall have been sporadic as they have not often been in the same division. In 1976 a Millwall fan, 18-year-old Ian Pratt, died after falling from a train at New Cross Station into the path of an express train. The subsequent inquest delivered an open verdict, as it was unable to decide whether Ian fell or was pushed out of the train. His mother clearly believed he had been the victim of murder by West Ham fans, and reportedly told the *Daily Mirror* later that year that her brothers and the rest of her family had vowed to get the perpetrators before the police.[208] She doubted whether they would have a quick death.

If people thought that the days of serious hooliganism were left behind in the 1970s and '80s, they must have been shocked when West Ham were drawn to play Millwall in the League Cup in August 2009. Hundreds and possibly thousands of people were involved in a night of violence, which started well over an hour before kick-off and carried on for hours after the game had finished. The trouble occurred in railway stations, in the streets around West Ham's Boleyn Ground, and in the stadium itself. A man was stabbed in the chest, bricks and bottles were thrown at rival fans, and pubs and other buildings were damaged. Riot police ran from one trouble spot to another only to be attacked themselves. The game itself was won 3-1 by West Ham but was stopped twice due to fans invading the pitch.

Mass football hooliganism did not originate in the 1970s, and local derbies in parts of the United Kingdom with divided communities have a long record of trouble. In Belfast, the divisions between local communities were crystal clear: the mutual antipathy between the Catholic and Protestant sections of the city. When regular matches got under way there in the 1890s, games between clubs seen as primarily Catholic or Protestant could degenerate into mob violence directed at players as well as at opposing spectators. One of the fiercest Belfast derbies was between Belfast Celtic and Linfield. When the clubs met at Celtic Park on 14 September 1912, tensions between Catholics and Protestants were very high following a series of recent incidents and political developments. The two teams had both started the new season in good form. The game started at the appointed time and the first half was fairly even, with Linfield going into the break 1-0 in front. The players had not got involved in any unseemly incidents; the football had been played in a clean and sporting way.

But when the players reached their dressing rooms, trouble began to break out on the terraces. Celtic's fans were mainly congregated at the Falls Road end of the ground, while Linfield's were at the Donegall Road end. Celtic's fans hoisted a green and white flag (the club's colours) and marched up to Linfield's end. The Linfield fans responded by raising a Union Jack. The taunting and jeering quickly gave way to scuffles, prompting a large contingent of Celtic fans to clamber over the iron railings bordering their enclosure. They ran to the Linfield end, picking up stones and other debris which was in abundant supply due to some ongoing ground improvements. A barrage of stones, bricks and clinker pieces rained down on the Linfield supporters, who if not hit, picked up the stones and threw them back at their adversaries. On the pitch many fist fights were in progress. Then revolver shots rang out amid the turmoil, fired from the Celtic supporters in the direction of the Linfield fans. Many in the Linfield section spilled out the back of the ground on to Donegall Road. The shooter jumped over a barrier into the Linfield section and fired more shots into the retreating crowd, blue smoke from the gun curling up into the air.

The Linfield fans who had made it out on to Donegall Road found makeshift missiles of their own, as the road had recently been ripped up in preparation for the building of a tramway. Using these materials, they forced the Celtic crowd back into their own ground. The police, who were hopelessly outnumbered, tried to get in between the opposing groups, opting to baton-charge each side in an effort to restore some order. Eventually more police arrived and the two sets of fans were herded away. When things had calmed down, it was possible for the few people still left in the ground to take stock. Scores of men and youths were either staggering around streaming with blood or lying unconscious on the ground. All the city's ambulances were employed in ferrying the wounded away to hospitals. Although the riot had only lasted for around half an hour, 60 people were taken to hospital. While many were treated for lacerations and heavy bruising, five people had gunshot wounds and a policeman had a serious eye injury. At least three patients had fractured skulls.

Despite the city's shock at these events, the *Belfast Evening Telegraph* advised against mass arrests, arguing that people had assembled solely for the purposes of a football match rather than to start trouble. The paper argued that under strong provocation 'any man of energetic and excitable temperament' might find himself swept along by the excitement of the moment into defending himself or participating.[209] This plea for leniency seems to have been followed as only a handful of arrests were made. But, except for a kind of truce during the Great War, the rivalry between Belfast Celtic and Linfield rumbled on until the events of December 1948.

Elisha Scott was born and raised in Donegall Road, part of a large Protestant family. His elder brother Billy played in goal for Linfield before leaving for Everton. Elisha also had a brief time with Linfield, but in 1912 he signed for Liverpool where he had become the fans' favourite and their longest-serving player. In 1934, though, he left Liverpool and took up the job of managing Belfast Celtic. He could hardly have been more successful, guiding the Hoops to ten league titles. In 1947 Scott persuaded the square-shouldered Jimmy Jones to leave Linfield and play for Celtic. Another Protestant, Jones had assumed his future lay with Linfield, but they had been slow to realise his potential. Linfield could only rue their misjudgement as Jones scored 62 goals in all competitions in the 1947/48 season, and Celtic beat Linfield to the league title by four points. The success of Celtic, combined with the perceived 'betrayal' of Scott and Jones, must have been extremely galling for the Linfield supporters, who were predominantly Protestant.

On 27 December 1948, Belfast Celtic travelled the short distance to Windsor Park, home of the Bluemen of Linfield. A crowd of 30,000 packed into the ground. In those days managers were not allowed to send on substitutes for injured players. By half-time Linfield had been reduced to nine men because of injuries, one of which was a broken ankle following a challenge by Jones. The second half was played in an equally forceful manner, with the referee sending off a player from each team. A penalty in the 80th minute gave Celtic the lead but the eight remaining Linfield players refused to give up and scored an equaliser with six minutes to go. After the final whistle, Linfield fans surged on to the pitch and instead of celebrating a draw, they attacked the Celtic players. Jones was trying to make his way to the dressing room but was waylaid on the terraces by enraged fans who repeatedly stamped on his right leg. The police drew batons and dispersed the crowd. Jones was taken to hospital with a fractured shin bone. No arrests were made, and Linfield escaped serious punishment by the Irish Football Association – just a ground closure for two games. Disgusted at the leniency of this sanction, the board of directors at the Celtic club withdrew the team from the Irish League at the end of the season. Belfast Celtic never played a competitive match again.

Of course, the charge of sectarianism is most famously made against the two teams involved in the Glasgow derby: Celtic and Rangers. Celtic were formed in 1887 by an Irishman called Andrew Kerrins from County Sligo in the west of Ireland. He was a member of the Marist Brothers Teaching Order and was better known by his religious name of Brother Walfrid (the Marists are an international Catholic community dedicated to educating disadvantaged young people). As headteacher of the Sacred Heart School in the Bridgeton area of Glasgow, Brother Walfrid had come up with a 'Penny Dinner' scheme to boost numbers at the school. The scheme provided a substantial meal for each pupil, at the purely voluntary cost of a penny. By 1886, Brother Walfrid had well over 1,000 pupils at his school, most of whom were getting their dinners for free. He needed to find a source of funds, so he started arranging charitable football matches which proved to be very popular with the local community and an excellent means of raising money. He was the driving force in setting up Celtic Football Club and trying to use the new club as a means of helping local charities in the area.

It is possible that Brother Walfrid also had other motives. In addition to their obvious humanitarian benefit, his penny dinners could be seen by the more cynically minded as promoting the Catholic cause, by reducing the numbers of people from Catholic families queuing up at Protestant soup kitchens. Undoubtedly, he was inspired by the Edinburgh club Hibernian FC, who had formed in 1875 as an openly Irish club and reputedly supported Irish Home Rule. Hibernian were a leading force in the 1880s, winning the Scottish Cup in 1887, and gave every encouragement to Brother Walfrid and his friends to set up a similar Irish club in Glasgow.

Whatever Brother Walfrid's motives were, the formation of Glasgow Rangers appears to lack any conscious political, cultural or religious purpose. Rangers were formed in 1872 by four young friends who had no other thought in mind than to form a football club. But after the Scottish Football League was set up in 1890, Rangers and Celtic quickly emerged in the following years as the major two clubs in Glasgow. By the time the two teams met in the 1904 Scottish Cup Final, Rangers had won the Scottish league championship five times to Celtic's four, while the Scottish Cup had been won four times by Rangers to Celtic's three. Before the 1904 game, a cartoon appeared in the *Scottish Referee*, a popular sports magazine, depicting a dishevelled man with a sandwich board, emblazoned with the message 'Patronise The Old Firm'.

This is clearly a satirical reference to the increasingly regular and highly lucrative meetings of the two clubs. The cartoon reflected a feeling among some Glaswegians that the financial success of Celtic and Rangers had come at the expense of other local clubs. Chief among those who had been left behind by the advance of the Old Firm were Queen's Park FC, who had been one of the top clubs in late-Victorian Britain but decided to keep faith with a purely amateur status.

Events at the 1909 Scottish Cup Final between Celtic and Rangers suggest another facet of the Old Firm tag. The final was fixed for 10 April at Hampden Park in Glasgow, and a crowd of 66,000 eager fans duly assembled, providing record receipts. The game was close, but Rangers were leading 2-1 with a few minutes to go when Harry Rennie, their goalkeeper, caught a shot from Joe Dodds. Having secured the ball in a vice-like grip, he then behaved as if he had forgotten where his goal line was and swung round, thereby scoring an own goal which put Celtic level and necessitated a replay. One newspaper report described this goal as 'a strange event', while another said it was 'curious'.[210]

A week later, 60,000 people turned up for the replay. This time the final score was 1-1. Incensed by the need for yet another replay and suspicious that the teams were fixing results to increase their income, fans of both clubs invaded the pitch. The dozen constables on duty were hopelessly outnumbered as thousands of frustrated supporters went on the rampage. The goalposts were torn down, and fences were smashed, piled on the pitch and set ablaze, the flames spreading to pay boxes and turnstiles. The few mounted police on duty found their horses attacked mercilessly with sticks and stones. When the first fire crews arrived, they were also attacked and hoses thrown on to the fire. The police tried baton charges but this only incensed the crowd further and stones and bottles were hurled at the constables. The police waded into sections of the mob wielding their truncheons without any apparent concern for the injuries they might be causing. The mob tried to get into the main pavilion which housed the players and club officials, but the attack was repulsed when a group of five mounted policemen arrived and managed to prevent the crowd getting into the building. Around 100 extra constables arrived together with fresh units of the fire brigade, some of whom turned their hoses on the crowd. The police tried to make arrests but were forced by the crowd to release their prisoners.

In all, the riot lasted for two hours before the police managed to establish perfect order. Thirty policemen were badly injured and at least as many spectators. It is notable though that the fans did not attack each other; their animosity was directed at the clubs and players. Indeed, the early relations between the two clubs had been friendly and cordial. But in 1912 the tense political situation in Belfast prompted Harland and Wolff to open a massive shipyard in the Govan area of Glasgow. At the time the company were the builders of the world's greatest ships, including the *Titanic*, and their workforce was overwhelmingly Protestant. The new shipyard in Glasgow prompted many embittered Orangemen to transfer from the Belfast workforce and gain their living on the Govan docks, a short walk from Rangers' Ibrox Stadium. This event is sometimes pinpointed as the reason that relations between Celtic and Rangers deteriorated. However, many Scottish Presbyterians resented the influx of Irish Catholics, so it was probably the growing political tensions raised by the Irish Home Rule Crisis in the years preceding the Great War that was the main reason for the rifts between the clubs and their followers. Rangers clearly avoided signing any Catholic players for many years; Mo Johnston became the first Catholic to play for Rangers since the Great War, when he signed in 1989.

The Glasgow derby has an intensity which is unequalled anywhere else in Britain. The fixture still holds the record for the highest attendance at a league match between two British football clubs, when in January 1939 118,567 fans packed out Ibrox. The passion, and often enmity, between the two sets of fanatical supporters sometimes spills over into violence. The people who are always blamed for such violence are the fans, which seems logical at first glance. But surely at least part of the blame must be laid at the door of those who decided to make these clubs into political footballs. It could have been different, and the next chapter illustrates how.

The Friendly Derby

A WEBSITE devoted to the history of Liverpool describes the origins of football in England and explains that: 'In the City of Derby the games between two rival villages would turn very violent with many people being killed. It is from this City that the phrase "local derby match" comes.'[211] The Derby Shrovetide games were undoubtedly rough, violent, and routinely resulted in serious injuries, but no murders were attributed to them. It is rumoured that deaths did occasionally occur as a result of injuries received or illnesses contracted during the games, but these were incidental, unintended deaths and not deliberate killings. Local derbies create a complex range of emotions, and several observers of the old Derby Game remarked on the good-natured spirit of many of the participants, as well as upon the keenness of the contests. So it is interesting to look at the games between Everton and Liverpool, which used to be called the 'friendly derbies'.

The grounds of the two clubs are less than a mile apart. A large green space, Stanley Park, lies in between. Everton started out playing their games on a corner of Stanley Park but soon found it unsuitable to accommodate all the people who wanted to watch. In 1884 they started playing on a site in Anfield, owned by a brewing family called the Orrell Brothers. At that time this was the northern edge of the city, a place where 20 years previously merchants and bankers had built a few villas in leafy surroundings, a few miles from their warehouses and offices down at the docks. The villas were soon to be engulfed in a tide of development as Liverpool boomed and proclaimed itself the second city of the empire. The site off Anfield Road had been pasture land and club officials, players and fans had to muck in, to turn it into a suitable arena.

Everton turned professional in 1888 and won their first championship in 1890/91. The owner of the Anfield ground was now another brewer called John Houlding. He was also club president, but many of the club's members felt he was increasingly acting in his own financial interests rather than those of Everton. Consequently, Everton decamped to a field on the north side of Stanley Park. This was to become Goodison Park. Houlding was left with an empty football ground, so he formed a new club called Liverpool FC, after his suggested name of Everton Athletic was turned down by the Football Association. The Dublin-born manager of Everton, William Barclay, stayed on at Anfield to manage the new club and later became the club's chairman. At least two former Everton players also stayed on at Anfield to play for Liverpool, while another three former Everton players signed up within a couple of years.

It looks like the close historical connections between the two clubs led to a friendly rivalry which was unusual for two big clubs in the same city. When Houlding's wife died in 1897, Everton sent a wreath to her funeral. At Houlding's own funeral in 1902, players from both clubs carried his coffin as a mark of their joint respect. The good interclub relations continued and the word 'Liverton' was coined to echo this togetherness. A report in the *Liverpool Echo* in 1918 was full of smug anticipation and self-congratulation; the writer clearly viewed the relationship as of long standing and a cut above the rest:

> We are in a great mood ... the first of the season's
> succession of Derby games promises to live up to the
> Liverton reputation of cleanliness and keenness. That
> is all we require. Merseyside for many, many years has
> been a pattern of clean sport, and the players of the
> day will, I am sure, see that there is no blot on the
> copybook.[212]

There were good reasons to praise this relationship, particularly given the events in Belfast and Glasgow described in the previous chapter. Even before the Irish famine of the 1840s, Liverpool already had a large Irish population. But when the famine forced more than 1.5 million people to emigrate from Ireland, the first principal port they arrived at was Liverpool. While migrants often stepped off a boat in Liverpool with the aim of moving on elsewhere in Britain, or of catching a ship to North America or Australia, many found they didn't have enough money to carry out their plans. In which case, they often stayed in Liverpool. Others were attracted to stay because of links to friends and family in the city, or by the availability of jobs on the docks. By 1851, the city's Irish-born population accounted for nearly a quarter of its inhabitants.

John Houlding was a prominent member of the Orange order, and George Mahon, who engineered Everton's move from Anfield to Goodison, was in favour of Irish Home Rule. So Everton and Liverpool could easily have become the English equivalent of Celtic and Rangers, one club for Catholics and one for Protestants. There may possibly have been a political as well as a financial disagreement between Houlding and Mahon. But there is no evidence that the two Merseyside clubs showed any inclination to be sectarian in nature. One reason is that Everton started out as a boys' club of a Methodist church called St Domingo's. The club played cricket in the summer and football in the winter. So, despite Mahon's political views,

Everton did not have Catholic roots. Houlding became Lord Mayor of Liverpool and appeared to be generally well regarded, and supportive of charities who worked across denominations.

Posts on some internet football forums claim that sectarianism was never much of an issue in Liverpool, and thus did not infect local football. However, given the Irish heritage of much of the population, it is hard to believe that somehow Liverpool was immune to sectarianism. Indeed, Liverpool contained the only constituency outside of Ireland to elect an Irish Nationalist as MP: Thomas Power O'Connor represented a large district based around the Scotland Road area of Liverpool at Westminster from 1885 to 1929.

One reason the two clubs were so interwoven was that there was no geographical divide in their support. Many families had members who supported different clubs. Indeed, in the early 20th century, the more affluent local football fan was likely to support both teams. This may be one reason that between 1904 and 1935 the two clubs used to produce a joint matchday programme. In January 1932, the *Liverpool Echo* announced that in a forthcoming Merseyside derby in the FA Cup, the two teams would come out together two-by-two as a 'token of sporting friendship' and that the game would 'bear the imprint of Merseyside decency'.[213] Two years later, the same paper included an article in which two characters, 'Mr Kop' and 'Mr Goodson', discussed the merits of their respective teams. Mr Goodson commented on an Everton player called Billy Cook: 'Steady, there, Billy, don't hurt 'em, bump 'em, but don't forget we never have harsh football in these Derby games. I'm not implying anything, I'm only reminding you newer players of this city that Liverpool stands for all that is best and fairest.'[214] As Cook had been transferred from Celtic, and was used to Old Firm derbies, this was probably helpful advice.

Everton's greatest ever player was surely William Ralph Dean, better known as Dixie Dean. He was born in

Birkenhead, and as a young boy during the period of the Great War he helped deliver milk to local families, getting up at 4.30am to fetch the ponies and milk floats. He was football-mad from an early age and reportedly lied to get admitted to a Borstal school for 'juvenile delinquents' so that he could play the game more. Leaving school at 14 years old, he followed in his father's footsteps and got a job on the Wirral railway. He took the night shift so that he could play football during the day. His single-minded devotion to the sport paid off and aged 16 he signed for his local club, Tranmere Rovers. Two years later he joined Everton and began to rewrite the record books. In the 1927/28 season he scored an incredible 60 goals, a feat that has never been beaten.

Dean combined power with athleticism and is especially remembered for his prowess in the air, his goals often being headed home. He was also targeted by opponents. He was kicked and battered but kept his composure, limiting his retaliation to verbal jibes. He was never booked, and never sent off. He just got on with the game. As captain of Everton, he encouraged his players to stay focused on the football and led by example. Off the pitch he had a lively sense of humour and a liking for more than just a drink or two. Indeed, his erstwhile Everton colleague Joe Mercer claimed Dean made George Best look like a choirboy in comparison. In his later years, he was landlord of the Dublin Packet pub in Chester, where he was known to his closest friends as 'Bill'. One day, according to the *Liverpool Echo*, a coachload of pensioners pulled up outside and entered the pub, 'and one old chap said to Billy "I remember when you came down Scotland Road with the FA Cup". At the time of course, there were thousands of people lining the route and Bill said to the old chap, "Did you see me? Funny. I didn't see you."' [215]

Dixie Dean was the most prolific English striker since the days of Derby County's Steve Bloomer. When Bloomer finished his playing career in 1914, he had scored a total of 352 goals in league games. With one game left in the 1935/36 season, Dean had reached 351. Anticipating the imminent fall of the long-standing record, the *Liverpool Echo* invited Bloomer up to Goodison Park for Everton's final game of the year, which was against Preston North End. Unfortunately, the *Echo* had not checked with Dean, who was injured and unable to play due to a broken collarbone. Nevertheless, with his arm in a sling, the embarrassed player took the trouble to meet Bloomer off the train and shared a few beers with him after the match. Suitably refreshed, he sent Bloomer home with a bottle of whisky for company. In the following season Dean went on to break Bloomer's record and ended up with a career total of 379 league goals.

Dean's amiability with Bloomer was typical of the man, and his friendship and rivalry with the great Liverpool goalkeeper, Elisha Scott, typified the relationship between the two clubs. When Scott arrived at Everton as a young man for a trial, he was a thin, weak-looking stripling. Everton did not think he would be up to the job of competing with burly forwards. Liverpool, though, saw his potential and by the time Dean arrived at Everton, Scott was the darling of Liverpool's Kop. He was renowned for his swearing and when Scott first met Dean in the tunnel at Anfield, he called him various epithets, in his distinctive high-pitched Belfast accent. Dean calmly replied that if he didn't score that day he would go back to working on the railway. Dean scored many goals at Anfield, and sometimes after netting would bow to the Kop in the manner of a matador.

The 1920s and 1930s saw many thrilling Merseyside derbies. Following the 0-0 scoreline of December 1919 there were 28 matches between the two rivals before another goalless draw, with five or six goals being commonplace and one match featuring 11 when Liverpool beat Everton 7-4 in

February 1933. The crowds of around 60,000 were clearly absorbed in these sporting contests, made more thrilling and unpredictable because neither club was able to dominate the other for very long.

In later life, Dean would declare that Scott was the greatest goalkeeper he had ever faced. But prior to a derby game he would send Elisha a box of aspirins, in apology for the headache he was going to give him. On the day itself they led their teams out side-by-side and commiserated or congratulated each other when the game was finished, as in the 1932 FA Cup tie when Scott walked off with his arms round Dean's shoulders after Everton's defeat. Dean and Scott would share pre-match cigarettes and meet up for drinks after matches. A common story is that when Dean was walking through Liverpool city centre, he spotted Scott coming towards him. He nodded to acknowledge his sporting adversary and Scott instinctively dived to the floor. In some versions of the story, Scott dived through a plate glass window while Dean calmly carried on his way. The story probably originated to reflect the way Scott kept continually on his toes during a match, ready to leap in any direction, and to show Dean's cool and unflappable style.

In 1934, after 468 matches as Liverpool goalkeeper, Scott decided to retire. Eventually a deal was done with Belfast Celtic and Scott moved there initially as player-manager. He was moving into the sectarian battleground described in the previous chapter. It is little wonder, therefore, that the amicable football family of Merseyside made him seriously consider joining Everton as an alternative, where his elder brother Billy had kept goal before the Great War. After their playing careers finished, Scott and Dean appeared together at many Liverpool functions, still joshing but full of mutual respect.

Looking back, the period between the two world wars looks like a golden era for the Merseyside derby, when the two clubs could play in an intense but sporting atmosphere. Everton won three First Division titles during this time and one FA Cup, while Liverpool won the First Division twice. No doubt there were occasional incidents on the pitch and fist fights between supporters off it, yet there was a genuine, if competitive, friendship between the two clubs and no mass crowd trouble at Merseyside derbies. The atmosphere at other local derbies during this period was sometimes very different. Consider the first game in the 1922/23 season between Tottenham and Arsenal where:

> Feeling [sic] ran so high ... that at one moment it looked as if the match would degenerate into a free fight, and extra police had to be hurried up in order to protect the Arsenal goalkeeper from a threatened attack on the part of the crowd.[216]

Arsenal achieved a 2-1 victory but 'at the expense of all that is decent and clean and sportsmanlike'.[217] Tottenham's right-winger Walden had to limp off before half-time and a brutal challenge on his team-mate Lindsay roused the crowd to a frenzy. Bliss for Spurs and Bradshaw for Arsenal came to blows. At one point the Arsenal goalkeeper ran to the halfway line to remonstrate wildly with the referee. The reporter for the *Westminster Gazette* considered both Bradshaw and the Tottenham crowd to be 'a disgrace to decent football', denouncing the Tottenham spectator as 'about the most biased and intolerant of his kind'.[218] The *Daily News* put the blame on the Tottenham supporters for their unfair and provocative treatment of Arsenal players and described the scene at the final whistle, 'A noise welled up from the crowd which was faintly reminiscent of the sounds one may hear at the zoo round about the lions' feeding time. The game had ended in pandemonium.'[219]

Amazingly, given the heated passions that often arise during local derbies, the legacy of the friendly relationship between Everton and Liverpool lasted well into the latter half of the 20th century. As a former resident of Liverpool, who used to live a few streets behind the Kop during the great days of Bill Shankly and Bob Paisley in the 1970s, I can vouch for the generally affable relationships between opposing fans at that time. In those days, Liverpool and Everton fans generally preferred to sort out their differences through verbal banter rather than violence, but in 1985 relations came under strain following the Heysel Stadium disaster.

Liverpool had reached the final of the European Cup and their opponents in Brussels were the Italian side Juventus. About an hour before kick-off, some Liverpool fans charged through a fence separating them from the Juventus supporters; a stampede resulted, and a concrete wall gave way, killing 39 people and injuring hundreds of others. Despite poor ticket allocation and the decision to host the game in a crumbling stadium, the blame was overwhelmingly directed at Liverpool fans and UEFA banned all English football clubs from all European competitions. This punishment, which lasted for five years, was felt particularly keenly by Everton fans, as their club won the First Division and the European Cup Winners' Cup in 1984/85. They won the First Division again in 1986/87, but UEFA's ban meant they were unable to compete in Europe while they were at their peak. (Liverpool were banned from European competition for ten years, later reduced to six years.)

Ironically, the Hillsborough disaster of 1989, which led to the deaths of 97 people as a result of the events at the FA Cup semi-final between Liverpool and Nottingham Forest, served to bring the two clubs closer together again. It was a case of the city's people closing ranks in solidarity, embodied by the intertwining of blue and red scarves to link the Anfield and Goodison Park stadiums across Stanley Park.

The relative lack of crowd trouble between the two sets of fans meant that, historically, strict segregation of rival sets of supporters inside the two grounds was long considered unnecessary. Sadly, in the last decade or so, an undercurrent of ill feeling has developed, possibly exacerbated by the popularity of social media, where it is easy for banter to escalate into something vile and shameful. Segregation inside and outside the grounds is now the norm. The rise in tensions off the pitch seems to have spread to the players. By 2017 the fixture had resulted in no less than 21 players being sent off since the formation of the Premier League in 1992. If Everton and Liverpool are going to rediscover the spirit of the friendly derby then the players and club officials will need to take a lead. Perhaps then, their wilder supporters might realise, like their counterparts learnt in the old Derby Shrovetide games, that rivalry should be tempered by a shared code of behaviour, which reflects a love of the game and curbs its worst excesses.

Part of Football Esperanto

THE PLEASANT coastal town of Irun lies in the very north-east corner of Spain, looking out over a river that forms the border with France. Behind it, to the south, are sparsely populated hills and forests. It would make a useful holiday base from which to explore the Basque country. But there must have been times after his move there in 1923 that Steve Bloomer looked around his hotel room and wondered what on earth he was doing.

In a career spanning 23 seasons, he had scored a record 352 league goals (293 for Derby County and 59 for Middlesbrough). He had also put away 28 goals in 23 matches for the England national team and become their longest-serving player. He was nationally renowned and was one of the first footballers to endorse items of football kit – his Lucky Goal Scorer boots had an image of himself embossed on the sole. In football circles, he had an international reputation. Yet in 1923, the truth was that while he may still have been a household name in England, and he could hardly walk down a street in Derby without someone wanting to get his opinion on Derby County's prospects, he needed to earn a living. Naturally modest and unassuming, Bloomer had gone through many jobs since retiring as a professional footballer in 1914. Indeed, he had taken an overseas position before, when he accepted a job as coach of Britannia Berlin 92. He had arrived in Berlin in July 1914, only for war between England and Germany to be declared a few weeks later. His contract was cancelled, but he found it impossible to get back to England. A couple of months later he was interned in the Ruhleben detention camp, where he spent the next four miserable years behind barbed wire fences in cramped and unheated blocks.

After the war he took up a job in Derby County's boot room in a supportive role to the manager. As is often the way at Derby, the club ran into financial trouble and at the end of the 1922/23 season they dispensed with Bloomer's services. Then the offer of a job at Irun came through. The motivation for the offer was local rivalry. Spanish football at that time was very much in its infancy, and matches were organised in regional championships. The winners from each of the eight regions then went on to play each other in a knockout cup competition, the Copa del Rey, or King's Cup. Real Unión de Irun Football Club, although from a small town, had won both the regional championship and the Copa del Rey in 1918. They won the regional championship again in 1921/22, but in the following season local rivals Real Sociedad took the title. Real Unión's president regarded this as shameful, and his resulting appointment of Bloomer, a name well known across European football, was considered a major coup. Bloomer was an instant success. Marshalling his team of amateurs, Real Unión won the regional championship and went on to beat Barcelona and Real Madrid to win the Copa del Rey.

Bloomer's second and final season with Real Unión proved more difficult, both on the pitch and off it. His letters back home suggest a man who is missing his wife and adopted town, and still struggling with a foreign language. But he was not the only ex-British footballer in the Basque country. A close friend, Fred Pentland, was manager at Athletic Bilbao. Pentland had been a team-mate of Bloomer's during his time at Middlesbrough and a fellow intern at the Ruhleben detention camp. Also, at nearby San Sebastián, the coach was former Derby team-mate Ted Garry. These men were just part of a wave of British footballers employed as coaches and managers by eager continental football clubs wanting to benefit from the experience of those who had played in the 'homeland' of football.

But the British influence on European and global football goes back much further than Bloomer and his friends. In the last decades of the 19th century and the first decade of the 20th, the British Empire and British business was at its global peak. Wherever the British went they took football with them, from Argentina to Zanzibar. While cricket and rugby tended to be the main sports favoured by the upper-class administrators of British colonies, association football was the favoured game of the sailors, managers, engineers and teachers who spread across the globe to foster new industrial communities.

In 1884, for example, Charles Miller, the Brazilian-born son of a Scottish railway engineer, returned to São Paulo from a Hampshire public school with two footballs, a Football Association rulebook and a love of the game. He organised the first known match in São Paulo when the railwaymen took on the gasmen, established São Paulo Athletic Club, and helped set up the first league in Brazil. The sport spread across the country like a new virus, infecting both the Brazilian elite and the working classes. Within a few decades Brazil considered itself 'o País do Futebol' or 'the country of football'. In neighbouring Argentina, Alex Hutton, a Glaswegian teacher, set up the Argentine Association Football League. The early years of the league were dominated by the Alumni Athletic Club, which consisted of old boys from the English High School that Hutton had set up in Buenos Aires. In Uruguay, British immigrants, particularly workers for the Central Uruguay Railway, helped spread football fever across the country, with

Albion Football Club in Montevideo being the country's first club specifically devoted to football.

Similar stories can be told in countless countries across the world, which were all seduced by this facet of British culture. Bloomer and his friends were at the end of a long line of football missionaries who had taken not only a game but a whole football lexicon with them. Words like football, goal, penalty, forward and score entered and stayed in global use. This footballing lingo became what the Uruguayan writer Eduardo Galeano called 'the Esperanto of the ball'.[220] A language that is understood by people of many nationalities. One word in that global language is 'derby'.

Many foreign football clubs that originated due to the efforts of British expats have died out, but in 1899 a meeting of Englishmen in a swanky Milan hotel led to the formation of one of the most famous clubs in the world, and inadvertently to the *Derby della Madonnina*, one of the world's most famous and colourful local derbies. Two men formed the main driving force behind the new club. Alfred Edwards was a Shropshire engineer turned businessman whose main sporting passion was cricket. Herbert Kilpin, who was much younger, was a football man. They and their friends set up the Milan Football and Cricket Club. The Italians never really took to cricket, but took to football like ducks to water. The club became Associazione Calcio Milan, or AC Milan.

Edwards was an influential man and used his connections in the business world to generate financial support for the club, such as securing the involvement of the Pirelli family, the famous tyre manufacturers. If Edwards was the 'head' of the new enterprise then Kilpin was the 'heart'. Kilpin was a butcher's son, born at the back of a shop on Nottingham's Mansfield Road. In 1891 he emigrated to Turin to work for a textile merchant with links to a Nottingham lace manufacturer, and in 1897 moved to Milan. He became the captain as well as the coach of the club. He was a slightly tubby chap, and by English standards of the time was not the most gifted of footballers, but his commitment to the cause was legendary. On his wedding night he received a telegram inviting him to play a game in Genoa against Grasshopper Club Zürich. He duly informed his bride that he would need to leave the next day. His wife may have had mixed feelings when he returned from the game the following night sporting a broken nose. He was another footballer with a liking for a drink and was said to avail himself during a game of a swig, or two, from a bottle of whisky kept in a hole behind the goal.

During Kilpin's association, AC Milan won three national titles. But there was a rift inside the club which seems to have been related to pressure to play more Italian players. In 1908 a new club, Football Club Internazionale, was formed. Its name reflected the aims of its founders to include foreign as well as Italian players. Inter Milan soon became a force to be reckoned with, winning the national title in 1910. The rivalry between the two clubs was instantaneous, with the more middle-class supporter gravitating towards Inter, and AC Milan attracting more of the working class. The intensity of the rivalry is unusual in that since 1947 both clubs have used the San Siro stadium as their home ground.

Milan's huge cathedral dominates a large square in the centre of the city. On the very top of the cathedral, which took over 500 years to build, is a gilded statue of the Virgin Mary, known by the Milanese as the *Madonnina*, or little Madonna. She looks down on a city which has become the economic powerhouse of northern Italy and one of the main economic hubs of Europe. More pertinently, the statue is the subject of a Milanese song, 'Oh mia bèla Madonnina', which ends on a rousing verse full of civic pride. At a typical *Derby della Madonnina*, fans make sure they are in the stadium well before kick-off, because ten minutes before time each end of the ground explodes into a wonderful display of flags, banners, chants, flares and fireworks. These are not haphazard spectacles, but carefully organised presentations. Thousands of spectators will raise coloured placards to create stunning effects, unfurl huge portraits of club icons or drape banners with special messages from the second tier of the stadium which may be taunts, boasts or plain insults to the opposition.

In Italy, these displays of football fanaticism are controlled by groups known as 'Ultras'. They are diehard supporters, usually with a recognised head or director, who supervises design and co-ordination of the pre-match displays. The Ultras, with their shaven heads and tattoos, look intimidating, and occasionally have been held responsible for violent acts. But in 1983, after a series of incidents at the *Derby della Madonnina*, the Ultras from Inter and AC Milan met and agreed to channel their antagonism into pre-match displays. Insults are regarded as acceptable but violence is not. By and large this has resulted in a more friendly derby, where excited fans can mix freely outside the ground, and where battles inside the ground have been replaced with bravado.

Sadly, such civilised behaviour is not a universal feature of derby games elsewhere in Europe. In Poland, the *Derby Krakovia* games between Wisła Kraków and MKS Cracovia have become known as the 'Holy War'. Like Liverpool and Everton, the two clubs are less than a ten-minute walk away from each other. The historic centre of Kraków is a truly beautiful place and the walk, or short tram ride, to Wisła's stadium could not be more pleasant in terms of its surroundings. The Jordan Park adjoins the stadium. It is named after a doctor, Henryk Jordan, who returned to Kraków from a spell in England keen to promote both sport and parks. Jordan set up the park in 1899, the first of its kind in Kraków. It was modelled on English landscape gardens and included several football pitches. Jordan introduced local teenagers to football, which quickly became popular. Organised football teams sprang up, and used the park and set the seeds for the Cracovia and Wisła clubs. The Henryk Jordan Park now separates the grounds of the two clubs. It forms an incongruous background for the confrontations between the rival sets of fans which have made the *Derby Krakovia* notorious.

The reasons for the hostility are deep and complicated. After the Second World War, Poland became one of the Soviet Union's satellite states. Polish football clubs were stripped of their legal rights and had to be sponsored by one of the organs of the state. As a result of Hobson's choice, Wisła Kraków came under the influence of offices of state concerned with surveillance and repression. Gradually the likes of spies and secret policemen wormed their way into managerial positions. This could hardly have endeared the club to many locals. In 1989, the Communist regime came to an end as Poland returned to independence. A succession of wealthy but rather dodgy owners then took control of the club, and an unhealthily close relationship developed for a time with an extremely violent 'firm' of Ultras, who had an interest in drug dealing and money laundering.

MKS Cracovia was given its name by Józef Lustgarten, Cracovia being the Latin name for Kraków. Lustgarten was Jewish, and the club's policy for signing players was not restricted by nationality or religion. Ludwig Gintel was one of Cracovia's Jewish players in the 1920s, and it was he who called the games against Wisła a 'Holy War'. During the Communist era, the Cracovia club was aligned with the city's transit authority but seems to have been starved of necessary funds. Despite the club's association with academics, it has its own set of hooligans, called the Jude Gang. According to the *Kraków Post* website one of the leaders of this gang came to a brutal end in 2011, when he was pulled from his car and beaten and hacked to death, by at least a dozen men wearing masks, and wielding machetes and baseball bats.[221]

Fatalities related to the rivalry between the clubs are not unusual. In March 2006, my youngest son visited the city as a member of a university study trip. After checking into his hotel, he was persuaded by other members of his group to go along with them to a football match. This naive little group set off for the Cracovia ground, their opponents being none other than Wisła. On arrival they were thoroughly searched by the police, and any possible items which might be used as weapons were confiscated. It is little wonder that the police were not taking any chances; in the preceding 12 months there had been at least eight fatal stabbings outside the Wisła and Cracovia stadiums. This part of the study trip, if ill advised, was certainly educational, as the students entered a cauldron of crazed supporters all keen to mark the 100-year anniversary of their rivalry with Wisła. Whipped up into a frenzy by a public announcer, the crowd waved thousands of red and white flags, and jumped up and down as if their lives depended on it. Although not the largest of stadiums, the crowd's chanting hits an ear-splitting level. At one point during the game a huge banner with red and white chevrons was unfurled which went around most of the ground. The game finished in a 1-1 draw.

Six months later, in October 2006, Wisła 'welcomed' Cracovia to their ground; again a 100-year anniversary. Nearly 1,000 police were ready and waiting equipped with water cannons and riot gear, while helicopters beat the air above. The ground is larger than Cracovia's, but the atmosphere generated is still electric and hostile. Flares go off, flags and huge banners are waved, and again virtually the whole crowd jumps and chants in unison. With the pre-match rituals completed, the game began. Wisła scored after a minute and police intervened to prevent a Wisła supporter from burning a Cracovia scarf. This provoked a battle between a section of the crowd and the police. The police managed to take the scarf away, but at half-time hundreds of Cracovia scarves were burnt along the fences by Wisła fans. The incensed Cracovia supporters tried to break out of their heavily fenced enclosure, but the police intervened. Chairs were then ripped out and hurled on to the pitch. The match finished 3-0 to Wisła – and a relatively quiet affair for a *Derby Krakovia* came to an end.

Although the centre of Kraków may be a magnet for tourists, there are areas of housing, away from the main thoroughfares, that are not so picturesque. On walls and gable ends the graffiti artists have been at work, their art often reflecting support for one of the Kraków teams and hatred of the other. Messages get posted on walls as derby day approaches: *'Derby Blisko, Tylko Wisła!'* The Derby is Near, Only Wisła! The street art often features emblems of the rival gangs: the Sharks of Wisła and Cracovia's Jude Gang. While there is no doubt that some of the fatalities are associated with the interclub rivalry, those who are more familiar with the local situation, such as region officials and the police, have suggested that drug trafficking and organised crime have become enmeshed in the relationship.

The *Derby Krakovia* may be one of the smaller derbies with an international renown, but there is no doubt that the *Paulista Derby* in Brazil's São Paulo is one of the biggest. While British influence on the formation of the Kraków clubs was largely indirect, there was a clear British stimulus behind the formation of one of the São Paulo clubs. In late-Victorian football there was a rumbling argument among British clubs and the Football Association about the growth of professionalism in the sport. With the advantage of hindsight, the success of those promoting football as a paid profession seems inevitable. But at the time it didn't appear that way, at least not to well-heeled gentlemen from the public schools, who considered football to be something one should play out of sheer love for the sport. For the aspirational footballing gentleman of the late-Victorian period, there was no better place for one's talents than Corinthian Football Club.

When Scotland thrashed England 5-1 in 1882 they recorded their seventh win since the inauguration of the annual fixture between the two countries in 1872. England had only managed two victories, with the other games being drawn. Corinthian Football Club was set up with the intention of getting the best English players together on a regular basis so that they could develop the necessary teamwork to put a stop to these yearly humiliations. That idea did not last long, but with the growth of professionalism Corinthians ended up as a prestigious amateur club for gentlemen, capable of playing against the best teams in the land.

Corinthians did not enrol in any league but were a touring side, organising friendlies in the north and Scotland. They loved nothing better than putting FA Cup winners in their place. In 1884 they handed out an 8-1 drubbing to Blackburn Rovers. Five years later they beat the Football League and FA Cup winners, Preston North End, 5-0. In 1903, Derby County lost yet another FA Cup Final, this time to Bury, who in turn were whipped 10-3 by Corinthians. The club was renowned for its principles of fair play and sportsmanship, an image reflected by its famous white shirts. Legend has it that if a penalty was awarded against Corinthians, their goalkeeper would merely lean against a goalpost and examine his fingernails while the opposition rolled the ball into the net.

Many Corinthians players also played for England. Being from the upper class, they often did not associate off the field with their working-class team-mates. Steve Bloomer recalled playing in an 1898 international against Scotland at Celtic Park, when his captain was the Corinthians player Charles Wreford-Brown. When Freddy Wheldon of Aston Villa put England a goal up, Wreford-Brown ran up and pressed a gold sovereign into Wheldon's hand. Bloomer scored England's second and the same thing happened to him, and again when he scored England's third. The referee kindly pocketed the sovereigns for safekeeping until the final whistle. After the match, Wreford-Brown graciously invited the rest of the team into his separate dressing room to toast their 3-1 victory with champagne.

As competitive English football grew stronger during the 1900s with the expansion of the Football League, British interest in Corinthians started to wane and the club concentrated on organising foreign tours, looking on themselves as football missionaries. They toured South Africa, Europe and North America, amazing spectators with their virtuosity. In 1910 they ventured to Brazil where they had been invited to play Fluminense in Rio de Janeiro. They were soon contacted by Charles Miller, who had played briefly for Corinthians during his time in England. He invited the tourists to play his side, São Paulo Athletic. Five local railway workers were so impressed by Corinthians during this game that they decided to form a team of their own and adopted the name of the club that had inspired them so much. Sport Club Corinthians Paulista was born.

Due to economic turmoil in their native country, at least a million Italians emigrated to Brazil between 1880 and the start of the Great War. Many ended up in São Paulo. In 1914 some young Italians decided to form a sports club that they hoped would unite Italian support, called Palestra Italia. This initiative found the ready support of the Italian Consulate. In 1917 Palestra played their first game, against Corinthians Paulista. Apparently there was considerable annoyance in the Corinthians camp prior to the first game, resulting from the number of members who had defected from Corinthians to join Palestra. But the confidence of Corinthians was high; after all, they had not been beaten for three years. To their astonishment, Palestra beat them 3-0. An enduring rivalry was born. During the Second World War, the Brazilian president banned any organisation from having names relating to the Axis Powers. Accordingly, Palestra Italia changed its name to Sociedade Esportiva Palmeiras. This made no difference to the rivalry and by 2017, the two clubs could look back on 100 years of derby matches. One of the reasons that the rivalry has not waned is that the record between the two clubs is so well balanced, with each side having a virtually identical number of wins to the other.

Although Palmeiras is the wealthier of the two clubs, the basis for the rivalry seems to be a sporting one rather than any inter-community hostility. São Paulo is a megalopolis of between 20 and 30 million people, depending on where you want to draw a line across its sprawling urban form. While many super-rich people live there, much of the population is poor, lacking a regular water supply or anything approaching decent housing, while crime is rife. Given this background, and the ebullient Brazilian spirit, it is no surprise that there has been a catalogue of incidents both on and off the pitch. As a result, since 2015 away fans have been banned from entry to stadiums hosting the São Paulo derby. The two football clubs have several supporters' groups. One of the largest of these is the *Gaviões da Fiel*, the Faithful Hawks. The Hawks have 115,000 members and have a samba school which competes against others in carnivals, in elaborate costumes sporting the black and white of Corinthians. The Hawks tend to go to matches wearing black shirts, while another fan group, *Camisa 12*, wear white. These various groups often have an extensive social calendar with barbecues and dances being regular events. These activities provide the poorest fans, who cannot afford match tickets, with the chance to show their allegiance.

Neither Corinthians nor Palmeiras is the biggest club in São Paulo, but their rivalry is recognised as the oldest and most intense. Many legendary footballers have played in the derby games: Roberto Rivellino, Ronaldo, Roberto Carlos, Rivaldo, Sócrates and Gabriel Jesus are just a few names from a long list of football 'royalty'. The largest attendance at a *Paulista Derby* was an estimated 120,000 fans who packed into the neutral Morumbi stadium in São Paulo to see the two clubs contest a championship final in 1974. But if any game sums up this sporting rivalry best, it is probably the 2000 semi-final of the Copa Libertadores, South America's equivalent of the European Cup. The semi-final consists of two legs. In the first leg, Corinthians scored three goals, only for Palmeiras to equalise on each occasion. But in the 90th minute Corinthians scored again, leaving them 4-3 winners. In the second leg, although Palmeiras were the first to score, they were 2-1 down at half-time, but finished the game with a 3-2 win. This meant the combined score from the two legs was equal at 6-6. Consequently, the game had to be decided by penalties. Palmeiras put five away in succession and Corinthians had replied with four of their own, when Marcelinho Carioca stepped up to take their fifth, only to see the keeper save his low shot with a spectacular dive. Palmeiras had won by the narrowest of margins.

The use of the word 'derby' to describe local clashes between football clubs is widespread across the globe, but the Spanish term '*clásico*' tends to be used in some countries to signify the biggest games of all. A clash between Boca Juniors and River Plate in Buenos Aires is referred to as a *Superclásico*, even though the two clubs are less than six miles apart. Perhaps this reflects the fact that most of the Argentinian nation supports either one club or the other.

Other countries have appropriated the *clásico* label for matches that are not local, but undeniably important. Barcelona versus Real Madrid games are known as *El Clasico* and a Bayern Munich versus Borussia Dortmund match is called

Der Klassiker. But the 'derby' tag is still used in connection with some of the greatest occasions in world football. The Cairo derby between Al Ahly Sporting Club and Zamalek is regarded as the biggest match in Africa, attracting crowds of 100,000 and is broadcast live to most Middle Eastern and North African countries. In India's Kolkata derby, ATK Mohun Bagan and East Bengal FC battle for supremacy in front of huge crowds in a fixture riddled with ethnic and economic divisions. In Istanbul, a game between Fenerbahçe SK and Galatasaray SK is known in Turkish as the *Kitalararasi Derbi*, the Intercontinental Derby. Although part of the same city, the two clubs originate from either side of the Bosphorus, a strait of open water separating Europe from Asia. There is also a legacy of class division. Fenerbahçe SK was associated with a mainly working-class origin and support. In contrast, Galatasaray emerged from a high school background with a stated desire to play together like Englishmen. The number of altercations between these two rivals is long and terrible. But one of the most infamous incidents was provoked by two Britons: a Scotsman and a former Derby County man.

Dean Saunders played 106 games for Derby County, scoring 42 goals, and followed in Steve Bloomer's muddy footsteps across Derby's Baseball Ground pitch. After leaving Derby, the Welshman had spells with Liverpool and Aston Villa before being transferred to Galatasaray. In 1996, the two Istanbul teams reached the final of the Turkish Cup, which was at the time played over two legs. Saunders put away a penalty to give Galatasaray a slim one-goal advantage to take into the return leg at Fenerbahçe's ground. At the end of normal time in the second leg the combined score was 1-1, so extra time was played. With only a few minutes to go Saunders struck again, smashing a shot into the top of the net. When the final whistle went, Galatasaray's Scottish manager Graeme Souness ran to his club's supporters, took hold of a huge flag in the club's red and gold colours and 'planted' it in the centre of the pitch. Incensed by the defeat and by this insult to their sacred ground, some of the Fenerbahçc crowd managed to scale the fences and Souness had a bang on the head and a tussle with a supporter before he managed to get down the tunnel.

When the cup was presented to Souness's team, they had to be surrounded by ranks of riot police to protect them from angry home supporters. Riots broke out across Istanbul and the rest of Turkey, requiring the military to restore order. It was roughly 150 years between this game fought between two halves of a great intercontinental city, and the final Shrovetide football match in the modest English town of Derby. Through a series of circumstances and shared passions, Istanbul's *Kitalararasi Derbi* is just one of many across the world influenced by a rough old game and a name that became part of the 'Esperanto of the ball'.

Afterword

IT IS clear that the term 'derby' is used on an almost worldwide basis to herald a football match between close, local rivals. It is also evident that very few people using the term know how it links to a game once played in a town in the middle of England. Modern football and Shrovetide football are very different games. The Derby Shrovetide events involved hundreds of players drawn from local communities. Their supporters were their relatives, friends, neighbours and work-mates and they assisted their sides with drink, refreshments, and care for the injured or exhausted, as well as with vocal support. They could even join in the fray if they wanted to. In contrast, the modern game is played by just a few players – most of whom are unlikely to be local – while spectators demonstrate their support or displeasure from the stands.

But for a time, in a local derby, players and fans share the same unity of purpose, the same strengthening of identity and togetherness, and the same ecstatic joy when their side scores a goal or wins a game. The fans talk about how 'we' scored a goal, as if they were personally responsible. It's the ability of football to confer shared belonging that is part of its appeal, and that shared sense of identity is strongest when 'we' are faced with 'them'.

The fervour which some fans assign to their football club is almost religious. Rightly or wrongly, there seems to be a trend to glorify founding members and turn them into icons of worship, with images displayed on flags and t-shirts, or statues unveiled to their memory. The city of Derby can certainly not be accused of glorifying its footballing past. The ball that was used in the 1845 Shrovetide match lies unseen in an old warehouse, where homeless people use the doorway as a toilet. At the time of writing, no mention of the game that was Derby's big annual event is made in any museum display. Most Derby people have no idea that well before it became a city, the town was once notorious for its Shrovetide football game, or that arguments raged for over 100 years about whether it should be stopped.

Many contradictions surround Shrovetide football and local derbies. They are events that both divide and unite at the same time. There is a shared love of the game and of the local derby as an event, but often a bitter hatred, sometimes temporary and sometimes longer lasting, of the other side, be they St Peter's, Millwall, or Galatasaray. This is especially odd given that the opposing teams generally have such a lot in common. They just happen to be on the other side of a brook, of a river, or a perceived social divide. In a rational world, the sight of a ball nestling in the back of a net should not provoke either ecstatic joy or utter despair. But the fact is that it does, and for many supporters across the world, it is the goals that are scored in derby games that matter most.

As a final point, it is interesting that the very word 'rival' derives from rivers. The Latin word *rivalis* means a person living on the opposite bank who uses the same brook or river as another. So it is fitting that at some point centuries ago, the original Derby Game was devised to pit people living north of the Markeaton Brook against those to the south. A few years before the final Derby Game, the brook's course through the centre of the town was culverted over. The removal of this landmark must have seemed very odd to people at the time. Today, like the game that once created mayhem in its streets, the brook's subterranean presence is largely unknown and unregarded. But on a Shrove Tuesday afternoon at least the game at Ashbourne still provides an echo of those forgotten days.

Acknowledgements

FIRST AND foremost, I would like to thank my wife Lynne for her constant support and for taking on the role of critical friend in reading countless drafts. I would also like to thank Spencer Bailey at the Derby Museum for letting me see and touch the old Shrovetide football and for his help in sourcing images. I am also grateful to Mark Young and his staff at the Derby Local Studies and Family History Library; much of the local research was carried out when social distancing and safe working practices were paramount due to the Covid-19 outbreak, but the helpful attitude of library staff enabled progress to be made. Special thanks are due to Anna Lord for her indispensable help with the Index. Finally, thanks to the amazing Bob Moulder for taking a few hazy ideas for a cover illustration and producing an image which brings those wild and wondrous days of Derby Shrovetide Football back to life.

Endnotes

CHAPTER 1: THE GAME

1   Mozley, *Reminiscences*, p. 303.
2   *Penny Magazine*, 6 April 1839, p. 131.
3   *Penny Magazine*, 6 April 1839, p. 131.
4   Defoe, *A Tour thro' Great Britain*, Vol.3, Letter 8, Part 2.
5   *Derby Mercury*, 7 October 1840, p. 3.
6   *Derby Mercury*, 17 September 1851, p. 4.
7   *Derby Mercury*, 15 February 1888, p. 2.
8   Mozley, *Reminiscences*, p. 303.
9   Hutton, *History of Derby*, p. 219.
10 Mozley, *Reminiscences*, p. 304.
11 *Sporting Magazine*, July 1830, p. 226.
12 Glover, *History of the County of Derby*, p .310.
13 *Derbyshire Advertiser*, 4 June 1909, p. 3.
14 *Derby Mercury*, 18 February 1885, p. 2.
15 *Derby Mercury*, 18 February 1885, p. 2.
16 *Derby Mercury*, 28 February 1827, p. 3.
17 *Penny Magazine*, 6 April 1839, p. 132.

CHAPTER 2: GET THE BLADDER AND BLOW

18 Quoted in Hornby, *Uppies and Downies*, p. 20.
19 Quoted in Hornby, *Uppies and Downies*, p. 19.
20 Quoted in Magoun, *History of Football*, p. 14.
21 Moor, *Suffolk Words and Phrases*, p. 64.
22 Cox, *Chronicles of All Saints' Derby*, p. 46.
23 Cox, *Chronicles of All Saints' Derby*, p. 46.
24 Cox, *Chronicles of All Saints' Derby*, p. 45.
25 Cox, *Chronicles of All Saints' Derby*, p. 46.
26 Cox, *Chronicles of All Saints' Derby*, p. 114.
27 Quoted in Magoun, 'Shrove Tuesday Football', p. 13.
28 Quoted in Hornby, *Uppies and Downies*, p. 23.

CHAPTER 3: FOLKLORE, FACT AND FICTION

29 Hutton, *Life*, p. 82.
30 Hutton, *History of Derby*, pp. 218-9.

239

31   *Derby Mercury*, 28 February 1827, p. 3.
32   *Manchester Courier*, 28 February 1891, p. 9.
33   *Penny Magazine*, 6 April 1839, p. 131.
34   *Derby Daily Telegraph*, 21 February 1928, p. 8.

CHAPTER 4: LEGENDS OF THE GAME
35   Glover, *History of the County of Derby*, p. 310.
36   Hutton, *History of Derby*, p. 219.
37   *Sporting Magazine*, July 1830, p. 225.
38   *Derby Mercury*, 18 February 1885, p. 2.
39   *Derby Mercury*, 28 February 1827, p. 3.
40   *Penny Magazine*, 6 April 1839, p. 131.
41   *Derbyshire Advertiser*, 4 June 1909, p. 4.
42   *Sporting Magazine*, July 1830, p. 228.
43   *Derby Mercury*, 28 February 1827, p. 3.
44   Wood, *History of the General Baptists*, p. 194.
45   *Derby Mercury*, 15 February 1888, p. 2.
46   Tunchy Williams Interviewed, 1885, p. 2.
47   Tunchy Williams Interviewed, 1885, p. 1.
48   *Bell's Life*, 16 June 1839, p. 4.
49   *Derby Mercury*, 2 August 1837, p. 1.
50   Tunchy Williams Interviewed, 1885, p. 2.
51   Tunchy Williams Interviewed, 1885, p. 4.
52   Tunchy Williams Interviewed, 1885, p. 6.
53   Tunchy Williams Interviewed, 1885, p. 6.
54   *Sporting Magazine*, July 1830, p. 225.
55   *Sporting Magazine*, July 1830, p. 227.
56   *Penny Magazine*, 6 April 1839, p. 132.

CHAPTER 5: MAYHEM AND MISRULE
57   *Pioneer*, 1 February 1834, p. 181.
58   Glover, *History of the County of Derby*, p. 310.
59   Glover, *History of the County of Derby*, p. 310.
60   *Sporting Magazine*, July 1830, p. 225.
61   *Derbyshire Advertiser*, 4 June 1909, p. 4.
62   *Sporting Magazine*, July 1830, p. 228.
63   *Sporting Magazine*, July 1830, p. 228.
64   *Sporting Magazine*, July 1830, p. 227.
65   *Derbyshire Times*, 2 November 1878, p. 5.
66   *Derby Mercury*, 15 Feb 1888, p. 2.
67   *Derbyshire Advertiser and Journal*, 9 April 1909, p. 15.
68   *Derbyshire Advertiser and Journal*, 9 April 1909, p. 15.
69   *Derby Mercury*, 9 February 1815, p. 3.
70   *Derby Mercury*, 9 February 1815, p. 3.
71   *Derbyshire Times*, 2 November 1878, p. 5.
72   *Derby Mercury*, 18 February 1885, p. 2.

73 *Derby Mercury*, 28 February 1827, p. 3.

74 *Derby Mercury*, 18 February 1885, p. 2.

75 *Derby Mercury*, 15 February 1888, p. 2.

76 *Derbyshire Times*, 2 November 1878, p. 5.

77 Mozley, *Reminiscences*, p. 304.

78 *Derby Mercury*, 15 February 1888, p .2.

79 *Derby Mercury*, 28 February 1844, p. 3.

CHAPTER 6: A TOWN IN TURMOIL

80 *The Examiner*, 9 November 1817, p. 3.

81 *The Examiner*, 9 November 1817, p. 3.

82 *Derby Mercury*, 19 October 1831, p. 2.

83 *Derby Mercury*, 19 October 1831, p. 2.

84 Derby Riots: Transcript of Trial of Eleven Persons 1831, p. 23.

85 *Derby Mercury*, 30 January 1839, p. 3.

86 *Northern Star*, 9 February 1839, p. 6.

87 *Northern Star*, 9 February 1839, p. 6.

88 *Northern Star*, 9 February 1839, p. 6.

89 *Northern Star*, 9 February 1839, p. 6.

90 *Derby Mercury*, 30 January 1839, p. 3.

91 Parker, *Life of Sir James Graham*, p. 325.

CHAPTER 7: A TOWN TRANSFORMED

92 Defoe, A tour thro' Great Britain, Vol.3, Letter 8, Part 1.

93 Defoe, A tour thro' Great Britain, Vol.3, Letter 8, Part 1.

94 Hutton, *History of Derby*, p. 15.

95 Quoted in Grattidge, 'Working Class Housing in Derby', p. 181.

96 Quoted in Grattidge, 'Working Class Housing in Derby', p. 186.

97 Mozley, *Reminiscences*, p. 232.

CHAPTER 8: OPPOSING FORCES

98 Glover, *History of the Borough of Derby*, p. 61.

99 *Derbyshire Advertiser*, 5 June 1909, p. 3.

100 *Derby Mercury*, 17 January 1844, p. 3.

101 *Derby Mercury*, 2 September 1846, p. 4.

102 *Derby Mercury*, 12 February 1845, p. 3.

103 *Derby and Chesterfield Reporter*, 7 February 1845, p. 3.

104 *Derby Mercury*, 12 February 1845, p. 3.

105 *Derbyshire Advertiser*, 5 June 1909, p. 3.

106 Craven, 'Exeter House', Derby', p. 25.

107 *Derby Mercury*, 13 August 1845, p. 4.

108 Simpson, *A Solemn Warning*, p. 19.

109 Simpson, *A Solemn Warning*, p. 18.

110 Simpson, *A Solemn Warning*, pp. 22-23.

111 *Derby Mercury*, 26 February 1845, p .3.

112 *Derby Mercury*, 26 February 1845, p .3.

113 *Derby Mercury*, 26 February 1845, p .3.
114 *Derby Mercury*, 26 February 1845, p .3.
115 *Derby Mercury*, 26 February 1845, p .3.
116 *Northern Star*, 9 February 1839, p. 6.
117 *Pioneer*, 1 February 1834, p. 181.
118 *Derby and Chesterfield Reporter*, 9 February 1832, p. 62.
119 *Derby and Chesterfield Reporter*, 16 February 1832, p. 70.
120 *Derby and Chesterfield Reporter*, 16 February 1832, p. 70.
121 *Derby and Chesterfield Reporter*, 1 March 1832, p. 86.
122 *Derby Mercury*, 1 February 1837, p. 2.
123 *Derby Mercury*, 6 March 1844, p. 3.
124 *Derby Mercury*, 6 March 1844, p. 3.
125 *Sporting Magazine*, July 1830, p. 227.
126 *Dundee Evening Telegraph*, 15 June 1886, p. 4.
127 *Manchester Courier*, 28 February 1891, p. 9.

CHAPTER 9: ATTEMPTS TO BAN
128 Derby Research Group, 'Derby Shrovetide Football', p. 65.
129 Hutton, *History of Derby*, p. 39.
130 *Derby Mercury*, 20 February 1746, p. 4.
131 *Derby Mercury*, 25 February 1796, p. 3.
132 *Derby Mercury*, 25 February 1796, p. 3.
133 *Derby Mercury*, 25 February 1796, p. 3.
134 *Pioneer*, 1 February 1834, p. 181.
135 *Pioneer*, 22 February 1834, p. 215.
136 *Derby Mercury*, 24 February 1844, p. 3.
137 *Derby Mercury*, 22 January 1845, p. 2.
138 *Derby Mercury*, 25 February 1796, p. 3.
139 *Derby Mercury*, 25 February 1796, p. 2.
140 *Derby Mercury*, 25 February 1796, p. 3.
141 *Derby Mercury*, 25 February 1796, p. 3.
142 *Derby Evening Telegraph*, 23 March 1964, p. 5.
143 *Derby Mercury*, 5 February 1845, p. 3.
144 *Derby and Chesterfield Reporter*, 7 February 1845, p. 3.
145 *Derby and Chesterfield Reporter*, 7 February 1845, p. 3.
146 *Derby and Chesterfield Reporter*, 7 February 1845, p. 3.

CHAPTER 10: THE FINAL GAME
147 *Derby and Chesterfield Reporter*, 6 February 1846, p. 3.
148 *Derby and Chesterfield Reporter*, 6 February 1846, p. 3.
149 *Derby and Chesterfield Reporter*, 6 February 1846, p. 3.
150 *Derby Mercury*, 18 February 1846, p. 2.
151 *Derby Mercury*, 18 February 1846, p. 2.
152 *Derby Mercury*, 18 February 1846, p. 2.
153 *Derby and Chesterfield Reporter*, 27 February 1846, p. 3.
154 *Derby and Chesterfield Reporter*, 27 February 1846, p. 3.

155 *Derby and Chesterfield Reporter*, 27 February 1846, p. 3.
156 Hibbert, *Corunna*, p. 71, and Burnham, *Wellington's Brigade Commanders*, p. 265.
157 *Leeds Mercury*, 28 February 1846, p. 5.

CHAPTER 11: AFTERMATH
158 *Derbyshire Advertiser*, 4 March 1846, p. 3.
159 *Derby Mercury*, 4 March 1846, p. 2.
160 *Derby Mercury*, 4 March 1846, p. 3.
161 *Derby Mercury*, 4 March 1846, p. 3.
162 *Derby Mercury*, 18 March 1846, p. 3.
163 *Derby Mercury*, 18 March 1846, p. 3.
164 *Derby Mercury*, 18 March 1846, p. 1.
165 *Derby Mercury*, 25 March 1846, p. 4.
166 *Derby Mercury*, 25 March 1846, p. 4.
167 *Derby Mercury*, 10 November 1847, p. 3.
168 *Derby Mercury*, 7 February 1877, p. 2.
169 *Derby Daily Telegraph*, 25 February 1922, p. 2.

CHAPTER 12: HELL FOR LEATHER
170 Wheathills website ('Wheathills team tactics' accessed 6 January 2022)
171 Alexander, 'Shrove Tuesday Football in Surrey', p.199.
172 Alexander, 'Shrove Tuesday Football in Surrey', p.200.
173 *Derby Mercury*, 24 April 1878, p. 3.
174 *Derby Mercury*, 24 April 1878, p. 3.
175 *Derby Mercury*, 5 March 1884, p. 5.
176 Glover, *History of the County of Derby*, p. 310.

CHAPTER 13: NAMING RIGHTS
177 Murray, *Oxford English Dictionary*, p. 496.
178 Idiom Origins website ('Local Derby' accessed 14 January 2022).
179 *Hull Packet*, 31 May 1861, p. 5.
180 *Daily Express*, 29 October 1900, p. 8.
181 *The Athletic News*, 2 October 1888, p. 5.
182 *Dundee Courier*, 15 October 1897, p. 6.
183 *Daily Express*, 9 March 1912, p. 6.
184 *London Saturday Journal*, 15 February 1840, pp. 100-101.
185 *Derby Mercury*, 18 February 1796, p. 4.
186 *Derby Mercury*, 22 January 1845, p. 2.
187 *Leeds Mercury*, 28 February 1846, p. 5.
188 Booth, *Father of Modern Sport*.
189 *Derby Mercury*, 18 February 1885, p. 2.

190 *Dundee Evening Telegraph*, 15 June 1886, p. 4.
191 *Manchester Courier*, 29 February 1891, p. 6.
192 *Pall Mall Gazette*, 15 February 1895, p. 10.
193 Hornby, *Uppies and Downies*, p. 30.

CHAPTER 14: PROMISED FURY
194 *Sheffield Daily Telegraph*, 28 December 1860, p. 2.
195 *Sheffield Independent*, 30 December 1862, p. 5.
196 *Derby Mercury*, 28 February 1827, p. 3.
197 *Derby Mercury*, 7 October 1840, p. 4.
198 *Bell's Life*, 12 February 1843, p. 4.
199 *Sheffield Daily Telegraph*, 28 December 1860, p. 2.
200 *Athletic News*, 1 December 1880, p. 5.
201 *Belfast Morning News*, 3 December 1880, p. 4.
202 *Athletic News*, 1 December 1880, p. 1.
203 *Grantham Journal*, 4 February 1880, p. 7.
204 *Dundee Courier*, 26 August 1898, p. 6.
205 *Yorkshire Telegraph and Star*, 5 November 1909, p. 18.
206 *Monmouthshire Beacon*, 24 December 1909, p. 26.

CHAPTER 15: TROUBLE AND STRIFE
207 *Woolwich Gazette*, 21 September 1906, p. 2.
208 *Daily Mirror*, 23 September 1976, p. 3.
209 *Belfast Evening Telegraph*, 16 September 1912, p. 6.
210 *Athletic News*, 12 April 1909, p. 8 and *Sporting Life*, 12 April 1909, p. 7.

CHAPTER 16: THE FRIENDLY DERBY
211 History of Liverpool website ('Everton and Liverpool History' accessed 28 August 2021).
212 *Liverpool Echo*, 4 October 1918, p. 3.
213 *Liverpool Echo*, 8 January 1932, p. 14.
214 *Liverpool Echo*, 9 February 1934, p. 14.
215 *Liverpool Echo*, 15 March 1980, p. 22.
216 *Westminster Gazette*, 25 September 1922, p. 10.
217 *Westminster Gazette*, 25 September 1922, p.10.
218 *Westminster Gazette*, 25 September 1922, p.10.
219 *Daily News*, 25 September 1922, p. 9.

CHAPTER 17:
220 Galeano, *Soccer in Sun and Shadow*, p. 30.
221 Krakow Post website ('Daylight Slaying Unsolved' accessed 25 November 2021).

Bibliography

Books and articles

Alcock, Charles, *Football: Our Winter Game* (London: Imperial Press, 1874)

Alexander, Matthew, 'Shrove Tuesday Football in Surrey', *Surrey Archaeological Collections,* Vol.77 (1986), pp. 197–205

Bandyopadhyay, Kausik, ed., *Face to Face: Enduring Rivalries in World Soccer* (Abingdon: Routledge, 2021)

Bates, Stephen, *Two Nations: Britain in 1846* (London: Head of Zeus, 2014)

Booth, Keith, *The Father of Modern Sport: The Life and Times of Charles W. Alcock* (Manchester: Parrs Wood Press, 2002)

Burnham, R., and McGuigan, R., *Wellington's Brigade Commanders: Peninsular and Waterloo* (Barnsley: Pen and Sword, 2017)

Butterton, Harry, *Dickensian Derby* (Derby: H. Butterton, 2001)

Cole, Michael, 'Holy War in the city of knives: anti-semitism and football in the streets of Kraków', (17 September 2020), Open Democracy website, accessed 24 November 2021

Campomar, Andreas, *¡Golazo!: A History of Latin American Football* (London: Quercus Editions Ltd., 2014)

Capp, Bernard, *Culture Wars: Puritan Reformation and its Enemies in the Interregnum 1649–1660* (Oxford University Press, 2012)

Cox, Rev. J. Charles, and Hope, W. H. St John, *The Chronicles of the Collegiate Church or Free Chapel of All Saints' Derby* (London: Bemrose and Sons, 1881)

Craven, Maxwell, 'Exeter House, Derby', *Country Images,* (February 2016), pp. 22–25

Craven, Maxwell, *The Illustrated History of Derby* (Derby: Breedon Books, 2007)

Curry, Graham, 'Up'Ards, Down'Ards and derbies: figurational reflections on intense enmity in pre-modern English football', *Soccer & Society*, Vol.19 Issue 5–6 (2018), pp. 645–656

Davison, Arthur William, *Derby: Its Rise and Progress* (London: Bemrose and Sons, 1906)

Defoe, Daniel, *A Tour Thro' the Whole Island of Great Britain, divided into circuits or journeys* (London: JM Dent and Co, 1927)

Delves, Anthony, 'Popular Recreation and Social Conflict in Derby, 1800–1850' in Eileen and Stephen Yeo (eds.), *Popular Culture and Class Conflict 1590–1914* (Brighton: Harvester Press, 1981)

Derby Research Group, 'Derby Shrovetide Football to be banned in 1731', *Derbyshire Miscellany*, Vol.20 Part 3 (spring 2014), p.65

Dewhurst, Keith, *Underdogs: The Unlikely Story of Football's First FA Cup Heroes* (London: Yellow Jersey Press, 2012)

Doidge, Mark, *Football Italia: Italian Football in an Age of Globalization* (London: Bloomsbury, 2015)

Dymond, David, 'A Lost Social Institution: The Camping Close', *Rural History*, Vol.1 No.2 (October 1990), pp. 165–192

Elliot, Paul, 'The Derby Arboretum (1840): The First Specially Designed Municipal Park in Britain', *Midland History*, Vol.26 Issue 1 (June 2021), pp.144–176

Elliot-Binns, L.E., *Medieval Cornwall* (London: Methuen & Co, 1955)

Ellis, Bob, 'William Eaton Mousley: Saint or Sinner?', *Derbyshire Miscellany*, Vol.22 Part 4 (autumn 2020), pp. 93–99

Falconer, Robert, 'Celebrating 175 years of Railway History', *Derbyshire Life*, Vol.79 No. 11 (Nov 2014), pp. 66–68

Galeano, Eduardo, *Soccer in Sun and Shadow* (London: Verso, 2003)

Garner, Edward, *The Last Football Game at Derby* (Durban: Just Done Productions, 2008)

Glover, Stephen, *History of the County of Derby*, Vol.1 (Derby: Henry Mozley and Sons, 1829)

Glover, Stephen, *The History and Directory of the Borough of Derby* (Derby: Henry Mozley and Sons, 1843)

Grattidge, Jonathan and Heath, John, 'Working Class Housing in Nineteenth Century Derby', *Derbyshire Miscellany*, Vol.12 Part 6 (autumn 1991), pp. 181–188

Harvey, Adrian, *Football: The First Hundred Years* (London: Routledge, 2005)

Heath, John E., 'The Borough of Derby between 1780 and 1810', *Derbyshire Miscellany*, Vol.8 Part 6 (autumn 1979), pp.181–197

Heath, John and Christian, Roy, *Yesterday's Town: Derby* (Buckingham: Barracuda, 1985)

Hendricks, Thomas S., *Disputed Pleasures: Sport and Society in Pre-Industrial England* (Westport: Greenwood Publishing, 1991)

Hibbert, C., *Corunna* (London: Batsford, 1961)

Hobson, James, *Dark Days of Georgian Britain* (Barnsley: Pen and Sword, 2017)

Hornby, Hugh, *Uppies and Downies: The extraordinary football games of Britain* (English Heritage, 2008)

Hutton, William, *The History of Derby from Remote Ages of Antiquity to the Year MDCCXCI* (London: J. Nichols, 1817)

Hutton, William, *Life of William Hutton* (London: Baldwin, Craddock and Joy, 1817)

Keith, John, *Dixie Dean: The Inside Story of a Football Icon* (London: Robson Books, 2001)

Koller, Christian, and Brändle, Faber, *Goal: A Cultural and Social History of Modern Football* (Washington DC: The Catholic University of America Press, 2015)

Lee, Chris, *Origin Stories: The Pioneers Who Took Football to the World* (Worthing: Pitch Publishing, 2021)

LoPatin, Nancy, *Political Union and the Great Reform Act of 1832* (Palgrave Macmillan, 1999)

Magoun, Francis Peabody, 'Football in Medieval England and Middle-English Literature', *American Historical Review*, Vol.35 Issue 1 (October 1929), pp. 33–45

Magoun, Francis Peabody, *History of Football from the Beginnings to 1871* (Bochum-Langendreer, H. Pöppinghaus, 1938)

Magoun, Francis Peabody, 'Shrove Tuesday Football', *Harvard Studies and Notes in Philology and Literature*, Vol.13 (1931), pp. 9–46

Malcolmson, Robert W., *Popular Recreations in English Society 1700–1850* (New York and London: Cambridge University Press, 1973)

Moor, Edward, *Suffolk Words and Phrases* (London: Printed by J. Loder for R. Hunter, 1823)

Mozley, Rev. Thomas, *Reminiscences: chiefly of towns, villages and schools*, Vol.1 (London: Longmans, Green and Co., 1885)

Murray, Bill, *The Old Firm: Sectarianism, Sport and Society* (Edinburgh: J. Donald, 1997)

Murray, J.A.H., and others, eds., *Oxford English Dictionary*. 2nd edition, compiled by J.A. Simpson and E.S.C. Weiner, Vol. IV. (Oxford: Clarendon Press, 1989)

Parker, Charles Stuart, *Life and Letters of Sir James Graham 1792–1861*, Vol.1 (London: John Murray, 1907)

Porter, Lindsey, *Shrovetide Football and the Ashbourne Game* (Ashbourne: Landmark, 2002)

Richardson, W. Alfred, *Citizen's Derby* (London: Oxford University Press, 1949)

Rippon, Nicola, *Derbyshire's Own* (Stroud: Sutton, 2006)

Roberts, Mike, *The Same Old Game: Volume One Before Codification* (Barcelona: Roberts BCN Publications, 2011)

Sanders, Richard, *Beastly Fury* (Bantam, London, 2009)

Scott, Les, *End to End Stuff* (Bantam, London, 2008)

Seddon, Peter, 'Shrovetide Football – the original Derby Game?', *Derbyshire Life*, Vol.80 No. 2 (February 2015), pp. 57–59

Seddon, Peter, *Steve Bloomer: the story of football's first superstar* (Derby: Breedon Books, 1999)

Simpson, Rev. Robert, *A Solemn Warning against the Theatre and Races* (Derby: Henry Mozley and Sons, 1829)

Sinclair, Sir John, The Statistical Account of Scotland, Vol.18 (Edinburgh: William Creech, 1796)

Stevenson, Graham, *Defence or Defiance – a people's history of Derbyshire* (Manifesto Press, 1982)

Sullivan, Paul, *Bloody British History: Derby* (Stroud: The History Press, 2011)

Wallis, Alfred, *The delectable ballad of the Derby Ram* (London: Bemrose and Sons, 1869)

Walvin, James, *The People's Game: A Social History of British Football* (London: Allen Lane, 1975)

Wood, J.H., *A Condensed History of the General Baptists of the New Connexion* (London: Simpkin Marshall and Co., 1847)

Websites

Ashbourne History: ourashbourne.co.uk

Ancestry UK: ancestryuk.co.uk

The Ba': bagame.com

BBC: bbc.co.uk

Belper Derbyshire: belper-research.com

Birmingham Live: birminghammail.co.uk

Bleacher Report: bleacherreport.com

Border Reivers: borderreivers.co.uk

British History Online: british-history.ac.uk

British Newspaper Archive: britishnewspaperarchive.co.uk

Business Live: business-live.co.uk

Chester A Virtual Stroll Around the Walls: chesterwalls.info

Chester-le-Street Heritage Group: chesterlestreetheritage.org

Daily Express Archive: ukpressonline.co.uk

Derbyshire Archaeological Society: derbyshireas.org.uk

Dictionaries of the Scots Language: dsl.ac.uk

Encyclopedia Britannica: Britannica.com

Football Pink: footballpink.net

Football Stadiums: football-stadiums.co.uk

Forza Italian Football: forzaitalianfootball.com

FourFourTwo: fourfourtwo.com

Google Books: books.google.co.uk

Historical Belfast: historicalbelfast.com

Historic England: historicengland.org.uk

Historic UK: historic-uk.com

History of Liverpool: historyofliverpool.com

History West Midlands: historywm.com

Idiom Origins: idiomorigins.org

The Guardian: guardian.com

Jewish Journal: jewishjournal.com

Kraków Post: krakowpost.com

Nottinghamshire History: nottshistory.gov.uk

Norfolk Record Office: norfolkrecordoffice.blog.org

Nuneaton and North Warwickshire Local and Family History: nuneatonhistory.com

Open Democracy: opendemocracy.net

Outside Write: outsidewrite.co.uk

The Pentrich and South Wingfield Revolution Group: pentrichrevolution.org.uk

Vision of Britain: visionofbritain.org.uk

Wheathills: wheathills.com

Wikipedia: en.wikipedia.com

Other sources

Derby Riots: The Trial of the Eleven Persons Charged with Breaking Open the Gaol of the Borough of Derby and Liberating the Felons and other Prisoners on Sunday 9 October 1831 and their Acquittal Taken in shorthand (Derby: Thomas Richardson; Google Books website, accessed 17 October 2021).

Hudson, Paul, The History of Derby Shrovetide Football (2005, booklet in Derby Local Studies Library)

Tunchy Williams, interviewed 1885 (Manuscript transcribed from articles in the *Derby Express* by Marion Johnson; held by Derby Local Studies Library). (Note: Tunchy Williams was also known as William Williamson and Tunchy Shelton.

Index